# Why Is the Stanley Cup in Mario Lemieux's Swimming Pool?

*How Winners Celebrate with the World's Most Famous Cup*

# WHY IS THE STANLEY CUP IN MARIO LEMIEUX'S SWIMMING POOL?

## How Winners Celebrate with the World's Most Famous Cup

### Kevin Allen

TRIUMPH
BOOKS
CHICAGO

Library of Congress Cataloging-in-Publication Data

Allen, Kevin, 1956–
    Why Is the Stanley Cup in Mario Lemieux's swimming pool?: how winners celebrate with the world's most famous cup/Kevin Allen.
        p. cm
    ISBN 1-57243-390-6
    1. Stanley Cup (Hockey)—Anecdotes. 2. Stanley Cup (Hockey)—History.
I. Title
GV847.7. A55 2000
797.962'648'09—dc21

                                                              00-060737

This book is available in quantity at special discounts for your group or organization. For further information, contact:

Triumph Books
601 South LaSalle Street
Suite 500
Chicago, Illinois 60605
(312) 939-3330
Fax (312) 663-3557

Printed in the United States.

ISBN 1-57243-390-6

Book design by Amy Flammang.

*To my friend Tom Schmieder,
who was to youth floor hockey
what Guy Lafleur was to the NHL.*

# Table of Contents

# Acknowledgments

This book was the best idea I never had. Credit for the creative notion of tying together the history of Stanley Cup celebrations through the eyes of the players belongs solely with Tracy Lovasz Sator. She is a former St. Louis Blues employee, the wife of former NHL coach Ted Sator, and an effervescent freethinker who has a passion for the game that tiptoes charmingly beyond normal fan boundaries. Having worked in marketing with NHL players for several years, Tracy observed that every Cup winner has a story to tell, and every nonwinner longed for the days when he would have a story to tell. It was a short leap for Tracy to convince me to write a book about their thoughts and feelings. She had me on "Will you . . . "

The vast majority of quotes from players, coaches, and general managers in this book (probably more than 90 percent) came from one-on-one interviews with the subjects. A few tales were gathered as part of larger media scrums during the 2000 Stanley Cup playoffs. A couple more were gleaned from newspaper accounts and, in those instances, the newspaper and/or writer is credited. Friend and colleague Bob Duff, a sports columnist for the *Windsor Star* and one of Canada's leading hockey historians, supplied a few yarns, including the delightful stories on Murray Gough and Frank McGee. He is also an incomparable hockey fact checker—a living encyclopedia of hockey knowledge. Gifted *Boston Globe* writer Kevin Dupont, another scribe destined for the Hall of Fame's writer's wing, supplied a couple of tales as well.

Thanks is also due to Mitch Rogatz, the lord and master of Triumph Books. In a publishing world that still hesitates to throw its weight behind hockey, Rogatz hasn't been afraid to grind in the corners to make a hockey book work.

My love and gratitude also goes to my children: Erin (sixteen), Kelsey (thirteen), and Shane (ten), who long ago learned that my book projects are family affairs. Near the end of this project each of my children took turns, without complaint, working to complete a Stanley Cup winners' list so their loony (but lovable) dad could finish in time to attend a family reunion. If that isn't an act of love, I don't know what is.

And of course thanks goes to my wife Terri, who always has the job of combing through my manuscripts to remove unsightly snarls.

An ironic aspect of working on this book project was that many of the players' stories weren't jocular. My original idea was to capture the hilarity and comical exploits of those who have won the Cup. But what I quickly discovered was that although players often explore their wild side after winning, their crazy antics aren't always what they remember. What they all seem to recall was that they momentarily drowned in their own emotions, washed over by a sea of feelings and a sense of fulfillment that only come with living out a childhood dream. Winning the Cup often resurrects the child buried deep within a player. In a sports world now compromised by pressure and money, the quest for the Cup is

ix

still a pure pursuit. How else can you explain the fact that multimillionaire athletes take so much pleasure in seeing their name highlighted on a five dollar engraving job?

No story I heard summed up the Cup's innocence and charm better than a tale Colorado Avalanche general manager Pierre Lacroix told me about Patrick Roy, who is the most winning playoff goaltender in NHL history. Lacroix was Roy's agent when he won the Cup with Montreal in 1993. "That's when they started having a bodyguard with the Cup," Lacroix recalled. "We were at his house and most of his friends and guests were gone." Seeing the bodyguard distracted by Roy's wife and a few friends, Roy looked at Lacroix and said, "Let's get a special look at the Cup." He grabbed the Cup and headed to his garage. "He took a screwdriver and unscrewed the bottom," Lacroix said. "He just wanted to see what was in inside. To him that was a very big deal. He was like a kid in a candy store."

With the Hall of Fame now more vigilant in guarding the Cup, it's become increasingly more difficult for players to gain that guilty pleasure. But Hockey Hall of Fame Director of Information and Acquisitions Phil Pritchard confirms that the inside areas of the Cup do contain various scratches and crude renderings that may or may not be letters or initials. The fact that million-dollar athletes want to carve their name inside the Cup like a schoolboy speaks to the Cup's mystique.

Here's my own confession: in 1988, another sportswriter and I returned to the Westin Hotel in Edmonton, Alberta, from a night of sampling hops and barley at an establishment called "Sherlock Holmes." It was after 3:00 A.M. and the Stanley Cup was on display in the Westin lobby, guarded by a young man who was utterly bored by that duty.

No one else was stirring in the hotel. After some small talk, we told the guard we wanted to get a closer look at the Cup and he gave us the "go-ahead" wave. We removed the Cup from inside the rope and took it to a nearby chair for an advanced inspection. We looked at all the great names of the past: Jean Beliveau, Gordie Howe, Terrible Ted Lindsay, Jacques Plante. My colleague suggested that we should scratch our initials in the bottom of the base so we could share eternity with some of the great heroes of hockey. The so-called guard was chatting with the clerk at the front desk. But we decided against it.

Or did we?

# Why Is the Stanley Cup in Mario Lemieux's Swimming Pool?

*How Winners Celebrate with the World's Most Famous Cup*

# Introduction

When the Stanley Cup finally belonged to the Dallas Stars at 1:37 A.M., June 20, 1999, Stars center Mike Modano's face was drowned in a wash of tears that only he and 975 others truly understood.

That's the number of people who had their names inscribed on the Cup in the twentieth century—the number of people who came closest to unlocking the mystery of its lure. The word "close" is apt in this case because everyone who has won the Cup seems incapable of offering words to translate the experience. To a hockey player, a Stanley Cup triumph is nirvana—a place where your mind is overwhelmed by a blend of joy and emotion that is truly indescribable. It would probably take a battalion of sports psychologists to accurately catalog the zigzagging range of feelings present in a player during and after winning the 107-year-old Cup.

"I don't think Mike ever understood the commitment it took to win until that moment," Stars coach Ken Hitchcock says about the memory of Modano unraveling in a flood of joy after the Stars defeated Buffalo to win the Cup. "He had put everything he had emotionally into it. Everything. His body melted and he reverted back to a little boy."

For a multitude of reasons, the Stanley Cup touches the child in all of us. The sporting arena is rich in historically significant symbols, including the Masters' Green Jacket, baseball's Cy Young award, tennis' Davis Cup, and yachting's America's Cup to name just a few. Yet an argument can be made that because its aura has overflowed well beyond the walls of its arenas, Lord Stanley's gift to hockey in 1893 has become the world's grandest trophy. The Stanley Cup has become a global symbol of sporting success. Tens of thousands of people have lined up everywhere from Sweden to Tokyo to the Czech Republic to Moscow's Red Square hoping to bask in its glow and understand its lure.

To assess the true value of the thirty-five pound Stanley Cup, a degree in psychology is far more essential than expertise in metallurgy. Frederick Arthur, Lord Stanley of Preston and son of the Earl of Derby, purchased the sterling silver cup for ten guineas in 1893. That was $48.47 at the time. Today, the Hockey Hall of Fame has insured the Cup for $75,000, and memorabilia experts surmise it would fetch up to three million dollars if it were ever sold at a Sotheby's auction. But anyone who has won the Cup, or desired to win it, will tell you that the Cup's value can't be defined in monetary terms. This is hockey's priceless 35 1/4-inch chalice—clearly the most exalted trophy in the professional sports kingdom. The Vince Lombardi Trophy is dime store hardware compared to Lord Stanley's legacy. Can you even name the World Series championship trophy or the hunk of metal awarded to the National Basketball Association champions?

Lord Stanley was Governor General of Canada when he commissioned the Cup to be forged as a challenge trophy to recognize the top hockey club in the Dominion of Canada. Lord Stanley had become smitten with hockey during his tour of duty in Canada. His two sons played the game and his daughter Isobel was among the first girls to play hockey in Canada. Lord Stanley's goal was to promote hockey through a national championship trophy, but it's unlikely he could have envisioned the impact his gift would have on the game and its people.

The Stanley Cup has become a symbol of passion and success even for those who don't follow the sport. Even some folks who can't name a single National Hockey League player know that the winner claims the Stanley Cup.

"This is really the people's trophy," said Minnesota Wild president Doug Risebrough, who won four Stanley Cup championships as a player with the Montreal Canadiens and one as an assistant coach with the calgary Flames. "It's a hugable trophy. It doesn't sit up in an elite cabinet. It doesn't look fragile. I looks like you can hug it."

The Stanley Cup is awarded to the champion, but those who have their name inscribed on the Stanley Cup say it's about so much more than a championship; it's about fathers and sons, vision quests, camaraderie, personal commitment, national pride, and a multitude of other ideals that are personal to each player. How else do you explain why New York Islanders captain Bryan Trottier once slept with the Stanley Cup beside him, or why Dallas Stars center Joe Nieuwendyk felt obliged to make sure a blind Cornell professor—his favorite instructor—could feel and touch the Cup? And what words can explain why Detroit Red Wings All-Star Brendan Shanahan and Dallas Stars veteran Guy Carbonneau both needed to take the Cup to their fathers' graves in recent years?

*Brendan Shanahan, one of the key members of the 1997 and 1998 Stanley Cup champion Detroit Red Wings, took the Cup on* The Tonight Show with Jay Leno *in June 1997.*

Part of the Cup's mystique is its tie to the past as well as its immortality. When a player wins the Cup, he knows his name will forever be engraved on one of the Stanley Cup's silver bands. It will stand in perpetuity as a reminder of his success. The quest for the Cup almost seems pure and unpolluted by the rapid flow of money that runs through the sports world. Hockey players seem to want to win the Cup with the same passion with which climbers want to conquer Everest.

The adventurous spirit that fueled Modano's quest for hockey immortality in 1999 was undoubtedly similar to what the feisty players of the Yukon Territory felt in 1904 when they challenged the Ottawa Silver Seven for the Stanley Cup championship. Starting out December 4, 1904, from Dawson City, legend has it that the Yukon players started their trip on dog sleds and covered about four thousand miles by boat, train, and on foot to arrive in Ottawa on January 12, 1905. The boisterous Yukon players lost the two-game series by a composite score of 32–4, but their trek added another layer of history to the Cup and another colorful story to a trophy that has far more tales than it has champions.

Today players don't travel by dogsled in their quest to win the Cup, but the journey isn't any less arduous. The players who have won the Cup may feel like they have completed an Iditarod. To win the Cup, a team must win sixteen times over two months with pressure blowing through at hurricane velocity. "You play eighty-two regular-season games and then you have two more months of work in order to become a champion," St. Louis Blues general manager Larry Pleau says. "Doesn't that discourage you right off the bat? We really haven't even started yet."

Given the amount of physical contact in hockey, players argue that no other sport comes close to matching the torturous grind of the NHL playoffs. It's like a two-month gauntlet during which players are clubbed, cut, and worn down by exhaustion. Modano says the two-month march to the Cup in 1999 was "the most emotional and physically draining experience I've ever had."

The grind takes its toll on the mind as well as the body. Bill Clement, who helped the Flyers win back-to-back Stanley Cups in 1974 and 1975, apologizes for using a war analogy, but says that it's the only thing he knows that can sum up the bond he felt with his teammates. "It was a foxhole mentality. You couldn't describe the bond we had. When we won, it was like the war was over."

When the Cup is won, tradition dictates that players should indeed celebrate like it's VJ day. With emotions colliding and jubilation uncorked, players have celebrated Stanley Cup victories with unbridled passion and zeal. If the Stanley Cup were allowed to tell its tale, it would be a story filled with raw emotions and zany twists. It would be a sweet story with many hardships weaving into happy endings. It would also be a comedic story of trips to strip clubs, booze-inspired dips into hotel pools, and a night spent alone on a street corner in Montreal. To many players, having the Cup is almost as important as winning it.

In days gone by, players only touched the Cup on the night they won it—on the ice and perhaps at the usually raucous postgame party. In 1995, NHL Commissioner Gary Bettman decreed that every player, coach, and member of management would be allowed a period of twenty-four hours in which to have the Cup in their possession for the purpose of celebration. But even before players

*Warren Rychel, a member of the championship Colorado Avalanche in 1996, strikes the classic Stanley Cup pose during a private party he held for friends and family near Windsor, Ontario.*

were unofficially allowed to take the Cup home, it unofficially made party stops in many different locales over the years. That's why New York Islanders great Clark Gillies was able to allow his pooch to enjoy supper out of the Stanley Cup in 1980. That's how it ended up in the bottom of Mario Lemieux's swimming pool in 1992. That's why Pittsburgh Penguins player Phil Bourque was able to sit in his living room and take the Cup apart to determine the source of a rattle.

Where a player chooses to take the Cup is a personal decision that may say more about the athlete than do his season statistics. Colorado Avalanche center Peter Forsberg was so smitten with the championship glow in 1996 that he took the Cup to Sweden. He was the first NHL player to party with the Cup overseas. Igor Larionov, Slava Kozlov, and Slava Fetisov took the Cup to Moscow one year later and stood in Red Square like conquering warriors displaying their plunder.

Wanting to share the Cup with fans, Detroit's Darren McCarty took it to Bob's Big Boy for breakfast, then to a cigar store, a golf course, and then to a corn roast for dinner. Dallas Stars center Joe Nieuwendyk sweet-talked the Hall of Fame into giving him an extra half-day so he could split time between his hometown of Whitby, Ontario, and his summer home in Ithaca, New York. In Whitby he drove downtown with his brothers hanging out the back of his Chevy Tahoe with the Cup in hand. In Ithaca he held a private reception at Cornell, where he let blind professor Dan Sisler lay his hands on the Cup.

To hockey players, winning the Cup means owning a piece of history that can't ever be lost or forgotten. The Cup has frequently runneth over with champagne and fine Canadian ale. That explains why the Stanley Cup has more battle scars than do veterans of foreign wars, and why Stanley Cup celebrations have stumbled into the wee hours and beyond.

Tradition demands that, at public gatherings, the Stanley Cup must be treated with a reverence and dignity that would usually be reserved for religious artifacts. The keeper of the Cup wears white gloves when he brings it onto the ice and it is always placed on a table covered with cloth. The Hockey Hall of Fame makes sure that the Cup's silver gleams with polish when it's on public display. Tradition also demands that winners have earned the right to treat the Stanley Cup as if it were an old wash bucket.

In many celebrations through the years, the Stanley Cup has been treated with some irreverence, or been at the center of horseplay. In 1905, for example, the Ottawa Silver Seven dropkicked the Stanley Cup into the Rideau Canal. The following year, the same Silver Seven were invited to dine with Lord Minto, Canada's governor-general, at Government House. Frank McGee, who had once scored fourteen goals in a Stanley Cup Final game against Dawson City, was the only member of the Silver Seven squad who grew up in affluent surroundings. His uncle was D'Arcy McGee, a famous Canadian politician. In addition to being the Silver Seven's most dangerous scorer, McGee was a notorious practical joker. As he prepared his nervous teammates for a fine-dining experience with the government dignitaries, he told them simply, "Watch me and do whatever I do. And don't worry about the forks. You are supposed to just use your hands." Not realizing that McGee was pulling off the best prank of his career, his teammates followed his lead right down the path to embarrassment. When the finger bowls arrived after dinner, McGee picked his up and slurped it noisily like a cup of tea. His teammates did likewise. The Governor General apparently had a heart of gold. Not wishing to embarrass his nation's best hockey players, he picked up his bowl and began slurping away. The name of McGee is synonymous with the Stanley Cup in its early years. His life was cut short when he was killed in action while fighting in France in World War I.

In 1924 Montreal Canadiens owner Leo Dandurand left the Stanley Cup on the curb after he had stopped to change a flat tire. Hall of Famer Red Kelly has told the story about how he put his infant son in the Cup's bowl one year; the child promptly peed in it. In the 1980s the Edmonton Oilers tucked the Cup in agent Mike Barnett's trunk after a night of revelry, and everyone except Barnett forgot where they left it.

The overflowing emotions of the victors may spill as much from a sense of relief as celebration. Those who enter the NHL do so knowing that, rightly or wrongly, players, especially top players, are made to feel incomplete if they haven't won a Stanley Cup. Marcel Dionne was an outstanding offensive player and ranked third all-time with 731 career goals, yet cruelly he is often remembered as the best player never to win a Cup. Although no one speaks about it, players all know Dionne's story; they also know that Gordie Howe, Wayne Gretzky, Phil Esposito, and Bobby Hull did all win the Stanley Cup. They know if they win, their names will be forever linked with the Cup.

In Canada in particular, youngsters dream of winning the Stanley Cup more than they do of becoming Prime Minister. Hockey seems intertwined with the country's self esteem. In Canada the Stanley Cup may be a metaphor for life and the struggles that accompany it. Gordie Howe, nicknamed "Mr. Hockey" during his glory days with the Detroit Red Wings, can remember growing up in Saskatchewan and going to a neighbor's house to hear the radio broadcast of playoff games. "All you heard about was the Stanley Cup," Howe says. "It became your dream. Playing hockey was part of being Canadian.

Tradition says that no player is allowed to lift the Cup until he has won it. And most players won't even touch it before then—as if the ghost of Lord Stanley might curse them for their act of insolence. (Hockey players are notoriously superstitious and it would be an easy leap of faith for many to believe that they might not ever win the Cup if they violated this unwritten rule.) In the 1950s Detroit's Ted Lindsay became the first player to lift the Stanley Cup and take it to the boards so the fans could have a closer look. Since then the hoisting of Lord Stanley's chalice has become the official beginning of the championship experience. It's fitting that Lindsay isn't quite sure what inspired him to do that, other than wanting to give the fans a better opportunity to see the Cup. It was just a triumphant, emotional moment.

Lord Stanley had intended that champions engrave their names in the Cup "at their own charge." One assumes that those who did their crude silver-smithing in the early years with a penknife, rusty ten-penny nail, or sharp instrument weren't any less thrilled to win the Cup than today's heroes whose names are engraved professionally by a Montreal silver expert. Through interviews with past champions, we discover that although the game and its trappings have changed dramatically through the years, the emotions have remained a constant that unifies the past with the present. Knowing that game stories and statistical scoring summaries provide an accurate historical record about how each Stanley Cup was won, this book's objective is merely to allow past champions a chance to reflect on how they felt about winning and what they did to celebrate that accomplishment.

To come close to understanding how players feel about winning the Stanley Cup, you need to accompany an underwear-clad Phil Bourque as he climbed a twenty-five foot waterfall at Mario Lemieux's home at four in the morning. You must know what he was thinking as he stood on that waterfall with the Cup raised above his head like he was king of the world. You must feel his exhilaration as he hurled the Cup into the pool with teammates reveling in the splash that he made.

About ninety players were interviewed for this book, a cross section from the 1920s to the present. The hope is that a glimpse at their thoughts and their celebrations might give us all a better understanding of why a Stanley Cup victory can reduce a stoic man to a sobbing boy.

# Chapter One

*Stories, 1928–1983*

# Murray Murdoch

When then–general manager Conn Smythe first sent Murray Murdoch a telegram in 1926 inviting him to join the fledgling New York Rangers, all he accomplished at first was to make Marie Murdoch suspicious of her husband.

"My wife wanted to know who the hell this Connie Smythe was and why she was inviting me to New York," Murdoch says, chuckling at a seventy-four-year-old memory.

When the new millennium began, Murdoch, then ninety-five, was the oldest living Stanley Cup champion, having earned his place in hockey championship lore as a member of the 1927–28 Rangers. Murdoch had actually moved from the University of Manitoba to Manhattan to join the first-year Rangers team in 1926, right after he and Smythe worked out what seemed like high finances in those days. According to Murdoch's memory, he had Smythe meet him in Minnesota where Murdoch was playing senior hockey. "He showed up and put fifteen one-hundred-dollar bills out there, figuring a small time boy would be impressed."

Murdoch didn't take Smythe's first bonus offer, although they came to terms soon afterwards and Murdoch ended up playing eleven seasons for the Rangers. To bring his historical significance into context, consider that Murdoch was playing hockey in New York when Babe Ruth wowed the world by smashing sixty home runs during the 1927 season, and he was there in 1929 when the stock market crashed and America plunged into depression.

"Hockey was well covered in the newspapers back then," Murdoch said by phone from his home in Hamden, Connecticut. "We drew very well. But it was sort of a high-class game in those days. The average public hadn't taken it up. It was a prep school game."

Murdoch apologizes for not recalling all the details of the Rangers' 1928 championship series against the Montreal Maroons or the 1933 series against the Toronto Maple Leafs, and yet his memory of the events that happened seventy-two years ago is quite remarkable. He recalls quite clearly the now-famous Game 2 in which forty-four-year-old coach Lester Patrick, grandfather of current Pittsburgh Penguins general manager Craig Patrick, had to enter the game to play goal when starter Lorne Chabot suffered an eye injury. During his playing days Patrick had been a defenseman, not a goaltender. The Rangers were down 1–0 in the series when Chabot was hurt and couldn't afford a loss in the second game.

"They wouldn't give us a goaltender," Murdoch said. "And Lester would play some goal for us in practice so he decided to go into the net. We didn't have assistant coaches so some of the [general] managers from the other teams came down to help behind the bench. [Detroit's] Jack Adams was one of them."

The Rangers ended up winning that game 2–1 in overtime on Frank Boucher's goal. "We tried to protect Lester the best we could, but they were shooting long shots at him and he was stopping them," Murdoch said.

That game was played in Montreal. In fact, every game in that series was played in Montreal because the circus was booked in Madison Square Garden. The circus always took precedence over hockey even in the playoffs—a tradition that lasted into the 1970s. Clowns and elephants had priority over wingers and defensemen in a ranking that wasn't close.

> "Funny that I don't even remember seeing the Cup."
>
> — *Murray Murdoch*

"You have to remember that the Garden was built for the circus and boxing," said Murdoch. "If you were at the top gallery on the side—unless you were in the first or second row—you couldn't see the complete rink. It was set up to see the center of the Circus Ring. We knew the circus took over for a month. That was one of the big events of the Gardens. Six day bicycle racing was another big event in the Garden."

Murdoch was a speedy, defensive-minded winger who was often assigned to shadow the other team's top scorers. He often infuriated opposing players because of his knack of covering them as if he were tethered to their torso. He lined up against all the great players of that era, including Howie Morenz. ("He was a terrific skater, very, very fast," Murdoch said.) Murdoch's longevity and continued decent health seem apropos considering that in the 1920s and 1930s he was considered one of the NHL's most durable athletes. He didn't miss a game during his NHL career, compiling a league record of 508 consecutive games that lasted until Johnny Wilson broke it on March 21, 1959.

Murdoch's memory of the 1928 celebration is a little hazy, although he does remember getting to meet New York Mayor Jimmy Walker. At that point, the Stanley Cup was already thirty years old. "Funny that I don't even remember seeing the Cup," Murdoch said.

He ended up winning the Stanley Cup again in 1933, and he remembers that. "You never remember all the wonderful plays," he says, laughing. "All I seem to remember is the mistakes I made."

# Milt Schmidt

*Boston Bruins, 1938–39 and 1940–41*

*General Manager, Boston Bruins, 1969–70 and 1971–72*

When Hall of Fame center Milt Schmidt thinks about the 1939 Stanley Cup Championship postgame revelry at Boston Garden, it's what he heard, not what he saw, that instantly comes to mind.

As NHL President Frank Calder tried to present the Stanley Cup to the Bruins after they had vanquished the Toronto Maple Leafs 3–1 in Game 5, the boisterous, appreciative Boston faithful wouldn't quiet down to allow the event to continue. The reason: their hero, Bruins' defenseman Eddie Shore, had inexplicably left the ice and headed to the dressing room. Schmidt remembers the noise level was deafening until Shore's teammates coaxed him out of the dressing room for the celebration.

"To think about that still gives me goose pimples," Schmidt says more than sixty years after the fact. "Only a couple of other times I dare say someone received as loud and lengthy an ovation as Shore got that night. When they retired No. 4 [Bobby Orr's number] and when they retired [Phil] Esposito's No. 7. It was really loud then, especially when Ray Bourque took his No. 7 jersey off and he was wearing No. 77."

Schmidt was twenty-one when the Bruins won in 1939. "To win that championship at that age was the greatest thing that ever happened to me in hockey," Schmidt said. "I had various All-Star nominations and the Most Valuable Player trophy, the Hall of Fame. But that championship was the best. When you think of all the great things this game has seen, and so many great players have come and gone, to have won the Stanley Cup championship is the best thing that can happen to you."

Young players, usually somewhat blind to long-range thinking, aren't supposed to savor the Cup's sweetness with the same level of understanding that a veteran player has. But Schmidt appreciated the magnitude of his accomplishment even then. He was indeed mature beyond his years. The Bruins signed him at age eighteen, but they really had wanted him in the lineup at age seventeen. He rejected their offer even after attending training camp. "Here I was in 1935 at training camp on the same ice surface with Eddie Shore, Dit Clapper, Tiny Thompson—all the guys I heard about on the radio," Schmidt. "I'm not ashamed to say they offered me $2,000 to sign. I didn't have an agent back then because your bus ticket would have been waiting for you if you had an agent. But I said 'I'm seventeen and I'm too young. I'm going back to play another year in junior hockey, and I can probably make that money working over the course of a year.'"

They did, however, convince him to join the team in 1936, and he ultimately wound up being part of two Stanley Cup championships. The feeling in the 1940s was that the Bruins might have actually won more titles had Schmidt and others not given up three years of their life to serve in the Royal Canadian Air Force during World War II.

Schmidt doesn't recall much about the Cup celebrations, other than he was happy just to be part of a group that included Shore, Clapper, and famed goaltender Frank Brimsek. He remembers the people better than the event.

"Eddie was kind of a loner. He liked to be by himself on the road, to get his proper rest because he played a lot," Schmidt remembers. "But when it came time to look after the younger players, he did look after us. He would say 'You are going out to dinner with me,' and we would all go."

Schmidt clearly would like to call Brimsek the best goaltender of that era, but he says he can't "because I never played against him." ("The best I ever played against," he said, "was Montreal's Bill Durnan.") But he remembers Brimsek was highly competitive, even in practice. "He and Clapper were close, and they would play a game after practice," Schmidt said "Clapper would take shots from twenty to twenty-five feet, and they would [bet] some kind of ice cream drink. Brimmy would always win."

When it comes to celebrations, Schmidt has more colorful memories of being general manager when the Bruins won in 1970 and 1972.

"We had this big parade, and when we got on the balcony at city hall, John McKenzie found a couple of seconds to pour a can of beer on Mayor White's head," Schmidt said. "That's one of my favorite memories."

Schmidt did end up with the Cup in his possession at 3:00 A.M. after one night of celebrating in 1970, and he couldn't make up his mind what to do with it in his house.

He and his late wife, Marie, finally decided to tuck it into a baby crib that was no longer in use in their home. "I couldn't think of any better place to put it than the sack," Schmidt said. "We tucked it in and it slept soundly through the night where it should be." Considering that the Stanley Cup usually parties with players through the night, Schmidt's action may have allowed Stanley the best night of rest it ever had.

# Clint Smith

*New York Rangers, 1939–40*

When the New York Rangers won the 1940 Stanley Cup championship at Maple Leaf Gardens, they were acknowledged with a round of silence.

"That's the way it was in those days in Toronto and Montreal," remembered Clint Smith. "When they scored fans would raise the roof two or three inches, and when we scored you could hear a pin drop."

This was a romantic period in hockey history when fans came to games wearing their Sunday best and NHL contests were considered high-class entertainment. "When I first got [to the NHL], fans used to come in tuxedos," Smith remembered. "It wasn't unusual to see top hats."

To win a Stanley Cup in a hockey mecca like Toronto added another level of distinction to an already glorious event. Smith doesn't recall the Stanley Cup trophy being central to the Rangers' celebration after Bryan Hextall had scored in overtime to down the Maple Leafs 3–2 in the deciding sixth game. What he remembers is that President John Reed Kilpatrick, called General Kilpatrick by players, came into the dressing room. That probably added as much distinction to the event as did the venue.

"I had never seen General Kilpatrick in the dressing room before," Smith recalled. "He said we were going to have a party at the Royal York Hotel. He said he wanted everybody there. It was like an order, and we obeyed."

Word must have spread around town about the Rangers' party because the room was jammed with bodies, including members of the Maple Leafs' team, plus a multitude of gate-crashing people that no one on the Rangers' organization even recognized.

"General Kilpatrick came up to Muzz Patrick and said 'If I was a younger man, I would take a few of these bottles [of scotch and whiskey] up to my room for later. It won't be long before they are all gone.'"

Smith and Patrick didn't need to be told twice; they squirreled away several bottles for safekeeping. The Rangers' celebrating went well into the night, and it was a haggard looking group of players that trudged across the street to the train station the next morning for their 7:00 A.M. departure. Given that it was a Sunday, players undoubtedly presumed they would sleep their way back to Manhattan in a no-alcohol environment. They were wrong.

"When I first got [to the NHL], fans used to come in tuxedos. It wasn't unusual to see top hats."

— *Clint Smith*

"Everyone had a little hangover," Smith said. "Things were pretty dull. Muzz was the first to bring out one of our bottles. He just wanted to liven things up."

By the time the train chugged into New York, the Rangers' celebration had reached the same level of enthusiasm that had been accomplished the night before in Toronto. "I don't think we had enough liquor left on the train to fill one bottle when we got back," Smith said.

On the train, players talked about making a run at a string of championships. The team was overflowing with dependable, team-oriented players such as Hextall, Babe Pratt, Alex Shibicky, Art Coulter, goalkeeper Dave Kerr, plus Muzz and Lynn Patrick, who had matched their father's accomplishment by getting their name on the Cup. The consensus on the party train that day was these Rangers would win again and again. "I thought we would win two or three more," Smith recalled.

What no one knew that day is that the world would soon realize that Adolf Hitler and Japanese imperialism needed to be stopped, and several of the Rangers would end up in the military. And no one could have dreamed on that day that it would be fifty-four years before the Rangers would again become champions.

Smith, making about $6,000 to play in those days, recalls that the players received $1,250 from the NHL for winning the Stanley Cup, and Madison Square Garden corporation "magnanimously" chipped in another $500. But he insists the joke was on the Garden. "We would have played for nothing back then," Smith says.

# Bud Poile

*Toronto Maple Leafs, 1946–47*

The Dallas Stars received $80,000 and a $10,500 ring for winning the 1999 Stanley Cup championship. In 1947, Bud Poile remembers he received $600, a silver cigarette case, and a cardigan sweater for helping the Maple Leafs capture the same Cup. But it was a damn nice cardigan.

"It was quite an honor to get that buttoned down sweater," Poile remembered. "It had that Maple Leaf crest on it. It really was quite a sweater."

Poile has donated that sweater to a museum in his hometown of Thunder Bay, Ontario (formerly Fort William). But Poile's pride in the sweater and its meaning may symbolize the Cup's charm and mystique as much as any fourteen-karat jewelry could. This was a time in hockey when a fan could still secure a gray seat in the upper reaches of Maple Leaf Gardens for ninety cents, and players' wages were more in line with common laborers than entertainment icons. Poile suggests that it probably cost some players money to compete for the Stanley Cup because players traditionally had summer jobs lined up to supplement their hockey income. "My first year with the Leafs I had to put a deposit on my skates," Poile recalled.

> "Being a Canadian winning the Cup in Canada was like winning the World Series for the New York Yankees."
>
> — *Bud Poile*

With only six teams in the NHL, only the world's 120 top players were afforded the opportunity to compete for the Stanley. Making it in the NHL was the Canadian equivalent of knighthood, maybe even sainthood. To play for the Cup as a member of the Maple Leafs or Montreal Canadiens was the hockey equivalent of praying in the Holy Land.

"Being a Canadian winning the Cup in Canada was like winning the World Series for the New York Yankees," Poile remembered.

Poile says he made "a little contribution" to the Leafs' championship. Actually he netted two goals in the six-game triumph against the Montreal Canadiens, and only Teeder Kennedy and Vic Lynn managed to score three goals. One of Poile's tallies came in Game 3 when the Maple Leafs won 4–2 to take a 2–1 lead in the best-of-seven series. The Maple Leafs had seven different scorers producing their thirteen goals in that series, and that result may have been a reflection of general manager Conn Smythe's philosophy more than coincidence. Smythe believed that the key to winning is making sure all hands are pulling on the rope at the same time. He was famous for coming into the room and saying, "We can't let another dog hunt in our yard."

The Maple Leafs turned out to be the bigger dogs in 1946 and '47, even though Montreal had the better regular-season record.

Poile and his Maple Leafs teammates were celebrities, but he doesn't believe the Stanley Cup hoopla was as crazed, scripted, or lengthy as it is today. For example, he can't remember having his picture taken with the Stanley Cup, except in the team picture that was taken at 12:20 the next day. He knows that because the Garden's clock is in the picture. He does remember being a "big wheel" that summer in his hometown, Fort William, especially at Armstrong's Pool Hall and Dom DePiro's Barber Shop. You weren't anyone in Fort William if you didn't frequent those two locales.

"Today they go to Disneyland when they win the Cup," Poile says. "If memory serves me, we did what we always did after weekend games. We went to Howie Meeker's house and had a few beers."

# Ted Lindsay

*Detroit Red Wings, 1949–50, 1951–52, 1953–54, and 1954–55*

When Detroit Red Wings captain Ted Lindsay picked up the Stanley Cup and carried it to the cheering fans at Olympia Stadium, it was the twentieth-century equivalent of the king's knight allowing the masses to inspect the crown jewel. It just wasn't done before Lindsay's moment of impulsiveness.

Photographs would seem to prove that Lindsay was the first to raise the Cup above his head in what is now the classic Stanley Cup pose. What did his teammates think of Lindsay's Cup raising? "They probably thought the idiot Lindsay is off on another tangent," Lindsay says, chuckling.

Lindsay's historically significant act wasn't premeditated. "I really didn't even think about it at all," Lindsay said. "You never know what you will do in your life that will turn out to be important. This was just one of those impulsive things."

After Red Wings owner Bruce Norris and general manager Jack Adams had received the trophy from NHL president Clarence Campbell, it was handed off to Lindsay for the traditional photograph. After that snap, he picked it up over his head and carried it to the boards. There was no Plexi-glass in those days, only chicken wire, and fans could actually touch the cold silver of the Cup.

"I was very public relations oriented," Lindsay said. "I knew who paid our salary. It wasn't the owners; it was the people. I just wanted them to have a closer look. I just went around the rink and let everyone see it. This is what we dream about, maybe from the time we're born—to be recognized as the best in the world. I wanted to share it with the fans."

Did Campbell say anything? "I don't think so, but I wouldn't have heard him anyway because the fans were pretty loud," he says.

"Terrible Ted" Lindsay was a man of the people, even if he played so aggressively that opponents couldn't stand him. The Detroit Red Wings were a dominant team in Lindsay's heyday, winning eight of nine regular-season championships in one stretch from 1948 to 1957. The Red Wings won four Stanley Cup championships during that period and it seems somewhat surprising that they didn't win more.

"Oh, we had a great team," Lindsay said. "But every year we had to hope that our farm teams in Indianapolis and Edmonton would go to their championship round because we knew that four, five, or six of those players were going to be brought up. They were supposed to be reserves in case we had injuries, but Adams always became a magician. They weren't good enough to play with us all year, but he would want to insert them in the lineup."

"And you had to give Toronto and Montreal credit at that time. They had good teams back then."

Lindsay had some classic playoff moments in that era, including one in 1955 when he became the second NHL player to score four goals in a Stanley Cup final game. He netted four in a 7–1 win against Montreal on April 5, 1955. Lindsay was as respected in that era as any athlete in Detroit, including young Al Kaline of the Detroit Tigers and Bobby Layne of the Detroit Lions. He settled in the Detroit area after the war, starting a manufacturing business with teammate Marty Pavelich. Lindsay has fond memories of winning the championship four times on Olympia ice.

After each championship the team would gather at the Book Cadillac Hotel on Washington Boulevard in downtown Detroit and party until 3:00 A.M. "Washington Boulevard was one of the premier streets in America back then," Lindsay said. "It wasn't like it is now. There were no parades. But we just had a very nice party with all of the players, their wives, and their friends. Management became very generous that night."

"We would have dinner and beers," Lindsay said. "Our parade was we drove home after that."

Players received no rings back then, and the players' lack of what Lindsay considered a fair financial reward became a major source of tension between Lindsay and the team.

"When we won the league championship we got $1,000," Lindsay says matter-of-factly. "When you won in the first round, you were supposed to get $1,000 and $500 if you lost, and when you won the Stanley Cup you were supposed to get $1,000. We should have gotten at least $3,000. When I went to school that's how the math added up. But when we got our checks they would be $2,365—not after taxes, before taxes. I could never find out where the other $700 or so went. That was one of my gripes that forced me to start up the players association. I didn't want people like Adams to control our money."

The Red Wings would eventually end up trading Lindsay, primarily because of his union activism.

Lindsay seemed to be at odds with Jack Adams, even when the Red Wings were winning. "When the Red Wings won, Jack Adams would say we won," Lindsay said, chuckling. "When we didn't, he would say, "It was you guys who lost it."

# Max McNab

*Detroit Red Wings, 1949–50*

Max McNab can be forgiven for believing that his job security on the Detroit Red Wings always boiled down to how ornery general manager Jack Adams was feeling on any particular day.

With World War II taking two years out of his career, McNab had only played about twenty junior games and part of one season with the Omaha Knights in the United States Hockey League before he was called up by the Detroit Red Wings in 1947. He was a lanky and raw twenty-three-year-old when he played his first game at Olympia Stadium. "I wasn't a guy who played with tremendous confidence," he admits now.

It certainly didn't bolster his confidence that Adams always threatened his players with a demotion after a loss. In 1950, McNab can remember Adams bellowing, "Those kids in Oshawa, [Alex] Delvecchio and [Lou] Jankowski, are going great in Oshawa. Gawd damn it, they are going to be ready. They are burning up the OHA."

McNab was a role player for the Red Wings in that era, and lasted parts of four seasons. He killed penalties with Marty Pavelich, and served as the understudy for Hall of Fame center Sid Abel who was the center on the famed Production Line. By 1950, Abel was a thirty-two-year-old playing on a line with a twenty-five-year-old and a twenty-two-year-old.

Ted Lindsay and Gordie Howe were such finely honed physical specimens that they could play ninety seconds without losing their wind. Abel would play more than a minute. "Then I would clean up the last twenty or twenty-five seconds," McNab remembered. "I would watch the puck cross in front of my nose between Lindsay and Howe. "

He learned from watching Abel. "Sid never blew his own horn, but he always knew everything that was going on out on the ice. He took those two kids Howe and Lindsay and made them a unit. Sid really couldn't skate with those guys, but he was an engineer. He knew where to go and how to get there. He directed traffic."

With only six teams in the NHL and a host of talented players in the junior and minor leagues, it didn't take McNab long to decide that playing in the league was a privilege. "There were five regular superstars on every team who were irreplaceable," McNab recalled. "The rest of the roster spots went to whoever worked the hardest."

That's why a half century later McNab still feels honored to have played for the Red Wings when they won the 1950 Stanley Cup championship.

"When you are playing you really don't understand the impact nationwide," McNab said. "All the people in my hometown of Watson, Saskatchewan, never slept because they got the game on the radio. But I remember the night we won the Cup it was like a crazy dream."

He recalls the party at the Book Cadillac, including odd details like the fact that the beer drinking hockey players arrived to find that only champagne was available to drink. "Everyone was totally fatigued and we were dehydrated," McNab remembered, chuckling. "You couldn't quench your thirst. Guys were popping champagne. Guys got horribly sick. It was an awful night."

But he makes it clear that it was really a wondrous evening. He remembers Red Wings scout Carson Cooper sitting at the head of the table poking fun at players who started to show signs of inebriation. "He was joking that the young guys didn't know how to drink," McNab said. "He sat there for a long time and never got up. When he did get up, he just hit the deck. He was out like a light."

As players said goodbye at the "break up party" a couple days later, McNab said it was a very emotional parting. As a fringe player, McNab had taught himself never "to look beyond the next week when I was with the big club." He certainly knew it was possible that he might not be back in the NHL, but he probably wouldn't have guessed that he would never play another regular-season game in an NHL uniform.

"It's like being in the service," McNab said. "You get close, and then you say goodbye and there are some tears. And everyone says there's going to be reunions and people are going to keep in touch forever. Everyone is going to write. Then everyone gets dispersed all over the country and everyone gets caught up in their own problems. That's the same with a hockey break up party. For the stars it was like another day at the office. Most of us left there not knowing what the future would hold for us.

The following season Glen Skov won the job that McNab had owned; McNab was demoted to the American Hockey League where he spent the entire season. He did get into two playoff games with the big club. A back injury dashed his hopes of joining the Chicago Black Hawks the following season and he ended up spending the rest of his career as a star in the Western Hockey League. He didn't get back to the NHL until he became general manager of the Washington Capitals. He also later served as general manager of the New Jersey Devils.

McNab was earning about $6,000 a season during his NHL career and his playoff share in 1950 was about half that. In that era, players didn't get a championship ring.

In 1983, his two young granddaughters, Shanon and Robyn, brought him a present from his family. He opened it up and it was an NHL championship ring. His son David (now Anaheim's assistant general manager) had come up with the idea and convinced family members to participate. David had gotten the NHL's cooperation to make sure the ring was like today's championship ring. It included the scores from the 1950 championship games. "It brought tears to my eyes," McNab said.

Shortly thereafter he ran into Tommy Ivan, who had been coach of that team. "My, that's a fantastic ring," Ivan said. "Is it your college ring?"

Impishness took over. "No, it's my Red Wings' championship ring," McNab said. "Didn't you get one?"

# Gordie Howe

*Detroit Red Wings, 1949–50, 1951–52, 1953–54, and 1954–55*

After Gordie Howe's mother and father died, he told his sister repeatedly that he didn't want anything from the old Howe homestead in Saskatchewan.

"I said take anything you want," Howe said, smiling at the memory. "She came up to me with this old flower pot and said you might want this. I said, 'Read my lips. I don't want anything.'"

Howe's sister turned over the flowerpot to show him the inscription. It read: "Stanley Cup champion, 1951–52."

"I changed my mind," Howe remembers saying sheepishly. "I will take that."

To the best of Howe's recollections that was the only keepsake "Mr. Hockey" received for winning any of his four Stanley Cup championships. He remembers giving it to his mother because a young bachelor didn't have much use for a flowerpot, regardless of its inscription.

Winning the Cup in the 1950s was far different than it is today. The playoff intensity was similar. The passion was similar, the pride was similar. But the celebration time was shorter, says Howe. It lasted a night or two at best. When the Red Wings won in 1952, Howe was anxious to get out of town because in the summer he played semi-pro baseball in Saskatchewan. His baseball team paid him more per game than the Red Wings did. He played first base and third base.

"Remember we had to work in the summer. It cost us money to play for the Stanley Cup because we had to pay another month's rent."

— *Gordie Howe*

After Howe was married, he remembers packing up the car quickly and heading off to Florida. "Remember we had to work in the summer," Howe said. "It cost us money to play for the Stanley Cup because we had to pay another month's rent."

Howe would attend the Red Wings' season-ending celebrations, although he confesses he didn't much like them for a couple of reasons.

"When you were there, you realized that some of the guys wouldn't be around the following season," Howe said. "It was sad."

He was convinced that All-Star defenseman Bill Quackenbush was traded before the 1950 championship season because of something he said at the 1949 season-ending party. "You shouldn't mix management with the players like that," Howe said. "Players are drinking, having fun, and getting a little cocky. They say things they shouldn't."

Goaltender Terry Sawchuk, who won three Stanley Cups with Howe (1952, 1954, and 1955), was always a candidate to say something he shouldn't. Sometimes Sawchuk came across as not being happy to hang out with his teammates. But Howe said Sawchuk was often misunderstood.

"He didn't like crowds, and this is a bad game to play if you don't like crowds," Howe said. "He would be at our gatherings but he would be in the background."

Sawchuk had a temper, but Howe said he got along with him better than most people did. They had one confrontation away from the rink. "He got mad at me and I told him to back off," Howe remembered. "I said I will get ten shots on you tomorrow in practice, and I can probably hit you between the eyes at least once. He moved on to another table."

The next day in practice Howe sent his first shot whizzing over his head. Sawchuk came out with his own personal brand of apologies. "He said he had too much to drink," Howe remembered. "I told him: 'Then don't have so much to drink.'"

Sawchuk's moodiness could be heightened during the playoffs. He would treat autograph seekers with disdain, even children. Howe remembered that other Detroit players would go over and make some excuse to the fan. Howe remembers one story in particular that sums up how Sawchuk perceived the world. While the Red Wings were in an airport, Sawchuk saw singer Nat King Cole. "He said 'That's one of my favorite singers,'" Howe recalled. "I told him to go get his autograph, or he would be kicking himself if he didn't do it."

Cole dutifully put down his bag and signed his name. But he really just looked straight ahead and didn't acknowledge Sawchuk's presence. Sawchuk tore up the autograph and said, "If that's how you feel about it, I don't even want it."

Sawchuk's volatility was another reason why a championship celebration was also a cause for Howe to be on guard.

Howe never gave too much thought to the fact that he wasn't showered with mementos when he won his Stanley Cup championships. But family members must have sensed that Howe regretted that he never received a championship ring. When son Mark was playing for the Philadelphia Flyers in the mid-1980s, he said frequently that if he won a Stanley Cup he was going to order a ring for his father. The late Tommy Ivan, Gordie Howe's second NHL coach, saw Mark Howe being interviewed. When he mentioned the possibility of getting his father a ring, Ivan decided to take action. Ivan, then working for the Chicago Black Hawks, was quite close to Howe.

"He [Ivan] did things that were disturbing, like pulling me out of the game," Howe said.

Early in his career he remembers he got into a scrap on the ice and when he came to the bench Ivan quizzed him about the encounter.

"Don't you like that guy?" Ivan asked.

"I don't like anyone out there," Howe replied.

After his career, he asked Ivan whether he had appreciated that answer. "You played all the time, didn't you?" Ivan said.

Says Howe, "I think he thought I came of age then."

What Howe didn't know was that after Ivan saw McNab's ring he vowed to have one made for himself, and "one for the man who made me a lot of money."

That was Gordie Howe.

A box showed up at the Hartford Whalers' office where Howe was still working in the 1980s. Whalers' general manager Emile Francis brought it to Howe, and both were stunned by its magnificence.

Said Howe as he tried it on: "I think he likes me."

"No," said Francis. "He's in love."

Howe is proud of his accomplishments, but it was the accomplishments of another Howe that gave him the most joy. Mark Howe never won a Stanley Cup in sixteen seasons as a NHL player. But he was a pro scout for the Detroit Red Wings when they won the Stanley Cup. "I was more excited to see Mark's name on the Cup than my own," Howe said.

# Marcel Pronovost

*Detroit Red Wings, 1949–50, 1951–52, 1953–54, and 1954–55*

*Toronto Maple Leafs, 1966–67*

Imagine what nineteen-year-old Detroit Red Wings defenseman Marcel Pronovost must have been feeling and thinking in 1950 when hockey's gladiator, "Black Jack" Stewart, came into the dressing room breathing fire at his teammates.

"If I have to hit players on both teams, I will," Stewart said. "You are going to play better or you will have to face me."

Defenseman Stewart called that meeting after the Red Wings had fallen behind 3–2 in the best-of-seven final against the New York Rangers. Fifty years later Pronovost still remembers the Stewart firestorm as if it happened yesterday. Not even revered captain Sid Abel had immunity from Stewart's wrath. Pronovost's memory is clear on that.

"That bag of bones Don Raleigh is making an ass of you," Stewart barked at Abel. "Do something with him."

In Game 6, the Red Wings trailed early but came from behind to win 5–4 on the strength of Abel's two goals, including the game-winner at 10:34 of the third period.

"Black Jack was one tough son of a bitch," Pronovost said. "He had a bad back, and we had the real hot liniment back then that he splashed on like it was aftershave."

Pronovost's memories of his Stanley Cup championships are rooted more in the camaraderie players shared in the battle than the beers they shared afterward. "I know I was on cloud nine when I won my first one," Pronovost said. "But what I tell everyone is that every Cup was special for different reasons."

After winning his first Cup at a tender age, Pronovost discovered all of his championships would be unique. He views them like a parent views his or her children, each one deemed special for a different reason.

1949–50: Winning at such a young age was a remarkable achievement, given that it was rare for young players to even make the NHL unless they were budding superstars. Pronovost got called up from Omaha after the regular season, meaning he made his NHL debut in the postseason.

1951–52: The Red Wings won eight consecutive playoff games to claim the Cup, with goaltender Terry Sawchuk giving up just five goals. Sawchuk gave up just two goals in the final, and none at home. "They called us Terry and the Pirates," Pronovost said.

1953–54: Tony Leswick scores a memorable overtime goal to give the Red Wings a 2–1 win against Montreal in Game 7.

1954–55: The Red Wings were three points back with ten games to go and passed the Montreal Canadiens in the stretch run. That year was memorable because of the Rocket Richard riot. The Red Wings were leading 4–1 in the Montreal Forum when rioting began (because of the fans' anger over Richard being suspended for the remainder of the 1955 season). That game was awarded to Detroit, and they won the next game against the Canadiens to win the regular-season championship by two points (95–93). They won the final in seven games.

1966–67: The Maple Leafs were a third place club when they captured the Cup in 1967. "We were a club going nowhere that year," Pronovost said. "King Clancy came in and coached a while. And we had a good group of veterans and some good kids. If you remember that was the year of Expo 67 in Montreal. They were going to put the Stanley Cup in the Quebec Pavilion. We made them put it in the Ontario Pavilion."

Pronovost understood the Stanley Cup's lure before he played for it. He was brought into the Detroit organization at age sixteen (he used to say he was "raised by Detroit") and actually was brought in to travel with the team in the playoffs the year before he was called up. He possesses vivid memories about all of Detroit's players in that era, particularly the late Sawchuk, whom he considered to be misunderstood.

"He was a real competitor," Pronovost said. "A lot of people had the wrong impression of Terry. He didn't like the limelight. In order to get rid of the limelight he got rude. But not to kids, he really loved kids."

Pronovost remembers one night in Toronto when one of his shots rose up just above the short glass and broke a youngster's nose. "They brought that kid into the dressing room after the game and Sawchuk grabbed his goalie stick and handed it to me and told me to give it to the kid," Pronovost said. "But he said, 'Don't tell anyone that I gave it you.'"

Although Stewart's tongue-lashing is prominent in Pronovost's collection of Cup memories, Stewart isn't on Pronovost's list of the toughest Stanley Cup competitors he knew.

"Ted Lindsay and Rocket Richard epitomized the desire to win," Pronovost said. "Of the people I see play today there is no one like them."

# Red Kelly

*Detroit Red Wings, 1949–50, 1952–53, 1953–54, and 1954–55*

*Toronto Maple Leafs, 1961–62, 1962–63, 1963–64, and 1966–67*

Hall of Famer Red Kelly doesn't mind letting the world in on a Kelly family inside joke connected with one of his championship celebrations with the revered Stanley Cup.

In 1964 Kelly was playing for the Toronto Maple Leafs and sitting as a member of the Canadian Parliament. The Maple Leafs defeated the Detroit Red Wings 4–0 in Game 7 of the Stanley Cup finals, and Kelly had to be carried out of the dressing room after passing out from pain. He had suffered a knee injury in Game 6 when he was crunched simultaneously by Gordie Howe and Bill Gadsby. The injured knee had been frozen to allow Kelly to play in Game 6, but the novocaine had long since worn off. He was standing in the shower when the pain just overwhelmed him. Goaltender Johnny Bower helped carry him out. To add further complication to his life, he had to fly to Ottawa by 2:00 A.M. the next day to fulfill legislative duties. He got some crutches at the hospital and did his civic duty.

*The Toronto Maple Leafs, with goaltender Johnny Bower to the left of the Cup, celebrate their 1967 Stanley Cup championship.*

"I never got a chance to celebrate," Kelly recalls. "At the time, [owner] Harold Ballard was a neighbor. I don't know what other owner would have thought of this. He was a strange character in many ways. But when I got back, he brought the Cup to the house with two bottles of champagne."

> "He did the whole load in the Cup. He did everything. That's why our family laughs when we see the players drinking champagne out of the Cup."
>
> — Red Kelly

A central figure in the Kelly celebration that day was Red's newborn son Conn, whose name is the subject of another inside joke. Famed Maple Leafs general manager Conn Smythe assumed that the child had been named after him, and gave him stock shares of Canadian Pacific as a birth present. It wasn't until later that Kelly told Smythe that Conn had actually been named after the first king of Ireland, who had been credited with winning more than one hundred battles. "I told Conn Smythe the story of the king and how the people he defeated often became his friends because he was actually a good leader," Kelly remembered. "He liked that story and began to tell people that's where he got his name even though I don't think he had ever heard that story before I told him."

Ballard never had a reputation for being overly generous with players ("You needed a magnifying glass to see the first diamond in our Stanley Cup rings," Kelly said.). But he apparently liked Kelly quite a bit because he went out of his way to make sure that Kelly's Cup celebration was special. He sent along a photographer so the Kelly family could have pictures of the event. Red put his three-month-old son Conn into the Cup for the picture and the infant chose that moment to relieve himself. "He did the whole load in the Cup,'" Kelly says, chuckling. "He did everything. That's why our family laughs when we see the players drinking champagne out of the Cup."

# Glenn Hall

*Chicago Black Hawks, 1960–61*

Glenn Hall remembers Noel Picard going around to all the expansion St. Louis Blues team members in 1967–68 and reminding them that their former teams had discarded them into the expansion pool.

"He was rabble rousing a little bit and he would yell, 'these are the teams that do not want you,'" Hall remembered.

Hall understood that sentiment, because in 1960–61 he led the Chicago Black Hawks to a Stanley Cup championship over the team that didn't want him. In 1957, Red Wings general manager Jack Adams peddled Hall and Ted

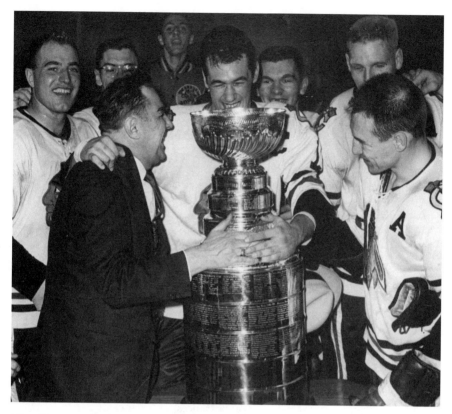

*The Chicago Black Hawks' Ed Litzenberger (center) accepts the Stanley Cup in 1961, with Randy Pilous (left) and Pierre Pilote (right) accompanying him. In the background is Al Arbour (wearing glasses); two decades later he would coach the four-time Stanley Cup winning New York Islanders.*

Lindsay to the Black Hawks for John Wilson, Forbes Kennedy, William Preston, and Hank Bassen. To appreciate what a slap that was, consider that Hall had led the NHL with thirty-eight wins the season before and the Red Wings had finished first overall. Just two seasons before, Hall had led the NHL with twelve shutouts. This wasn't just a hockey trade; it was an effort to punish Hall, and particularly Lindsay, who had stirred up players to form a Players Association. Before being traded, Hall remembers seeing a pension society report that showed that the Black Hawks had the NHL's smallest payroll at $156,000. The Montreal Canadiens were ranked first in payroll at about $300,000.

"I didn't like Jack Adams any more than he liked me so it was nice to get away from that situation," Hall said. "I always said my loyalty was with whoever was signing my paycheck."

That thought not withstanding, Hall admits there was a little more satisfaction in beating the Red Wings for the Stanley Cup in 1961. "It really didn't matter who we beat," Hall says, honestly. "But I suppose it's satisfying to beat the team that didn't want you."

The Hawks downed the Red Wings in six games with Hall playing terrifically in the 5–1 clincher in Game 6. It was a 2–1 game entering the third period. Bobby Hull, in his fourth NHL season, was the Black Hawks' big gun in the playoffs, leading all scorers with eight goals. "He was just starting to become explosive then," Hall said.

Hall remembers receiving a ring for the championship. "I don't know, but that might have been the beginning of the rings," Hall said. "I know the Maple Leafs got them for the Cups they won after that."

He recalls a parade "or at least they stopped traffic for us." He knows that the Black Hawks didn't open their vault to reward players for their championship performance.

"[Black Hawks player] Reg Fleming told me he asked for a raise, and they said, 'No,'" Hall recalled. "He said, 'But we won the Stanley Cup,' and they said, 'Oh, you've already been paid for that.'"

> "The best team will win the Stanley Cup. The goaltending needs to be good. But it's not always the best goaltender that wins the Stanley Cup."
>
> — Glen Hall

When Hall went home to Western Canada, local youth hockey groups wanted him to share his championship aura. He says he was more than happy to do it, and he turned down all offers of money from the youth organizations because the Black Hawks had a policy of giving players ten dollars for their public appearances, and ten cents per mile. During the spring and summer he accumulated about $250 worth of appearances. He turned his invoice in to the Hawks and much to his amazement they refused to pay.

"General manager Tommy [Ivan] said we didn't tell you to go," Hall remembered. "No they didn't, but that was the agreement. I said call to make sure I went. He said that wasn't the point. I said OK, but see if I ever represent the Black Hawks again. Even when you won the Stanley Cup back then, they would nickel-and-dime you. They weren't pouring a bunch of money out. Had things been a little fairer then, maybe they would be fairer now. Now it's too bad because it's gone the other way and the fans are getting stuck. It's the fan being kept out of the arena because of cost."

With Hull and Stan Mikita still young and Hall still in his prime, the Black Hawks believed that championship would be the first of several. But they lost in the final to Toronto the following year and haven't won since.

"Remember, Toronto had the best team defensively and that's how you win the Stanley Cup," Hall offers. "That's how you win any championship, whether it's football, baseball, basketball, or whatever. You win by defense. I believe the Edmonton Oilers [in the 1980s] were the only team to disprove that theory. They had the offense that could overcome their poor defense."

Considered one of the best goaltenders in NHL history, Hall believes goaltenders have always gotten too much credit for wins and too much blame for losses.

"You hear that the team with the best goaltending will win the Stanley Cup and I disagree totally," Hall says. "The best team will win the Stanley Cup. The goaltending needs to be good. But it's not always the best goaltender that wins the Stanley Cup."

The fact that Hall only won one Stanley Cup supports that contention.

# Stan Mikita

*Chicago Black Hawks, 1960–61*

Officially, the Chicago Black Hawks won the 1961 Stanley Cup in Detroit with a 5–1 thumping of the Red Wings in Game 6. However, Stan Mikita would argue that the Black Hawks' only championship in the last sixty years was probably won two weeks earlier when Chicago defeated Montreal in the semifinal.

"The Detroit series was anticlimatic as far as we were concerned," Mikita remembered. "We had to play them, and they had some great hockey players. But we didn't think that beating that team was as big a deal as it was beating the Montreal Canadiens."

Mikita's memory speaks to the notion of how awestruck the hockey world was of the Canadiens' championship aura. Remember, the Canadiens had won five consecutive titles coming into that season and beating them in Montreal was like breaking into the palace and stealing the king's nightshirt. The Hawks had finished seventeen points behind the regular-season champion Canadiens that season.

Many consider the Montreal-Chicago 1961 semifinal as one of the real classics with a triple-overtime game won on Murray Balfour's goal in Game 3 and Glenn Hall posting back-to-back shutouts in the final two games of the series. With Jean Beliveau and Henri Richard leading the way, the Canadiens' offensive output was far superior to every other team of that era. "What really impressed me was the play of Glenn Hall in the playoffs," Mikita said. "The way he played in that series, we felt this could go on for quite a while."

Of course the Black Hawks haven't won since. Perhaps an omen of that came the night they won in Detroit but were then snowed in and couldn't fly out. They were stuck in the airport for two hours and then finally went back to the hotel, where they celebrated. But the delay in returning home took some steam out of the city's celebration.

"We had a little victory parade and I think we rode on fire trucks," Mikita said. "But what I really remember was that we weren't prepared for the weather and we froze our asses off in the parade. You have to remember the Stanley Cup used to get over in April, not June, back then and it was very cold that day."

But whether the celebration was large or small didn't change how players felt about the accomplishment, says Mikita. "Maybe winning the Cup meant even more back then," Mikita said, "because there wasn't as much moving players around back then. There was more loyalty from the players to management and management to players back then."

# Johnny Bower

*Toronto Maple Leafs, 1961–62, 1962–63, 1963–64, and 1966–67*

When Maple Leafs goalkeeper Johnny Bower walked into Maple Leaf Gardens for practice for Game 6 of the 1967 Cup final, he spied two armed guards posted at the dressing room door.

"I thought there had been a shooting or something," Bower remembered.

But when the guards waved him into the room, instead of a crime scene what he saw was a table in the middle of the room covered with cash. It looked as if someone was in the midst of counting the loot from a successful bank heist. Stacks of every denomination were present, including $100 bills.

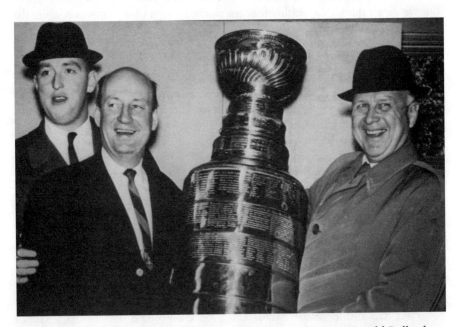

*Toronto Maple Leafs coach Punch Imlach (center) and owner Harold Ballard (right) were two of the most colorful figures in the NHL during the original six-team era.*

According to Bower, when coach Punch Imlach came into the dressing room, he said, "That's $10,000 there and that's how much money you can make if we win the Stanley Cup."

Bower said "I headed for that table and I was ready to take that money. If Punch thought it would get us excited, it worked."

Few players appreciate the trappings of Stanley Cup lore more than Bower. Having earned a "second chance" at the NHL at age thirty-four, Bower didn't put on a Maple Leafs' uniform with illusions of becoming a four-time NHL champion and a member of the Hall of Fame. He hadn't even been sure he wanted to leave the Cleveland team in the American Hockey League when the Maple Leafs selected him in the interleague draft . After failing to stick during an NHL trial with the New York Rangers in the mid-'50s, Bower had settled in Cleveland. The hockey was good in the American League and the fringe benefits were better. Especially after he hit age thirty, Bower was very realistic about his chances of playing in the NHL.

"There were very good players in the minor leagues," Bower said. "But there were only six teams, and they carried one goalie. How was I going to beat out [Turk] Broda, or Charlie Raynor, or Bill Durnan? I had to wait until they got old. But I got old too."

When the Maple Leafs summoned Bower in 1958, he had thirteen years of service in the minor leagues.

"When I heard about it, I said I don't know if I can help Toronto or not," Bower remembered. "They [Cleveland management] told me if you don't go, they will suspend you. I didn't want to be suspended. So they put in my contract that if I didn't make the National Hockey League, I could come back to Cleveland. That was what I wanted."

Reasonably sure he would return to Cleveland, Bower went to Toronto without grand expectations. "They only wanted me a couple of years at best because they were developing some young goaltenders," Bower recalled. "Gerry Cheevers was there. And I was going to be their goaltending assistant. But I fooled them. I was thinking Punch has a pretty good hockey team here, and I'm not going to give this up."

With Bower in goal, the Maple Leafs won three consecutive Stanley Cup championships from 1962 to 1964 and Bower's goals-against averages in those postseason runs were 2.28, 1.60, and 2.12.

He says the 1962 title was the sweetest because "having my name on the Stanley Cup was my dream, and I never thought it would happen."

To play hockey for the Maple Leafs in that era was an honor that is difficult to describe, Bower insists. The thrill of Toronto winning the Cup for three consecutive seasons was almost matched by the thrill of Montreal not winning the Stanley Cup in those years. "We were as big as the Montreal Canadiens," Bower said. "I didn't know when I first got to Toronto what a rivalry the Maple Leafs had with Montreal. The Canadiens had won more Stanley Cups than Toronto and the Maple Leafs' fans were getting pretty perturbed. [President] Conn Smythe hated to lose."

That may be why the Leafs' 1966–67 championship also has a special place in Bower's memory. The Maple Leafs defeated the Canadiens in six games to win that crown. Bower (teamed with Terry Sawchuk in goal that season) played four games in the Stanley Cup final and posted a 1.94 goals-against average.

That 1966–67 Toronto team had only finished five games above .500, and seemed to struggle at times. Bower remembered the team being a mixture of older and younger players. "We had quite a few meetings," Bower said. "George Armstrong would say to me, 'What's going on with your goaltending?' I would tell him, 'I'm fighting the puck,' or 'I've lost my angles,' or 'I am giving up stupid short-side goals,' or 'I'm in a slump. But I'm working on my negatives.' Then George would go to Allan Stanley and Tim Horton, and everyone would get it off their chest. Then we would go out and have a couple of good practices and we would start to play well again."

What Bower remembers most about the postchampionship celebration was the parade down Yonge Street, in particular all the banners and pennants that flew from the buildings along the route. "I'm glad I didn't have the job of picking up all the papers that were thrown down during that," Bower recalled. "When you win the Stanley Cup, your whole body just goes numb from the excitement. It really is hard to explain."

When the Maple Leafs won the 1961–62 Stanley Cup, owner Harold Ballard had championship rings made for team members. When the Maple Leafs won again in 1962–63, he recalled all the rings.

"I wondered what the heck was going on," Bower said. "What he did was he had the diamond removed and put a larger diamond in. And he said when we won again, he would take the diamond out again and put in a little larger one."

Ballard had a reputation for being a skinflint at worst, and a man who was tight with his money at best. When the Leafs won again in 1963–64, Bower dutifully turned in his ring and when he got it back he turned to Armstrong and said: "I could swear this diamond is getting smaller."

Armstrong laughingly suggested that Bower should go tell Ballard that.

"No, no, you are the captain," Bower insisted. "You go tell him, and don't mention my name."

# Doug Risebrough

*Montreal Canadiens, 1975–76, 1976–77, 1977–78, and 1978–79*

*Assistant Coach, Calgary Flames, 1988–89*

Legendary coach Toe Blake retired after the 1967–68 season, but he shared in the Montreal Canadiens' postseason successes into the 1970s.

Doug Risebrough says a big part of the Canadiens' 1970s Cup celebrations was the ritual of taking the Stanley Cup to the Toe Blake Tavern the day after it had been reclaimed. Blake had won eight Stanley Cup championships as coach of the Canadiens, and players honored his success by bringing him the Cup first. It was like schoolboys showing off their accomplishments to their favorite teacher.

"He had a back room that was full of old hockey pictures," Risebrough remembered. "We would get there around noon, even if we had been up half the night celebrating. Toe would be sitting at a table or desk and we would talk hockey, laugh, joke, discuss the playoffs for three, four, five, six hours. Toe could reflect back on eight Stanley Cups. There was always a great reflection upon the history of the team. Toe would laugh, 'I can tell you another story about that.' And he would."

Everyone came to Toe's Tavern for a bonding session that none of them has ever forgotten. It was in Toe's Tavern that players truly understood what it meant to be a member of the Canadiens' grand tradition. It was in the tavern that the past was brought together with the present. It was in that tavern that the Stanley Cup took on an even greater meaning, if that was even possible.

After spending the afternoon at Toe's Tavern, the party was shifted to Henri Richard's bar. "If anyone had Cup stories to tell, it was Henri," Risebrough says. "He won eleven of them."

A five-time winner himself, Risebrough found that his awareness of the experience grew each time he added another title. "After you have won the Cup a couple of times, you start to feel more happy for everyone who can share it with you," he says. "Your family, who watched you grow up in hockey, your neighbors, the people around the rink. The Cup is something that glues people together. You just can't believe how much a championship cements your relationship with the guys."

> "The Cup is something that glues people together. You just can't believe how much a championship cements your relationship with the guys."
>
> — *Doug Risebrough*

It would be difficult for Risebrough to say that he enjoyed one Stanley Cup experience more than another, although he will say that serving as an assistant coach for the Calgary Flames in their championship run in 1989 wasn't the same as winning the Cup as a player.

"I couldn't believe the satisfaction of being involved in a Cup as a member of the management of the team," Risebrough said. "There weren't many of us in Calgary who had the experience of winning before. We were trying to tell people what it was like to be a first-time winner. I can remember people saying to me that it was exactly as I had described it to them. As a player, you are thinking if I do my job, I will be fine. But when you are in coaching, you are trying to work through people. You are trying to motivate people in tough times. You are hard on people in tough times. You are trying to instill confidence in some who don't have confidence. Like I say, I couldn't believe the satisfaction I got from that."

# Jean Beliveau

*Montreal Canadiens, 1955–56, 1956–57, 1957–58, 1958–59, 1959–60, 1964–65, 1965–66, 1967–68, 1968–69, and 1970–71*

Jean Beliveau's parting gift to hockey in 1971 was the launch of a grand tradition that more than likely will be among the Stanley Cup's most sacred rituals through this millennium and beyond.

Le Gros Bill, as French Canadian fans knew him, is clearly one of the most beloved players in hockey history. He is remembered as one of the NHL's most elegant athletes, a 6'4" center who played his position with a curious blend of grace, dignity, and dominance. It's almost fitting that it is Beliveau who is credited with beginning the tradition of the team captain skating around the rink with the Cup raised above his head and teammates following behind in an informal parade line.

One irony of the moment was that it came in Chicago Stadium, not in the Montreal Forum. The Canadiens had just defeated the Black Hawks 3–2 in Game 7 to win the Cup when Beliveau unexpectedly began what could be called his "farewell tour" around the ice.

"Why did I do it?" Beliveau asks rhetorically. "What comes to mind today is that I just wanted to bring the Cup closer to the fans."

As Beliveau, then forty, circled the ice, he knew this was to be his last NHL skate. At the end of the 1969–70 season he wanted to retire, but management had talked him out of it. However, he made it clear before the 1971 playoffs that there would be no change of heart. Beliveau admits that he felt a great sense of satisfaction that night in Chicago, not surprising considering that the Cup triumph was his tenth. In that playoff year he set an NHL record (since broken) of sixteen assists in postseason play. He is tied for second place on the all-time list with former teammate Yvon Cournoyer; they trail only Henri Richard, who has eleven Stanley Cup victories. When Beliveau stepped off the ice that night, he held the NHL record of ninety-seven postseason assists and 176 postseason points.

"Maybe there was some connection to my [pending] retirement when I did what I did," Beliveau said. "But really I think it was a spur of the moment thing. It was just a natural reaction and I wanted everyone to enjoy the Cup."

Beliveau wanted the fans, even the rival Chicago Black Hawks fans, to enjoy the trappings of winning the Stanley Cup as much as he always had. Beliveau, always stately in appearance and speech, waxes almost sentimental about the grand Stanley Cup championship receptions at the Queen Elizabeth Hotel. "They invited all of the Canadiens' employees, the secretaries, all the people behind the scenes."

His other fond memories of that storied era in Canadiens' history was Montreal mayor Jean Drapeau insisting that the Canadiens' triumph should be celebrated each time with a parade to city hall. "Sometimes on those parades up St.

*Montreal Canadiens great Jean Beliveau in a postvictory parade.*

Catharine Street we would barely be able to move because there were so many people."

Today Beliveau admits he enjoys watching the on-ice Stanley Cup victory celebrations because many memories flood into his mind. He says his first Stanley Cup in 1956 is probably his favorite because he reached the final in each of his first two playoffs in 1954 and 1955 only to lose to the Gordie Howe–led Detroit Red Wings.

"When you are a little boy growing up in French Quebec your first goal is to play with the Canadiens," Beliveau said. "Secondly, you want to be on a Stanley Cup championship team. To finally win one after coming close the first two years made it more special."

Beliveau pauses as if he is searching for the right words. "When I look at some of the great players like Ray Bourque, Jean Ratelle, Rod Gilbert, who have never won a Cup, and Bill Gadsby played twenty years without winning one I just feel fortunate to have joined the Canadiens at the right time."

His decision to carry the Stanley Cup around the ice was perhaps the best possible illustration that Beliveau understood the relationship between fans and their teams.

"Quebec fans identified themselves with the Canadiens," Beliveau said. "When you have great success, it makes it their success."

# John Ferguson

*Montreal Canadiens, 1964–65, 1965–66, 1967–68, 1968–69, and 1970–71*

John Ferguson enjoyed a sporting moment that only Jimmy Brown, Michael Jordan, and a few others can truly understand.

"I went out on top," Ferguson said.

Ferguson might be the only player in NHL history who retired literally minutes after winning the Stanley Cup championship. Amid all the hugs and back-slapping in the visitor's dressing room after a dramatic Game 7 win in Chicago Stadium in 1971, he told teammates Yvon Cournoyer and Ralph Backstrom that he was becoming a civilian at age thirty-two. He made it official by giving his skates and sweater to a good friend named Shakie Louie, a horseplayer who was also buddies with Montreal's Serge Savard.

Revered by many as the top tough guy in NHL history, Ferguson had tried retiring the season before because he was making more money as a business-man than he was making in hockey. But he was talked into playing again twenty games into the 1970–71 season. Ferguson considered his fifth champi-onship his sweetest, maybe because no one expected the Canadiens to win that season or maybe because he knew when entering the playoffs that he planned to retire for good this time. He didn't score on his last shot a la Michael Jordan, but he did assist on a goal in Montreal's 4–3 victory in Game 6 of the series against the Black Hawks. He pro-duced ten points in eighteen games in the 1971 playoffs—the highest postseason production he ever had.

**"You got a few photo-graphs with the Cup in the dressing room and then you didn't see it again until next year."**

*— John Ferguson*

With five Stanley Cup champi-onships to his credit, Ferguson's celebra-tion memories have been melded together over time. He remembers one year going to Bernie "Boom Boom" Geoffrion's restaurant for a celebration that lasted until daylight. "We also had a ritual of visiting Toe Blake's tavern on St. Catharine Street," Ferguson said. "It was always standard to spend the day after with Toe at the tavern."

"You got a few photographs with the Cup in the dressing room and then you didn't see it again until next year," Ferguson said. Ferguson's words speak to the confidence the Canadiens' players and management had in this era; they expected to see and win the Stanley Cup every year. Montreal players were Mon-treal's celebrity class. They moved about the city like they were royalty, particu-larly in the summers after winning the Cup. When the Stanley Cup ended up at city hall there was no need to give players a key to the city, because the door of every business was always open to a Canadiens player.

"The best way to say it is that I can still walk down the streets of Montreal [almost thirty years after his last championship] and people know who I am," Ferguson said. "We were the toast of the town."

One of Ferguson's memories of the final Cup win in Chicago was the excitement level of rookie Bobby Sheehan. The Canadiens' roster didn't turn over much in those days and most of the players were veterans of multiple championships. This was twenty-year-old Sheehan's first and only NHL crown.

"I think Bobby Sheehan was so happy, he missed the plane back from Chicago to Montreal," Ferguson joked. "He was very happy."

# Phil Esposito

*Boston Bruins, 1969–70 and 1971–72*

Seconds after Bobby Orr scored one of the most spectacular, graceful goals in NHL history, Boston Bruins teammate Phil Esposito enjoyed a klutzy moment that summed up the bedlam of the moment better than words ever could.

As a photographer was capturing the airborne Orr, frozen in time after netting the series-clinching overtime goal against the St. Louis Blues, the Bruins bolted from the bench like they had been sitting on an ejection seat. Esposito remembers that he was so excited that his leg caught on the top edge of the bench. "I felt flat on my head," he said, laughing.

Esposito didn't notice for several hours that he actually had a lump on his noggin from the mishap. Esposito was having too much fun to notice he had been wounded during the Bruins' charge to the ice, burying Orr in a pile of teammates. Ken Hodge kept picking up the 220–pound Esposito. "He wouldn't let me leave the ice," Esposito remembered. "He wouldn't leave me alone. It was just so exciting."

The pandemonium in the Boston Garden enveloped Esposito to the point that he remembers being happiest for John Bucyck, who had been with the Bruins since 1957 without winning until then, as well as for Ed Westfall and Ted Green, both of whom had been with the Bruins since the early 1960s.

When the Bruins finally made their way into the jammed dressing room, Esposito remembers that it seemed like a father and son banquet. His own father, Pat, was there, and he recalls the fathers of Fred Stanfield, Derek Sanderson, Bobby Orr, and Hodge being there as well. The players wanted to throw the parents into the showers. Bobby Orr's dad went willingly, Esposito recalls.

"But there wasn't anyone big enough to throw my dad into the shower," Esposito said, chuckling. "He said 'Don't even think about it.' But to be in there with my dad, talking to the players and their parents, that's my fondest memory."

The Bruins hadn't won a Stanley Cup since 1941, and the fans' uncorked enthusiasm poured freely over the Boston players.

The summerlong celebration in Boston seems a bit hazy to Esposito three decades later. "We had a lot of parties," Esposito said. "Sometimes they were two or three days. Sometimes they were four or five days. Sometimes they were a week. I remember waking up in Florida and not knowing how I got there. Eddie Johnston and Bobby Orr were with me."

After a night of revelry, some teammates brought him home just after dawn and essentially dumped him on his lawn. "I fell asleep," said Esposito, laughing at the memory. "The next thing I remember is the sprinkler system coming on around me."

Esposito wears his 1970 Stanley Cup championship ring and stores his 1972 ring. Originally Esposito had given one of his rings to his father. But days before the elder Esposito died in 1984 he summoned Phil for a chat. "Look, Phil," he said. "I want you to take the ring back when I die." Phil didn't want to talk about that, but his father insisted.

"I don't want to be in the casket with that ring," he said. "I'll take the All-Star watch with me because you have plenty of those."

Phil agreed he would take care of it.

At the funeral the family was the last to leave; the last thing Phil did before closing the casket was to slip the ring off his dad's finger. It was certainly one of the hardest things he ever had to do.

*The championship 1969–70 Boston Bruins team. In the center, wiping away a tear, is Ted Green, a defenseman who suffered a fractured skull in a preseason game and missed the entire season; his name was therefore not inscribed on the Cup along with the rest of his team.*

# Bobby Orr

*Boston Bruins, 1969–70 and 1971–72*

Bobby Orr's best moment with the Stanley Cup probably came twenty years after he actually won Lord Stanley's prize for the first time.

In 1990 the Bruins gathered for their twenty-year reunion and former Bruins player Ted Green, then an assistant coach with the Stanley Cup champion Edmonton Oilers, managed to convince the Oilers (and presumably the Hall of Fame) to allow him to bring Lord Stanley's chalice to the Bruins' party.

Most of the Bruins can barely remember having the Cup in 1970 because in that era it was whisked in and out of the city rather quickly. Most of the Bruins really never had an opportunity to inspect the Cup and stare at their names on it until that party.

To Orr, that reunion was special because it reminded him of how it took every last Bruins' player to win that first championship.

"When you look at teams that win championships it is the guys you don't hear much about that make a real difference," Orr says. "There are always MVPs that you don't expect. Every team has guys that you know what they are going to do. You could look at our team and expect certain performances out of guys like Esposito or [Gerry] Cheevers and I guess myself. But the other team always has their stars. You also know what to expect from them. That's why it's the guys you don't always read about that become the key guys. We had guys like Derek Sanderson, Eddie Westfall, Wayne Carleton, and Ace Bailey. And Dallas Smith and Don Awrey played solid for us on defense. These guys all played the best hockey of their careers."

> "The parents were more excited than the players, for God's sake."
>
> — *Bobby Orr*

Orr doesn't remember much about the on or off-ice celebration, particularly at the moment he was buried by teammates after netting the series-clinching goal. That tally now lives on in perpetuity thanks to the famous photo of Orr flying through the air, parallel to the ice, after scoring against Blues' netminder Glenn Hall. Orr had no understanding of how magnificent that goal was when he was in the midst of scoring it. This is how Orr described it: "The puck came off the board. I went in to try to cue it in. I knocked it back in the corner to Derek Sanderson. I went to the front of the net. He gave me a perfect pass. I was really just trying to get it on net. As I was moving across and as I shot it towards the net and I was moving across, Glenn Hall, the goalie for St. Louis at that time, had to move with me. As he moved across, his legs opened. Now, I would like to say that I turned it up on its edge, I saw his legs open, and I shot it. That's not how it happened at all, guys. I put it on net and I was lucky. He opened his legs because he had to move across with me a little bit, and it went between his legs.

How did he become airborne? "I jumped and Noel Picard, the St. Louis defenseman, helped a little bit with a stick under one of my legs, and he lifted me up out of frustration. But most of it was a jump for me, because I looked back over my shoulder and saw it going in."

Orr recalls his father, Doug, being there that night, along with the fathers of the other players. "The parents were more excited than the players, for God's sake," Orr says, laughing.

He adds another element to the famous story of John McKenzie pouring the beer over Mayor Kevin White. "As I recall the next time we won [in 1972] he poured one on Johnny," Orr said.

It is the fun-loving nature of the Bruins that Orr remembers. That's why the reunion was so special. Says Orr, laughing, "The guys hadn't changed much except they were a lot quieter."

# Harry Sinden

*Coach, Boston Bruins, 1969–70*

Harry Sinden had one of the best seats in the Boston Garden for Bobby Orr's dramatic, series-clinching goal in 1970, but he wasn't watching.

"My eyes were looking around to make sure that everyone else was in the right place," Sinden says, laughing. "Remember Bobby came in from the point and Eddie Westfall came back to cover up for him. I was coaching as Bobby was scoring because it was overtime and I wanted to know Westfall was back there."

When the Bruins won that day, it was the franchise's first Stanley Cup championship in twenty-nine years. It was also Mother's Day.

"I remember telling everyone to thank their mothers for their first pair of skates because look what it led to," Sinden recalled.

Sinden's memories of the Cup celebration are of the parade and the overflowing crowd that was present on that hot day in May. The players were transported in convertibles but since the streets are so narrow and there were so many people there, no one could move. Cars overheated and the Bruins had to walk back to the Boston Garden.

"On the way back a couple of our guys got into a fight," Sinden says, chuckling "I think it was Wayne Carleton and Ace Bailey."

That wasn't uncharacteristic for this team. Not to suggest that the Bruins didn't get along, but this roster was highlighted by passionate, talented, and colorful characters who all had a penchant for outlandish behavior.

Sinden certainly wasn't shocked when John "Pie" McKenzie doused the mayor with beer during his speech on the wonders of the Bruins' team.

"He kept saying all these nice things about us and McKenzie poured it right on him," Sinden said. "He kept talking. He didn't care."

This was Bobby Orr's team; his electrifying talent fueled it. Phil Esposito was a close second to him in terms of impact. But Sinden views Derek Sanderson as one of the unsung heroes of this championship team.

"I think Sanderson got a lot of notoriety off the ice, but he was a tremendous hockey player," Sinden recalled. "He was often overlooked because we had Orr, Esposito, and Gerry Cheevers [in goal]. And we had Ken Hodge scoring goals. But behind Orr and Esposito, Sanderson was probably our best player."

Sanderson's strong play on the ice was often overlooked because of his wild behavior off the ice. He was hockey's playboy, his long flowing hair a calling card that was perhaps the symbol of his free spirit.

"Most of that BS was promoted by Derek himself," Sinden said. "When he first came to the Bruins he was a saint. He became a bit of a cult figure in town and tried to take advantage of it. I don't think he was nearly as bad as he wants to believe he was."

Sanderson was hockey's Joe Namath. In fact, he actually became Namath's partner in a Bachelor's III club in Boston, modeled after Bachelor's III in New York.

"I'm sure Derek did some wild things," Sinden said. "But on the ice he could play the game."

One thing that has been lost through the years because of all the publicity surrounding the photo of Orr soaring through the air is the fact that there was no drama associated with that goal. The Bruins swept the St. Louis Blues and clearly were the best team in the game.

"Even Cheevers says he was just prolonging the suspense," Sinden says. "There was never any doubt we were going to win that series."

# Derek Sanderson

*Boston Bruins, 1969–70 and 1971–72*

The late Harold Sanderson earned about $22 take-home pay per week in the late 1950s when his son, Derek, came in and asked for a pair of Tack skates that retailed for $116.

"They were state of the art at that time," Derek Sanderson recalls. "They had kangaroo leather back then. That was before it was banned. They were the best. If you wore Tacks you were a player."

The Sanderson household wasn't flush with cash, but Harold Sanderson carefully pondered his son's request. He certainly knew his son was a top player. The Bruins had given the Sandersons $100 to put him on their protected list at age eleven.

"I will give you the Tacks," Harold Sanderson told his son. "But you have to promise me that I get the ring when you win the Stanley Cup."

The promise was made and quickly forgotten until the Bruins were celebrating their Stanley Cup on the ice after finishing off the sweep of the St. Louis Blues. The fans were on the ice. Bodies were everywhere. It was a joyous riot of emotions and craziness. Derek Sanderson had to bully his way through fans just to get back to the dressing room. Slipping and sliding to maintain his balance, Derek caught a glimpse of a fan coming at him and lifted up his shoulder to protect himself. He caught the man squarely in the jaw and decked him.

"Remember the ring—the ring is mine," Harold Sanderson said, grinning as he looked up at his son.

> "The champagne part is all made up. It's sticky. It stings. It's a mess. Don't spray me with champagne."
>
> — *Derek Sanderson*

Sanderson laughs at the memory. "He never brought up that ring one time until the night we won the championship," Sanderson said.

When Sanderson remembers the 1970 and 1972 Stanley Cup championships, he focuses on the team's cohesiveness, bolstered by how much fun the Bruins had off the ice. He thinks the team would have had a long run of success had the Bruins not allowed coach Harry Sinden to walk away over $1,500. After coaching the Bruins to a championship in 1970, Sinden wanted a raise and didn't get it. He left to sell prefabricated housing.

"The day Harry retired, I said in the newspaper that it just cost us the Stanley Cup," Sanderson said.

The Bruins did not win in 1971 without Sinden. "Harry was the best coach I ever had," Sanderson said. "He just knew how to handle twenty very odd characters. He brought the best out of all of us. He handled the egos well. You got to remember in that day you had no assistants. You had one coach and a trainer. Harry did it all. He thought about the game around the clock and he got us thinking the same way. He was a master at controlling the players, but Bobby Orr controlled the room."

According to Sanderson, Orr's ability to inspire others to a higher performance has been overshadowed by his greatness as a player.

"If you weren't playing well, he would just stare at you," Sanderson said. "And you would think, 'Oh, oh.' If you didn't know how you were playing, you would look at Bobby. If he was looking at you, you were dead."

Sanderson views Orr as a man who puts loyalty at the top of his lists of desirable attributes in a friend.

"If you have done something that isn't classy, or something that wasn't the right thing to do or you have embarrassed a friend of his, he does not forget," Sanderson said. "He is extremely loyal and he expects others to be just as loyal."

Sanderson viewed Esposito "as a big happy bear."

"He loved life and he took a big bite out of it every day," Sanderson said. "He was extremely talented and a lot better defensively than anyone ever gave him credit for."

Sanderson's highlight of the 1970 Cup run was setting up Orr for the game-winner. "It was Bobby who led us to the championship," Sanderson said. "It was fitting that he scored the goal. No one ever resented Orr's success. I've seen superstars on other teams come and go and I've seen people talk about them. Often teammates try to get in a little snipe or a little rip. But Bobby was a leader and we never questioned it."

What Sanderson remembers about the play was that he was careful with the pass because if he missed Orr's stick "it would have been three-on-none going back the other way."

"There was no one behind Orr," Sanderson said. "It crossed my mind that Orr was taking a hell of a gamble. Bobby timed it and snapped it quickly. I saw it hit the mesh and I was kind of mesmerized by the label of the puck spinning and I thought, 'Holy shit, we just won the Cup.'"

Hustling over to his close friend Orr, he found him with his arms open. Sanderson jumped on him. "We just laughed," Sanderson said.

Sanderson doesn't think much about the hijinks that followed the Bruins' championships. "Celebrations are all very anticlimatic," Sanderson said. "I used to look around at the Super Bowl and World Series and the camera would always be on some jerk shaking up the champagne. The champagne part is all made up. It's sticky. It stings. It's a mess. Don't spray me with champagne. I don't want to hear about how you drank champagne. I always watched the guy in the background who is content, happy, and just smiling."

According to Sanderson, that's the face of a man who understands winning. "Winning is about delivering and not choking," Sanderson said. "When it's over there's an empty feeling."

He pauses. "Really it is all about the ring," he says. "Athletes make enough money. You play for the ring. That's not made up. You want the ring because not many people have won. That's what you play for."

Harold Sanderson was quite proud of the Stanley Cup rings his son gave him, although Derek was flabbergasted one year when he found out where his father was keeping them. He discovered the secret hiding spot when he took his girlfriend back home to meet his family. He wanted to show her the rings, and he asked his father to get them.

Moving back the couch, Harold Sanderson started playing with the hem of the living room curtains until he extracted the rings from a small pouch within that hem.

"What the hell are they doing there?" Derek asked his father.

"Well, I can't wear them because I didn't earn them," Harold said. "That would be a little pretentious. And I don't want anyone to steal them."

Harold Sanderson has since passed away and Derek has now given his sons, Michael and Ryan, his two rings. It was a highly meaningful gift to his children because Sanderson treasures those rings.

When he reviews his career Sanderson thinks it was a godsend that he gave his father those championship rings. Otherwise they might not have survived his party years. This was the 1970s and Sanderson was a symbol of the excesses of the decade. He stayed out too late, lived too hard, and found himself in situations that weren't in his best interest. He will be the first to admit that today. He went broke, even though he signed a big contract to jump to the World Hockey Association. (The Bruins' hope of a dynasty was killed by five key players defecting to the WHA, including Sanderson and Cheevers.) At the wildest point in his life, Sanderson owned a farm and had to use a Rolls Royce to transport hay because he was forced to sell his truck to pay bills. He lived on the edge in those days.

"If I had those rings during my crazier period," he says, "I might have sold them. I'm thankful I still have them."

# Terry Crisp

*Philadelphia Flyers, 1973-74 and 1974-75*

*Coach, Calgary Flames, 1988–89*

As bedlam engulfed the Spectrum after the Philadelphia Flyers defeated the Boston Bruins 1–0 to win the Stanley Cup, player Terry Crisp remembers that he had focus amid chaos. "I went behind the net and picked up the puck, and I still have it," Crisp says. "And even in the midst of that pandemonium I wanted to make eye contact with my mom and dad [Nibs and Toots Crisp] and my wife Sheila. Just to say it was all worth it."

Crisp, then thirty-one, probably appreciated the sweetness of the Cup as much as, if not more than, anyone in the Philadelphia uniform that afternoon. He was a journeyman player with his fourth organization; he was a role player, a checker, and a penalty killer who never lost sight of what he needed to do to stay in the game. He never scored more than thirteen goals in one season, and the ten he scored that season for the Flyers was the second–highest total of his career. He scored two goals that postseason; but one had been in Game 3 of the finals. The game was tied 1–1 when Crisp netted the go-ahead and eventual winning goal in a 4-1 win.

"When you are a fringe player and never know whether you are ever going to play in the NHL, and then to reach the pinnacle, I was ecstatic," Crisp said. "If nothing else ever happens good for you, you know you still have this."

What Crisp didn't know was that he would win another Cup as a member of the Philadelphia Flyers the following year and then come back in 1989 to win the Cup as coach of the Calgary Flames. He joined a select number of men such as Cy Denneny, Al Arbour, Art Ross, and Toe Blake, who won hockey's grand prize as both a player and a coach.

As a player, what Crisp remembers was the pure joy that was present in Philadelphia when the Flyers won the Cup. He remembers with great delight the fans pouring onto the ice and the mass of humanity that stood between him and the dressing room. It may have been as difficult to navigate through the crowd in the postgame celebration as it was for the Flyers to pick their way through the Bruins' strong defense. "There was no such thing as security when it was over," Crisp remembered.

Crisp's memories of his first Stanley Cup center on the length of the celebration. "Hell, we didn't go to bed for three days," he says, laughing. "I told my wife to put out some clean shirts and clothes and I will be in and out frequently. For the next three days, whenever you would get a call to go somewhere for a party, off you would go."

Fourteen years later, winning the Stanley Cup was far different because he was the coach, instead of a player.

"When you are the coach you worry and fret over twenty-three guys," Crisp said. "It's the mother hen vs. the little hen in the parade. The mother hen has to worry about them all and the little hen just worries: Am I in the right line to get food?"

The Flames won their Stanley Cup victory on the road in Montreal, and the plane ride home stands out in Crisp's mind. "I think the Cup was flying the plane for a while," Crisp recalled, chuckling. "The pilot and copilot got their picture with the Cup. It might have been the first time that Lord Stanley was at the helm of a plane. Imagine them calling in and saying: "This is Lord Stanley coming in for a landing.""

His regret is that the NHL didn't allow players to take the Stanley Cup to their hometowns like they do today. "I'm still a little bitter about that," Crisp said.

Crisp would have liked just twenty-four hours more to savor his triumphs with his friends and family. "Everything happens so fast, so quick when you win," Crisp said. "You have these intense meetings and games and then you win 1–0 against Boston [in 1974]. You have the Cup and suddenly poof, it's all over. It's a blur. All that fun blends together. When you win, it's almost as if you say: Now what?"

One of the most famous quotes in NHL history was the late Flyers coach Fred Shero telling his team, "If we win tonight, we will walk together forever," before the Stanley Cup clinching game on May 19, 1974.

But Crisp recalls another sliver of Shero wisdom after the 1–0 win against Boston that now rings prophetic to him. When Shero addressed his champions after they clinched the first Stanley Cup in franchise history, he told them "You will not realize what you have done until ten years down the road."

"You know what, he was dead on right," Crisp says. "That night we thought utopia would last forever. We won again in 1975, but then you take it for granted. It is ten years later before you realize what you've done. I'll tell you when the memories come flooding back. When you are sitting in your living room watching Buffalo and Dallas play for the Cup and you are thinking 'I reached that point once.' Fred Shero had it dead on."

# Bill Clement

*Philadelphia Flyers, 1973–74 and 1974–75*

In the spring of 1974 the city of Philadelphia seemed like an infertile sports landscape where championship-caliber teams simply wouldn't take root.

The Philadelphia Eagles were 5–8–1 in 1973, which actually had been an improvement from the 2–11–1 mark they posted the season before. No one in the National Football League was fearful of an encounter in Philadelphia. In baseball, Philadelphia pitcher Steve Carlton intimidated opponents, but no one took the franchise all that seriously. Carlton had posted twenty-seven of the team's fifty-nine victories in 1972, and in 1973 the Phillies were twenty games under .500. The Philadelphia 76ers, meanwhile, were an NBA doormat. "The city was so ripe for an injection of B-12 into the self esteem vein," says Bill Clement, who played for Philadelphia from 1971 to 1975.

That may explain why Philly fans went several degrees beyond letting their hair down when the Philadelphia Flyers won back-to-back Stanley Cup crowns in 1974 and 1975. The intensity of the two years of celebrations certainly is among player Bill Clement's vivid memories of his two championships.

The second Cup was captured in Buffalo, and the Flyers chartered back to Philadelphia. Although it was after 1:00 A.M. when they landed, players immediately headed to the Ovations club in the Spectrum to join the fan celebration.

"When we first got there we got greeted with 'Hey, way to go, you won another Cup, but did you hear that Mary Jones got laid on table No. 6?'" Clement says. "That was the buzz when we came in."

Legend has it that a woman known to many Ovations patrons, Mary Jones (not her real name), and an unknown man became so carried away during the Flyers' celebration that they comingled in a carnal way right there in full sight of other celebrating fans. Whether the story is true or not, it certainly provides a glimpse of how fans may have released some pent-up emotion during the Flyers' championship run.

"I understand the impact it had on the city now more than I did then," Clement said. "I still live in the area, people are always coming up to me and saying I skipped school to be at the parade and their parents faking being mad at them because they really understood why the kids needed to go. I've heard that some classes had four students in them and that teachers didn't show up. Companies locked their doors. It was as if the war had just ended."

He remembers that the parade down Broad Street was dotted with craziness, including women taking off their shirts and streakers. In that era it was a fad to run nude through a big event.

When the parade finally arrived at JFK Stadium, Clement remembers being in awe of how many fans were jammed into the stadium when the two floats carrying the Flyers' players entered.

"Then this guy runs bare-ass naked from goal post to goal post," Clement says. "All I can say is that it was like a cross between a rock concert and the celebration that would accompany the end of a war."

Each of the Flyers' championships has its own unique flavor in Clement's mind. He has plenty of pride about the first title because he played through the final with the excruciating pain of a partially torn medial collateral ligament in his left knee. He suffered the injury in the semifinals against the New York Rangers, and sat out the first two games of the Stanley Cup final against Boston before asking doctors to take him out of the cast ten days earlier than expected. He was dismayed that he was still limping and felt he couldn't skate well enough to play Game 3.

He remembers sitting in the whirlpool before Game 4, angered about his injury, when team captain Bobby Clarke approached him. According to Clement, their conversation went something like this:

Clarke: "How are you feeling?"

Clement: "Awful."

Clarke: "We have guys called up from the minors who can't do what you can do. If you could just kill penalties, it would help us."

Clement: "I'll be out there."

Clement retells that tale often when he gives motivational speeches because he believes it shows why Clarke was a great leader and why people should never underestimate the value of positive reinforcement in the workplace.

He played Games 4, 5, and 6, even scoring a goal in Game 5. "I really wouldn't have been in uniform if Clarke hadn't made me feel as if the team couldn't win without me," Clement said. "I think that many things can be accomplished when you make someone feel as if he or she is vital to the outcome. My head was spinning after Clarke talked to me. I wondered: Can I really do this? But when I look back at the videos I played OK. I'm happy with the way I played. Today I must look at Bob Clarke objectively with the work he does as a general manager, but when he played I would stack him up with some of the greatest leaders of all time."

On the night of May 19, 1974, Clement kept his jersey on for four hours after the game in a dressing room overflowing with well-wishers. Clement was glad that he opted not to strip off his jersey because many of those who did found after the room was clear that they had been pilfered.

Eccentric Flyers coach Fred Shero often said and did things that simply couldn't be forgotten. When Clement tries to sum up the late Shero's relationship with players during the championship celebration he is drawn to a scene that played out earlier in the playoffs.

This was the 1970s, when many people, including star athletes, ignored the surgeon general's warning about the evils of cigarette smoking. Clement recalled that about half the team smoked, including himself. Even Shero could be seen regularly puffing on Lucky Strike cigarettes. But as common as it was, smoking during a game was taboo to the point that players felt obliged to sneak into the bathroom to catch their puffs between periods. During one playoff game intermission, Shero came in and started sniffing at the air as if he were trying to determine the odor.

"Don't think you are fooling me," Shero said. "I know you are going into the bathroom to smoke." Shero kept pacing back and fourth. "I don't like that very much," Shero continued.

The players prepared themselves for a tongue-lashing. Then Shero said simply, "You are going to ruin your skates in there. For God's sake go sit on the couch and be comfortable."

The players all started to laugh. "He was a master at keeping us poised," Clement remembered.

The Flyers team was as close as any group of men could be. "It was a foxhole mentality," said Clement. "You almost cannot describe the bond we had."

After the first Cup triumph, Clement remembers he only slept from 6:00 to 8:00 A.M. "I got up and had to go to my neighbors to borrow a six pack because I was all out," Clement said, laughing.

The second Flyers Cup was captured on the road in Buffalo. Not even the wives came along because the Flyers were preparing themselves for the possibility of a Game 7. After defeating the Sabres 2–0 the Flyers discovered that this would at least start out as a different kind of celebration. "It was almost as if we had quiet time together as champions before we opened the doors to the rest of the world," Clement said. "We flew home together and spent time together."

One of Clement's fondest memories was the parade after the first Cup win in 1974. Literally a million fans turned out to salute their warriors, many of whom were primed with celebratory alcohol and suffering from sleep deprivation.

Players were divided between two floats, with Clement in the back float. As the parade crept along Broad Street, Clement recalls he had a pressing need to find a urinal to pay the price for too much beverage intake. Spying a service station up the road, Clement scaled the side of the float and commenced his journey. After working his way through the horde of onlookers trying to shake his hand or pat him on the back, he finally arrived at the service station's bathroom only to find it was locked. By the time he received the key and relieved himself, he realized he had a more daunting task in front of him. The parade had not stopped to accommodate Bill Clement's bladder. About four thousand people were between Clement and his float, which was now a block up the road.

"When I came out of the bathroom two cops were waiting for me," Clement said. "They told me I was never going to make it back. But they put their billy clubs in the shape of a V, and they began to barge through the crowd. They told me to grab the back of their belts and hang on."

Much to even the police officers' surprise, they were able to get Clement back to the float. They both grabbed an end of a billy club to give him a ladder to climb back onto the float. He had just climbed back on the float and was in the midst of accepting his teammates' congratulations for surviving his journey when the parade came to a halt.

"The little staircase rolls down off the float and Bernie Parent steps out and the crowd parts like it's the Red Sea," Clement remembers. "Bernie has to piss.

He walks to a typical row house where a little lady is standing there—obviously honored that Bernie is going to whiz in her commode."

The crowd kept the path clear for Parent, who exited the house still fussing with the belt on his pants.

"The stairs come out, Bernie goes up. The stairs are rolled up and off we go," Clement says, laughing. "I'm sitting back there going, Yeah, right. You got to be kidding. The parade stops so Bernie can whiz after I had to fight my way through four thousand people."

Clement laughs about the old story that the lady had the toilet seat bronzed.

"I tell people jokingly that I have this recurring nightmare that I'm stranded outside the service station with the owner not believing who I am and not wanting to give me the key," Clement said. "In the back of my mind, I see people throwing coins into this shrine which is the commode that has been bronzed and put on Broad Street and called the Bernie Parent shrine. "

> "It was a foxhole mentality. You almost cannot describe the bond we had."
>
> — *Bill Clement*

Actually Clement wasn't the least bit upset that Parent, the team's star player, got the red carpet treatment during his potty stop.

"I didn't begrudge him his piss, because I knew that I wouldn't have had the opportunity to piss in that situation had Bernie not been Bernie," Clement said. "My kidneys wouldn't have been backed up if Bernie wasn't in our net."

Clement has two championship rings and both of his jerseys from those championship teams but he doesn't treasure the tangible evidence of his success as much as his memories. "I wouldn't trade the memories for anything," Clement said.

# Dave Schultz

*Philadelphia Flyers, 1973–74 and 1974–75*

A war of words doesn't traditionally decide the outcome of a Stanley Cup championship, but one ill-timed bellow by a Boston Bruins fan may have been the catalyst for one of the most memorable moments in Philadelphia Flyers' winger Dave Schultz's career.

It was about eleven-plus minutes into overtime of Game 2 of the Final in Boston when an anonymous fan yelled at the Flyers' bench, "Hey, put Schultz out there so we can score a goal." Coach Fred Shero then almost instantly shouted, "Schultz, Flett, and Clarke, get out there."

Schultz recalls being mildly surprised because he hadn't played the final ten minutes of regulation and hadn't seen any action in overtime. Schultz was one of the league's most intimidating fighters and had led the NHL in penalty minutes that season with 348. He had also netted twenty goals that season. But he wasn't really the first player that came to a coach's mind when the game was tight. Up until the moment the fan yelled it didn't appear that Shero was thinking much about him at all.

But shortly thereafter, Schultz gained control of the puck near the boards and, with Terry O'Reilly coming after him, fed the puck back to the high slot. The late Bill "Cowboy" Flett then sent the puck toward the net where Bobby Clarke knocked it home with his second swipe to win the game at 12:01.

"That was probably the biggest goal in Flyers' history," Schultz said. "If we hadn't won that game I don't know if we would have won the series."

The Flyers had lost Game 1 by a 3–2 decision on Bobby Orr's timely tally with twenty-two seconds remaining in the third period. Another loss in Boston, particularly in overtime, would have been a broadside blast to the Flyers' psyche. Winning Game 2 seemed to give rise to the thought that the Flyers' were a team of destiny.

Who knows whether the late Shero put Schultz on the ice in response to the fan or whether it was simply time, in his estimation, to put fresh legs on the ice? Regardless, the move may have altered the course of Flyers' history.

"Sometimes you get lucky," Schultz says. "I could say I saw the man and made a great pass. But I just went in the corner and threw it out to the deep slot."

> "That was probably the biggest goal in Flyers' history."
>
> — Dave Schultz

But that's the moment that has stayed with Schultz more than any other in the quarter century since the play occurred. He scored an important goal in Game 4, but that memory doesn't seem as vivid as the assist in Game 2. What fans remember about Schultz in 1974 was the whipping he laid on New York Rangers' defenseman Dale Rolfe during a fight in Game 7 of the semifinal. The Flyers won that game 4–3, with some believing Schultz had set a tone with his triumph.

"People always talk about that fight. Why didn't some of the Rangers' jump in? What happened? I've heard it all," he said. "But I never thought it had any effect on the game. Actually, one of our assistants said, 'If you get a chance, hit Rolfe. He's playing well.' What happened was he was tussling with Orest Kindrachuk. And I came over. Remember, if you came over back then, a lot of guys would think, 'Here comes Schultz, I guess I will have to fight.' He basically started it, or at least responded without much [prodding]."

In retrospect, Schultz has the common athlete's lament of wishing he spent more time soaking in the moment of the championship, particularly when the Flyers won their first Cup on home ice in 1974.

"What I remember was being upset because they had opened the doors and let everyone in the building after we won. People who weren't even at the game ended up on the ice," Schultz said. "Where were those people going? They were going to go on the ice. And they did. The glass wasn't as high as it was today. It was easy to get over. And then people who were at the game saw that and they came on the ice. We couldn't skate around in our own building with the Cup because there were so many people on the ice."

But through the years he has come to understand why fans reacted the way they did. "My appreciation of what we accomplished is one hundred times greater today than it was when we won," Schultz said. "The reaction of the fans in the Delaware Valley was unreal. People today can still tell you where they were when we won."

Schultz, president of the Flyers' Alumni association, says twenty-six players played on one or both of the Flyers' Cup winners. Two of those players (Flett and Barry Ashbee) have died, and eighteen of the remaining twenty-four still live in the Philadelphia area. "That tells you how special we have been treated," he says.

# Bobby Clarke

*Philadelphia Flyers, 1973–74 and 1974–75*

Boos as well as cheers provide testimony to Bobby Clarke's standing as one of the most exalted playoff warriors in NHL history.

A quarter-century after his last Stanley Cup championship, at the dawn of the new millennium, Clarke goes to the podium in Calgary to make a draft choice and fans greet him with heartfelt boos. It's the year 2000, and yet to them it is still 1975 and Clarke is still captain and main villain on the league's most despised team—the Philadelphia Flyers. Clarke's greatness rests in the fact that no one, particularly his adversaries, can forget how viciously he played. No one can forget his take-no-prisoners approach to winning. No one can forget the way his intensity burned through opponents like a laser.

He played in four different Stanley Cup finals and posted nine goals and twelve assists in twenty-two games. When a title was at stake, Clarke was always at the center of the fray. His leadership savvy will be remembered as much as his goals or assists.

"To be honest, I never really thought about being a leader," Clarke said. "I really never thought about it. I didn't plan anything. Whatever I felt was good for the team, I tried to do it."

He says it's always hard for him to even remember what he did after winning the Cup in 1974 and 1975. He remembers the Stanley Cup being at owner Ed Snider's house for a party, and other than that he has no recollection of being with the Cup. "Back then you were just lucky if you got to put your arms around it or got your picture taken with it," he says, chuckling. "You saw it at the team party, and then you never saw it again."

Clarke does remember the parades. "There were 2 million people there, both years," he says, pride hanging from his words.

But what Clarke remembers most about his championships was a feeling of togetherness that he hasn't felt since, even though he has remained in the game as a general manager.

"I was twenty-three or twenty-four when I won, and it was the highlight of my career," Clarke said. "What sticks out in my mind is the commitment that everyone makes to win. It's so hard to get everyone on the same page. That's what you are always trying to do. And it's so hard. You have to get breaks. And you always think you are going to win another, to get back there. And yet I'm still trying."

# Guy Lafleur

*Montreal Canadiens, 1972–73, 1975–76, 1976–77, 1977–78, and 1978–79*

Hall of Fame right wing Guy Lafleur is remembered as one of the most dynamic, crowd-pleasing performers in NHL history. He could steal a game with one dazzling dash up the ice.

But perhaps the slickest, most flamboyant move of his hockey career came the night he stole the Stanley Cup.

It was May 22, 1979, the day after his Montreal Canadiens had defeated the New York Rangers 4–1 to claim their fourth consecutive Stanley Cup championship. The "Flower," as he was often known, had cause to explore his mischievous side. He had run amuck yet again in the postseason, netting ten goals and adding thirteen assists in just sixteen games. For the third consecutive season, he had finished the postseason with no other player owning more points than he did. In 1979, he and teammate Jacques Lemaire had tied for the playoff lead.

Lafleur's plan for the heist was as well thought out as any move he ever made on the ice. Knowing Canadiens' vice president of public relations Claude Mouton would be entrusted to safeguard the Cup while it was in Montreal, Lafleur schemed to separate Mouton from the Cup while the team was all gathered at Toe Blake's tavern.

Having ridden with Mouton to Blake's establishment, Lafleur pretended to have forgotten something in Mouton's automobile. Mouton didn't suspect anything when Lafleur asked for his key. He hustled outside and gave the keys to a friend who had a duplicate made. Later that day, when Lafleur knew the Cup was in the trunk, he put his plan into action.

"Yes, we stole the car," Lafleur says, laughing. "Actually we just borrowed it, but he did have to report it stolen with the Cup in it." The car actually was taken to the parking garage right across from the Montreal Forum, and the Cup went home with Lafleur.

It didn't take all that long for word to filter back to Mouton that Lafleur probably was in possession of the stolen property. Lafleur and friends had taken the Cup to several clubs in downtown Montreal.

According to Lafleur, the late Mouton finally reached Lafleur via the telephone and the conversation went like this:

Mouton: "You've got the Cup."

Lafleur: "Which Cup?"

Mouton: "You had better bring it into my office Monday or I'm in trouble and you are in trouble."

Lafleur: "I will try to find it and bring it in."

In hindsight, Lafleur was simply fifteen years ahead of his time. The motivation for his Cup thievery was just to share the championship experience with his family and friends, something players now have the opportunity to do. One of Lafleur's favorite pictures features his then-five-year-old son watering the Cup with a hose on his front lawn.

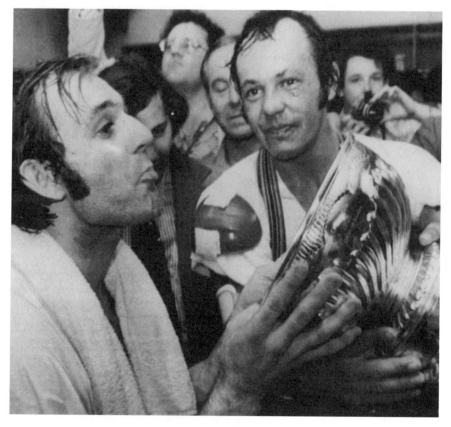

*Guy Lafleur sips champagne from the Stanley Cup with teammate Yvan Cournoyer waiting his turn.*

He also took the Cup to the Thurso, Quebec, home of his parents, Rejean and Pierrette Lafleur.

"It was unbelievable," Lafleur remembered. "Old people were crying and kissing the Cup. They couldn't believe the Cup was there. The Cup means a lot to them, especially when they could see it and touch it. They were never able to approach the Cup before. My sister had had a baby, and she put the baby in the Cup and took pictures. It was something special."

> "Old people were crying and kissing the Cup. They couldn't believe the Cup was there."
>
> — *Guy Lafleur*

Mouton eventually received his car and the Cup back, and Lafleur has a bundle of memories that players from his era simply don't have. Lafleur was among the few who understood the true significance when the NHL decreed in 1995 that all members of the NHL championship team would be able to have the Cup for twenty-four hours without resorting to crime to acquire it.

"For the players, it is great, great prestige and honor to win the Cup," said Lafleur. "When they have opportunity to show it to friends and family it means a lot to them."

# Brian Engblom

*Montreal Canadiens, 1976–77, 1977–78, and 1978–79*

The Stanley Cup is the NHL's symbol of excellence, but when Engblom thinks about his three NHL championship experiences he thinks about Toe Blake's fedora.

"I called it his Eliot Ness hat," Engblom said. "It was really right out of *The Untouchables* television series."

For Engblom the visits to Blake's tavern after a Stanley Cup triumph was a treasured highlight of his three championship memories. But Engblom was younger than most of the Canadiens, and the impact Blake's aura had on his experience seems even more pronounced. He can describe in rich detail Blake's long, narrow office and Blake sitting at his desk at the end of the table as if he was a CEO at a meeting with major stockholders. In actuality, Blake was the CEO of the Canadiens' mystique. He certainly had helped create it with eight Stanley Cup titles as a coach and three more as a player (1934–35 with the Montreal Maroons and 1943–44 and 1945–46 with the Canadiens).

A multitude of classic old photos adorned the walls from the 1930s, '40s, '50s, and '60s, a virtual history of the Canadiens, most of which Blake was in.

"There was the odd color photo," Engblom said. "But it was the black and white ones that caught your eye."

Blake was like an aging chief to the Canadiens' tribe; he seemed to feel as if it was his duty to pass along the Canadiens' history and traditions.

"Just to be in that room when he spoke was an honor," Engblom remembered. "He had a gravelly, raspy, deep voice, but not much volume to it. So whenever he would talk everyone would just shut-up whether it was Kenny Dryden, or [Serge] Savard, or one of the young guys. We all listened."

He would regale the Montreal players with vivid stories from the years when he played or coached. Players listened as if Blake was giving them secrets to immortality. Perhaps in a way he was; the idea of "once a Canadien, always a Canadien," certainly was propagated by Blake's presence and stories.

"Another thing about Toe was that he also loved to sit back and listen," Engblom said. "He wasn't one to command everyone to listen to him. He wasn't there to put on a show. He loved to hear the other stories."

Blake had no official capacity with the Canadiens back then, but he was viewed with so much respect that no one thought it strange that Blake would travel with the team in the playoffs. "You have to remember how [coach] Scotty Bowman felt about Toe," Engblom said. "I'm sure Scotty loved having him around and I'm sure he put his two cents in now and then."

He had a stately presence that no one mocked, although Savard once pushed the outside edge of propriety when he cut V-shaped gouges into the brim of Blake's famed hat. "That really pissed off Toe," Engblom said. "Serge thought it was hilarious, but you could see that Toe wasn't happy."

A younger player would never have dreamed of doing anything that brazen, even though Engblom earned the respect of his teammates with a noteworthy NHL debut. During the 1976–77 season, he played in Nova Scotia, not believing he had any shot to make the parent team, not when it had seven talented defensemen. But flu went through the team during the playoffs and injuries hit hard. With only four healthy defensemen available, Engblom was first to make his NHL debut in a playoff game against the St. Louis Blues.

He played in the second and third round, but everyone had regained their health for the final and he watched from the stands. It never occurred to him until later that he wouldn't get his name on the Cup because he didn't play in the final or didn't have the requisite forty games played in the regular season. Fortunately for Engblom he was playing for a team that expected to win more championships, and it did.

One regret about that first Cup was that he didn't step back and soak up even more of the atmosphere. To Engblom, the first Cup celebration was played at fast-forward speed. "It's all a flood in your mind," Engblom says. "It all blends together. The clock ticks down. Everyone piles on the ice. People are everywhere. One minute you are next to the Cup, and the next minute it's on the other side of the ice. Everyone piles on again and there's more pandemonium."

Other memories of his Cups include sitting next to Bowman at one of the Stanley Cup championship banquets. He felt like a child being forced to sit next to the teacher.

"Scotty doesn't make small talk during the season," Engblom said. "You didn't have a conversation with him that wasn't about hockey. When he said something to you it was short, sweet, and to the point. Then you went on your way."

When Bowman started making casual conversation with Engblom he almost wanted to make sure he was really talking to him. "He asked me what I was going to do in the summer and I was so surprised I almost didn't know what to say," Engblom said.

Engblom owns only one photo of himself with the Cup. He remembers seeking out fellow Winnipeg, Manitoban, Cam Connor in 1979 to make sure they had their picture together. Connor didn't play in the final that year, but he was a Canadien and Engblom treasures the photo. Engblom went home to Manitoba after the first Cup but after the next Stanley Cup he stayed in Montreal to soak in the atmosphere and afterglow that go with the championship. He wanted to be able to walk down the street and have people congratulate him for the championship.

Beyond his memories of the moments with Blake, what Engblom recalls is the feeling of camaraderie that was present in the dressing room. He says he feels fortunate to have played with players like Guy Lafleur, Larry Robinson, and Bob Gainey among others whose legends weren't even fully developed at that point. "Nine guys I played with are in the Hall of Fame," Engblom says.

He believed in the Canadiens' mystique—and still does in some respects. All the plaques listing the members of the championship teams that hang in the dressing room, along with the faces of great Canadien heroes like Rocket Richard, Jean Beliveau, and others, were a daily reminder of the hallowed nature of being a Canadiens player.

"All of those faces on the wall," Engblom said. "It really does affect you. People can say it's corny. But it's not when you are in there. You look at the faces and it's all part of being a Montreal Canadien. There is a rich history in winning. Any organization or business is smart to use their history. Why would you ignore it? Remember we had Rocket Richard, Toe Blake, and Jacques Laperriere coming around all the time. It made a difference."

Engblom believes that the mystique weighed on everyone's minds.

"A lot of it was the Forum," Engblom said. "Young kids get overwhelmed by it. I was. You grow up watching the Canadiens every Saturday on *Hockey Night in Canada*. You start thinking this place has been around forever and all of these great players played here. You are in awe."

The Canadiens, particularly Scotty Bowman, worked to magnify the mystique. He always made sure that at the morning skate, when he knew the opposing team would be in the building watching, he would run a snappy, high tempo practice with plenty of high speed passing. Lafleur would always be zipping around at top speed.

"There was a saying that we had about how some teams lost to us at the morning skate," Engblom said. "They would see us get on and off the ice in a hurry, and some teams were overwhelmed and it was just 11:00 in the morning."

Every Canadien had a sense that he was carrying the torch for his teammates as well as those who had come before him. Even today, when championships are far more infrequent, the championship Canadiens of yesteryear are treated like megastars.

"Al Langlois played in the 1950s with Dick Moore and Jean Beliveau, but they can't walk down the street in Montreal without being recognized," Engblom said.

Engblom said his glory years with the Montreal dynasty has given him an identity—a special kind of fame that at least means his name will never die in Canadiens' lore. That's what those meetings with Blake were all about, cementing the bond, unifying past and present.

> "Being a Canadien is like being a New York Yankee or a Boston Celtic. No matter what age you are, people keep track of you."
>
> — *Brian Engblom*

"From what I've read and seen," Engblom said, "being a Canadien is like being a New York Yankee or a Boston Celtic. No matter what age you are, people keep track of you. You never lose your identity of being a Canadiens' player."

# Henri Richard

*Montreal Canadiens, 1955–56, 1956–57, 1957–58, 1958–59, 1959–60, 1964–65, 1965–66, 1967–68, 1968–69, 1970–71, and 1972–73*

Henri Richard was only six years old when his brother Maurice played his first National Hockey League game with the Montreal Canadiens, but his father used to tell folks that Henri would end up being the best player in the family.

"That wasn't true," Richard said, laughing. "But it certainly was nice for him to say that, and it gave me a lot of [confidence]."

Although Maurice "Rocket" Richard's stature was legendary, the Richard brothers' father may have been prophetic if one views only championships as the measure of success. Henri Richard's eleven championships as a player stand as an NHL record that may never be broken. To appreciate the immensity of that accomplishment, consider that Mickey Mantle and Babe Ruth won only seven World Series championships each while with the New York Yankees. With eleven titles in twenty NHL seasons, Henri Richard was a champion 55 percent of his career. His brother's championship percentage (eight in eighteen seasons) was 44.4 percent. Wayne Gretzky's championship percentage was 20 percent

*Henri Richard holds the NHL record for winning the Stanley Cup as a player—eleven times.*

(four in twenty seasons) while Mark Messier's is 28.5 percent (six in twenty-one seasons). Today, in a league that boasts thirty teams, players hope for just one title in the course of a career. Richard's consistency was at the heart of the Canadiens' dominance in the 1950s and 1960s.

"I just feel fortunate to be on so many good teams," Richard said. "I was in the right place at the right time."

Richard couldn't pinpoint one particular celebratory moment that stands out over the eleven years, although he remembered that winning for the fans of Montreal was almost an honor for a native Quebec son. His favorite Cup triumph may have been his last in 1970–71 because it was one of his toughest seasons. He had feuded with coach Al MacNeil, calling him the worst coach for whom he had ever played.

"I didn't mean it when I said it," Richard said. "You just say things when you are frustrated."

What made that Cup win special was that Richard scored the Cup-winning goal in Montreal's 3–2 victory in Game 7 of the Stanley Cup final in Chicago Stadium. "That was special," he said.

One sad footnote of Richard's championship aura is that his championship rings were swiped in a house robbery. "But they didn't get the one that was on my finger," Richard said.

# Frank Mahovlich

*Toronto Maple Leafs, 1961–62, 1962–63, 1963–64, and 1966–67*
*Montreal Canadiens, 1970–71 and 1972–73*

Frank Mahovlich's six Stanley Cup championships haven't blurred his perspective about which title was the most memorable of his career.

When the Canadiens traded for thirty-three-year-old Mahovlich in 1971, it was essentially a rescue mission aided by his younger brother Peter's lobbying. Already a four-time champion, Mahovlich knew he wasn't going to return to the winner's circle soon if he stayed in Detroit. The Red Wings were the league doormat that season, and eventually endured the insult of finishing behind the expansion Vancouver Canucks and Buffalo Sabres. Even when he arrived in Montreal there was no guarantee of success. The Canadiens finished behind Boston and the New York Rangers in the regular-season standings.

The Canadiens beat the odds to win the 1971 championship, and Mahovlich was Montreal's offensive catalyst. He led all NHL scorers in the postseason with fourteen goals and twenty-seven points. In the final against the Chicago Black Hawks, the Canadiens lost Game 5 to fall behind 3–2 in the best of seven. In Game 6, Frank Mahovlich scored the tying goal and set up his brother for the game-winner in the 4–3 victory that forced Game 7.

But it wasn't the individual glory that Mahovlich remembers most, but rather sharing the championship with his brother, who was eight years his junior.

"My brother won four Stanley Cups and I had six. We have ten between us," said Mahovlich, now a member of the Canadian Senate. "Only the Richards have more [with nineteen]. I'm proud of that."

# Ron Caron

*Assistant General Manager, Montreal Canadiens, 1970–71*

Ron Caron tasted the ambience of the Montreal Canadiens' championship success a few years before he would play a significant role in creating more of it.

In 1964–65 he was a scout for the Montreal Junior Canadiens and was being groomed for a larger role within the organization. He was a member of the Canadiens' family and when the Canadiens defeated Chicago 4–0 in Game 7 of the Stanley Cup final on Gump Worsley's shutout, Caron was one among the first at the party at the Queen Elizabeth Hotel.

To appreciate the intensity of a Canadiens' celebration, it is crucial to remember that the Canadiens approached the postseason as if embarking on a religious pilgrimage. In fact, during the playoffs, the Canadiens would sequester players miles outside of town. "They were like monks forming a family," Caron said.

Vows of silence weren't necessary to be a member of the Canadiens' organization in postseason, but a myopic focus on hockey was a minimum requirement. "Everyone knew that they had to continue on to win the Stanley Cup to call it a good year," Caron remembered.

When the Cup was finally won, the Canadiens management shared the experience with all of the franchise's employees—everyone from Jean Beliveau to the Zamboni driver was invited to the celebration party. The night after the glorious victory against Chicago, Caron remembered the official party went until about 3:00 A.M. and then players and special guests headed to the Laval home of Henri Richard's cousin for an after-hours party. That started at about 4:15, and by 5:30 the champagne had run out. "So we switched to the champagne of the poor," Caron said.

The beer didn't run out, and Caron chuckles at the memory of Claude Larose asking Caron to borrow his car at 7:30 in the morning. "I told him if you want to throw up, you are going to have to throw up in your own car," Caron remembers vividly.

He also remembers that a priest was among the all-night revelers. It was Father Aquin, known as the chaplain of the cab drivers. The Cup had been won on a Saturday night and, in the wee hours on Sunday, Father Aquin had a special message for the players, many of whom were Catholic.

"He said, 'I will give you the blessing and you won't have to go to Mass,'" Caron said.

Caron slept two hours that night and then got up to hit some golf balls with members of the organization. "Then it was time to get ready for another party, and that continued for six straight days," Caron recalls.

The seeds of Caron's ambition were sewn long before the Canadiens' 1965 title romp, but those special nights nurtured it through the addition of a heavy dose of inspiration. In that short period Caron had acquired a taste for success. That would serve him well as he worked his way up into the Canadiens' hierarchy. By 1968, he had become chief scout and one of general manager Sam Pollock's chief lieutenants.

The following season the Canadiens' aura had begun to lose its power. Montreal missed the playoffs, and when the 1970–71 season started it appeared the Canadiens' struggles might be long-term. By December, Canadians' boss David Molson had told Pollock that he had to replace Claude Ruel.

What Caron says no one ever knew was that he had been Pollock's first choice to replace Ruel as coach. Caron had been summoned to drive with Pollock to Quebec City on December 2, 1970.

"He told me 'I have made up my mind that you will coach the Canadiens,'" Caron recalled. "I told him, 'Sam, you are under pressure. I would be honored, but I think that Al MacNeil should be given a chance to take over.'"

That suggestion seemed to satisfy Pollock, but he quickly decided that Caron would become the team's assistant general manager. Pollock didn't fly, and

Caron was told that he would have to be at every game home and away. "Sam didn't believe in listening to games on the radio," Caron said. "So it was my job to call him from the road. If we won, I would let Al call. If we lost, I would call. He knew as soon as he heard my voice that we lost."

Caron clearly views the 1970–71 season as one of the highlights of his NHL career. There is considerable pride in his voice as he talks about convincing Pollock to make a trade to land Frank Mahovlich from the Detroit Red Wings. "Detroit was confused and I thought we could get Frank. Sam said he didn't know whether Frank Mahovlich still wanted to play," Caron said. "I told him we can find out in a minute because his brother Peter was on the team. Peter was always jovial, and when I asked him how long Frank was going to play he said, 'As long as there is money.'"

The Canadiens gave up Mickey Redmond, Billy Collins, and Guy Charron to get Mahovlich. The Canadiens were a better team with Mahovlich, but they still finished third in the league—twenty-four points behind the Bobby Orr–led Bruins. The Canadiens were always a confident organization, but Caron still looks at the team picture taken a few weeks before the start of the playoffs "and no one is smiling."

The Canadiens played a wild card late in the season that seemed to change the game. Rookie goaltender Ken Dryden was 6–0 at the completion of the regular season.

The Bruins had won the 1970 Stanley Cup championship and they had plenty of talent beyond Orr, including Gerry Cheevers in goal. No one was surprised Cheevers won Game 1, and everyone was stunned when Eddie Johnston was chosen to be the Bruins' goaltender in Game 2. Seven minutes into the game Boston led 5–1, but Caron still felt they could come back against Johnston. They came back to win that game 7–5, and suddenly the Canadiens began to believe they could win the series. Caron remembers that the Canadiens had two small strategy moves that helped in the victory. Caron had suggested that Jacques Laperriere play the point on the power play even though a hairline fracture prevented him from shooting. This move was made to combat the possibility that Orr might break up the ice shorthanded. Caron believed that Laperriere was best suited to deal with Orr. Pollock also noted that Ferguson, a little older now, didn't seem to enjoy playing against Ken Hodge. He told MacNeil to keep Ferguson away from Hodge. Small factors? Absolutely, but it demonstrated how the Canadiens analyzed and re-analyzed every element in the playoffs. They finally beat the Bruins in seven games.

"Talking to him was like talking to my dad," Caron said. "I always gave him respect, but he gave me respect."

The Canadiens needed six games to dispose of the Minnesota North Stars, and the triumph didn't come without controversy. MacNeil had benched Henri Richard and John Ferguson during the third period of a loss, and Richard had called him the "worst coach" he had ever played for. Ferguson reportedly broke a door on his way out of the dressing room. Once that was smoothed over, the Canadiens defeated Minnesota to set up the Stanley Cup final meeting with the

Chicago Black Hawks. This was a hotly contested series, with the Black Hawks winning the first two at home and the Canadiens winning the next two in Montreal. Chicago won again at home to make it 3–2 and Peter Mahovlich scored the game-winner in the Canadiens' 4–3 win at Montreal in Game 6.

At all of the games in Chicago Stadium, Caron always sat next to Pollock and behind Mayor Richard Daley. Caron remembers Daley always had a religious person next to him, either a priest or a nun. Chicago Stadium was alive that day in 1971. "You have to be confident when you are a winner," Caron says. "You couldn't let the fear get to you. That was the Montreal way. But I can't tell you what goes on in your soul in a Game 7. It was unreal what I felt."

The Black Hawks claimed a 1–0 lead on a late first period goal by Dennis Hull and then made it 2–0 at 7:33 of the second period on Danny O'Shea's tally. Caron remembers Daley and he talked only about ten seconds per period, but Daley felt obliged midway through the second period to do some crowing. "You are invited to taste the champagne after the game," Daley supposedly said.

Caron countered that it was a little early to be taking bows. "Ten seconds later I had the greatest moment of my life," Caron says.

Jacques Lemaire came over the red line and whistled a shot that Hall of Fame goaltender Tony Esposito inexplicably fumbled; the puck fell into the net to make it 2–1. About four minutes later Henri Richard scored to tie the game.

> "I can't tell you what goes on in your soul in a Game 7. It was unreal what I felt."
>
> — Ron Caron

"Lemaire is a very special person," Caron said. "He's brainy. He's timid in terms of ambition and achievement. But he knows the game big-time."

Early in the third period, Richard netted another goal to give Montreal a 3–2 lead. "Then God was on our side," Caron said. Bobby Hull hit two goal posts in the third period and Jim Pappin rang a shot off the crossbar. Meanwhile, Ken Dryden played the third period as if he was invincible. As time wound down, Caron invited Mayor Daley to enjoy some of Montreal's champagne. When the game was over, Caron remembers bounding down eight steps carrying the two-hundred-pound Pollock with one arm.

"This is the feeling that you want to translate into this book," Caron said. "The joy and sense of achievement that comes when people believe you have no hope of doing it."

No one was happier to win the Cup than MacNeil. He had been forced to move his family out of his home after receiving a death threat presumably because he had benched Richard during the Minnesota series.

True to his history, Pollock didn't fly during the Canadiens' postseason. His chauffeur drove him to Boston, Minnesota, and Chicago during the championship run. He put 10,600 miles on the automobile. At some point after the championship was won, Pollock told Caron that the 1971 title had provided him with the most joy of any he had won.

As the players boisterously celebrated their victory in the Chicago Stadium visitors' dressing room, Caron remembers asking Pollock if he would be at the parade the following afternoon. "No, it's a nine-hundred-mile drive," Pollock said. "But I will be at the party tomorrow night."

# Scotty Bowman

*Coach, Montreal Canadiens, 1972–73, 1975–76, 1976–77, 1977–78, and 1978–79*
*Coach, Pittsburgh Penguins, 1991–92*
*Coach, Detroit Red Wings, 1996–97 and 1997–98*

The Stanley Cup is so intertwined with Scotty Bowman's life and career that it seems appropriate that he and wife Suella named one of their children Stanley.

In 1973 Suella was within a month of her due date when Bowman was trying to capture his first Stanley Cup as the young coach of the Montreal Canadiens. "We decided if we won and had a boy, we had to call him Stanley," Bowman said.

The Canadiens won that Cup by beating the Chicago Black Hawks, completing the task with a 6–4 win at Chicago Stadium on May 10. In June, Suella gave birth to a boy named Stanley. At that time, no one would have guessed that Bowman would coach seven more NHL championships, nor could anyone have guessed that Stanley would someday end up sharing the championship feeling with his father on the same ice where his name became official.

Scotty Bowman witnessed his share of championship celebrations. "The first I heard of anyone taking the Cup anywhere was when Guy Lafleur took it home," Bowman says, chuckling. "One story I heard about that was that after the party a neighbor called him to tell him that the Cup was still in his backyard."

Bowman surprised his players and defied convention when he slipped on skates to join the Detroit Red Wings' Cup celebration in 1997. As with most everything else in his life, Bowman viewed the situation with logic. "That's one thing I had never done before," he said. "And I knew teams were starting to go around the ice more with the Cup. Before they would go around once. Now everyone gets to go around once with the Cup. I didn't feel comfortable walking around the ice. I had the trainer bring me my skates with a minute or two to go in the game."

One of his favorite Cup moments was attending the impromptu party captain Mario Lemieux threw in 1992 after the Penguins, coached by Bowman, won their second consecutive championship. Bowman has a fondness for that 1992 championship because his children were older then and were able to share in the success.

Bowman and family members witnessed Phil Bourque set a distance record for the Stanley Cup throw at the Lemieux party. He hurled it into Mario's pool in one of the memorable moments of Stanley Cup history. That incident will be discussed later in this book. "He threw it from way up," Bowman said. "It could have hit the deck. He was lucky."

Winning that 1992 championship had more special meaning for Bowman because it happened in Chicago—the site of his first championship and the place where it became official that his son would be named Stanley.

"Nineteen years later in Chicago he was on the ice after we won," Bowman said. "He was just finishing school and he was able to come to the game."

# Bill Torrey

*General Manager, New York Islanders, 1979–80, 1980–81, 1981–82, and 1982–83*

Bill Torrey knows precisely where he was May 25, 1980, at about 6:30 A.M.

He and a friend were floating around in his backyard pool, sipping champagne, while the Stanley Cup floated about on a lounge chair between them. The early morning dip seemed like the fitting poetic ending for what may have been the best party ever thrown in the sleepy Long Island hamlet of Coal Spring Harbor. About ten hours before Torrey thought he had invited just his players and their families to his home to celebrate the first NHL championship in Islanders history.

"But I think half of Long Island marched through my damn house that night," Torrey said, chuckling.

He lived on a main street in Coal Spring Harbor, and he had to call the local police to come in and coordinate the flow of automobiles into the area. Traffic was backed up for miles. Early that afternoon Bobby Nystrom become a permanent figure in NHL playoff lore by scoring at 7:11 in overtime to beat Philadelphia 5–4 in Game 6 of the Stanley Cup final. There was a small amount of relief mixed in with the pride when the celebration began late in the afternoon. Given that the Flyers had won Game 5 by a 6–3 score, Torrey had packed his bag for Philadelphia before Game 6, figuring it was highly possible that the pesky Flyers could force Game 7.

A league party was held at a Long Island hotel, but the Islanders understood their exuberance needed a landing place that had no curfew. "We swiped the Cup and took off," Torrey remembered.

He hadn't anticipated that the party would go all night, and he certainly hadn't figured on seeing many people in his home that he didn't recognize. He had anticipated it would be crazy; at one point, Clark Gillies put his dog in the Stanley Cup, and at various points "the Cup got very wet."

"But we rescued it right away," Torrey said. "I think we went into the pool to keep ourselves awake. You don't sleep much in the playoffs."

After his early morning Stanley Cup "float-a-thon," Torrey took inventory of his home. There were several items missing, including a handwoven rug with the Islanders' logo in the middle that had been given to him by a native American woman he had befriended. "I remember walking through the house that morning and it was a shambles," Torrey said.

The Islanders were ahead of their time when it came to recognizing players' desires to have the Cup in their possession to share with their families. The Islanders didn't give back the Cup right away; players didn't get to take it to their hometowns, but it did end up at their Long Island homes. Bryan Trottier reportedly slept with it the night it was in his possession.

Trottier was just one of the Islanders' impressive top players, including Mike Bossy, Denis Potvin, and goaltender Billy Smith. But as Torrey thought back to the Islanders' run of four consecutive Cups, the player he often thinks about was defenseman Ken Morrow, who joined the team after helping the United States win the 1980 Olympic gold medal at Lake Placid.

"People talk about the deal to get Butch Goring as the key, and it was because it opened things up for Trottier and Bossy," Torrey said. "We had a great second line. But I couldn't have done that deal if I hadn't watched Ken Morrow at the Olympics."

On March 10, 1980, Torrey had traded Billy Harris and Dave Lewis to Los Angeles for Goring. Even though Morrow had just joined the Islanders a couple of weeks before, Torrey was comfortable that he could replace Lewis on the Islanders' blue line. "I had noticed that [coach] Herbie Brooks played Morrow all the time against the big Russian line. He was so good defensively. Right from the get-go we used Morrow like he was a ten-year veteran. He was such an underrated player on our team."

> "When you have the Cup for that long, you start to think it's yours."
>
> — *Bill Torrey*

That was part of what Torrey shared with his friend as they floated around his pool that morning.

The celebrations of the second, third, and fourth Cups may have matched the intensity of the first, but Torrey can't be sure because they weren't at his home. What he remembers about the second, third, and fourth was the debate about whether the Islanders should get a ticker tape parade.

"The joke was that we should have our parade on the Hempstead Turnpike," Torrey recalled. "But it was thought that we should get a parade down Broadway because we represented all of New York. We were the New York Islanders, not the Long Island Islanders."

But the Islanders never got the ticker tape parade in the city. It did actually go up the Hempstead Turnpike. "The mayor said the city couldn't afford it and that New York was Ranger country," Torrey said. "That just made the rivalry that much better."

Interestingly, Torrey almost recalls the heartache of losing the Stanley Cup more than the joy of winning it, the feeling he had when the Edmonton Oilers won the Cup with a 5–2 win against the Islanders at Northlands Coliseum in 1984.

"I remember how depressed I was," Torrey said. "It took me a long time to get over that. When you win nineteen consecutive playoff series before losing the twentieth, it is an amazing team. I remember how tough that flight home was. That was a huge letdown. I tell this story to show how you feel about winning it. When you have the Cup for that long, you start to think it's yours."

# Denis Potvin

*New York Islanders, 1979–80, 1980–81, 1981–82, and 1982–83*

In Canada, hockey is about fathers and sons as much as it is goals and assists. Denis Potvin understood that, which is why his most emotional Stanley Cup championship moment doesn't involve any of his fifty-six postseason goals or the wild celebrations accompanying any of the Islanders' four titles under his watch.

On the day after the Islanders won their fourth consecutive Stanley Cup in 1983, Potvin took the Cup to visit his cancer-stricken father.

Armand Potvin had been a high-caliber junior hockey player in the late 1930s for the Perth Blue Wings. He often lined up against Maurice "Rocket" Richard, who played for Verdun. Potvin was talented enough to earn a tryout with the Detroit Red Wings. However, he broke his back in training camp— effectively destroying any hope he had of playing in the NHL.

Neither father nor son had to say anything to know what it meant to both of them to have the Cup in such an intimate setting. Armand had been diagnosed with cancer a year before and the family suspected that he was fighting a losing battle against his disease.

"That was kind of the ultimate," Potvin recalled. "Just to have my dad be able to touch the Cup, to feel it, to share it with me. He had come to the rink before and seen the Cup. But not like this. "

Potvin treasures the pictures he has of him and his father with the Cup. "It was very emotional and very important to me," he says. "To me the beauty of winning the Cup is the emotion that goes with it."

In that era, NHL players were not officially allowed to have the Cup in their possession for individual events. But Potvin, Trottier, Mike Bossy, Clark Gillies, and perhaps others defied convention during their four-Cup run. No one spirited it away to his Canadian hometown, but several Islanders had private moments with hockey's chalice.

"It's always asked of me which is the most important," Potvin says. "I always say obviously the first one is the most important because it is the first one. You never know whether you will get another. So the first is the ultimate because all of the emotions come to the forefront because all of your dreams as a kid are being realized. But then when you win four, it's almost like having children. You love them all equally, and they each have a different story to them."

Potvin's father survived the following 1983–84 season, but it was clear his time was short during the playoffs. He died while the Islanders were in the midst of defeating the Washington Capitals in the second round. Denis Potvin's uncle Andre relayed that shortly before Armand died he had asked whether the Islanders had won their fifth consecutive Cup. He was told that the Islanders did win the fifth Cup, even though the playoffs were far from over.

In fact, the Islanders lost the battle for the fifth Cup to Wayne Gretzky's Edmonton Oilers.

"I never believed in my own heart that my dad actually believed that we had another Cup," Potvin says. "Even though he was at the stage he was losing everything, I still today believe that my dad knew we hadn't won, even though he was told we had."

# Ken Morrow

*New York Islanders, 1979–80, 1980–81, 1981–82, and 1982–83*

Defenseman Ken Morrow was one of the hardest-working warriors of the United States's Olympic gold medal triumph at the Lake Placid Winter Olympics in February, 1980, and he thought he would never again know such an emotionally draining experience. He was wrong.

Three months later he was a regular on the New York Islanders blue line and playing an equally significant role in helping the Islanders win the first Stanley Cup in franchise history. He is the only player in hockey history to win an Olympic gold medal and a Stanley Cup championship in such a compressed period of time. Before joining the U.S. team Morrow was at Bowling Green. He was considered a good prospect, and after watching him perform, particularly against the vaunted Soviets, the Islanders decided he was ready to play a vital role on their team.

"Winning the Stanley Cup was a completely different experience," Morrow said. "It's such a grueling, demanding grind. You win one series and you go right to the next. At the end it's almost a relief when you finally do win it. You're just physically and emotionally spent."

The Americans had to beat the Germans, Czechs, Soviets, and Finns to win the gold medal. The Islanders had to win sixteen games to win the Stanley Cup. When the Americans won at Lake Placid there was a sweetness and a thrill to their success. When the Islanders won the Cup, Morrow initially felt more like a survivor than a champion. Even though he had been a member of the team for only a couple of months, Morrow understood that this team felt pressure to win now.

"The Islanders had been trying to win for many years and they had experienced such disappointment—losing to Toronto in the quarters [in 1978] and to the Rangers in the semis [in 1979]," Morrow said. "I think if they hadn't won that year [in 1980] they would have been broken up. That's why I think there was such a huge celebration when they finally won it."

When the United States won the gold medal, family and friends were brought into the locker room for a quiet celebration. Morrow remembers how touching those moments were.

"You couldn't do something like that immediately after winning the Stanley Cup," Morrow said.

When the Islanders won, it was like army buddies celebrating an armistice. The partying was nonstop on the island, but what Morrow remembers most was the forty-eight hours he had with the Cup in his possession. This was before the Hall of Fame demanded that the Cup be accompanied by one of its Cup babysitters. "There's an aura about it," Morrow said. "When you walked into the room with it, I loved the look on people's faces. They couldn't stop smiling. Their mouths fell agape, like kids looking inside a candy store window."

Having the Cup in one's possession is like having a passkey to every door in the city. "The Stanley Cup is a great way to set yourself up in the community," Morrow said. "You bring it to a restaurant and you eat for free. You bring it to a bar, you are drinking for free."

His Olympic and Stanley Cup experiences were so unique that Morrow says it's impossible to compare the two. But he allows himself one comingling of the two greatest accomplishments of his hockey career.

Says Morrow, "I did take some pictures of the Cup with the gold medal hanging around it."

# Mike Bossy

*New York Islanders, 1979–80, 1980–81, 1981–82, and 1982–83.*

Mike Bossy may have been one of only a few young boys in Quebec who grew up rooting against the Montreal Canadiens in their glory years; still, he doesn't undersell what that storied franchise meant in the development of his drive to succeed.

"You just got sick and tired of seeing them win all the time, and you rooted for someone else to win," Bossy said "But one of the reasons I wanted to play hockey was that I had watched them celebrate so much in my childhood. It was always in the back of your mind that you would like to celebrate like you watched them celebrate."

Few players have earned the right to celebrate with the same panache and productivity that marked Bossy's NHL postseason career. During the Islanders' four Stanley Cup celebrations, he netted sixty-one postseason goals. He captured the 1982 Conn Smythe Trophy after generating seventeen goals and eighteen assists for thirty-five points in seventeen games. He led the NHL in playoff goals for three consecutive years.

"After we won our first Cup the confidence level of everyone on the team seemed to leap," Bossy recalled. "We just always knew that there wasn't a situation that we couldn't get ourselves out of it."

That attitude would be useful in 1982 when they had to rally to erase a two-goal deficit in the final five minutes to beat Pittsburgh in overtime on John Tonelli's goal.

"I remember clear as day that in that overtime Pittsburgh had a 2-on-1 break and I was the second guy backchecking and their guy had an open net and shot wide or hit the post," Bossy said. "We came back and scored a minute later. You got the sense that someone was looking down on you."

According to Bossy, "After we got over that hurdle we did seem to be invincible."

In today's hockey market it's difficult to keep top teams intact, since older players have so much more freedom to peddle their talents in the League's open market. To appreciate how different the financial landscape was in the early 1980s consider that Bossy's salary in his second season worked out to about $925 per goal.

*"After we got over that hurdle we did seem to be invincible."*

*— Mike Bossy*

"I made $65,000 the second year when I scored sixty-nine goals," Bossy said. "Then my third year I think I got $200,000 and $250,000."

After the Islanders won their second Stanley Cup, Bossy boldly asked for $5 million over six years. "They ended up making it $5 million for seven years," Bossy said. "I gave in on the last year because I knew they weren't going to budge."

Bossy's memory about what happened in the game is sharper than what he remembers about his moments with the Cup.

"I really don't remember one being more special than the others with regard to the celebrations," Bossy said. "But I do remember the fourth being very satisfying."

That was the sweep against Wayne Gretzky's Edmonton Oilers. Going into that playoff year there was a prevailing thought that the Great One and his buddies were ready to take the title away from the champ. As it turned out, the champ wasn't ready to relinquish the crown.

"We had gone three in a row and they were supposed to dethrone us," Bossy said. "They were a young, brash team with a lot of stars and they were supposed to be ready to win."

Bossy says he can still remember "the clear disappointment on all of the Oilers' faces at the end of that series."

But Bossy has always admired the Oilers for learning from that experience. In 1984 they knocked out the champ in five games. They outscored the Islanders 19–6 in the final three games. That was the first of five Cups the Oilers would win in a seven-year period.

"I have found that no matter what aspect of work you are in, when you make a mistake the most important thing is to learn from it," Bossy said. "I think they learned a lot from us that year, and what they did afterward certainly proved that."

As Bossy rummaged through his memory banks about the four Stanley Cup celebrations that he experienced, he seemed amused to report that what stands out most in his mind is that his wife slept through the first one.

While all the Islanders and their wives and girlfriends were all gathered at the fraternity house–style party at Bill Torrey's house after the 1980 Cup triumph, the usually security conscious Lucie Bossy was "conked out" on her couch with her door wide open. She had been the victim of lapping up too much of the first celebration at the arena after Bob Nystrom had scored the Cup clincher.

"She was a little tipsy and decided not to go to Bill's house," said Bossy. "She reminds people of that because everyone who knows her knows that it was highly unusual for her to do that. When we first went down to Long Island, the idea of being alone there wasn't her idea of fun. When I would go on the road, I was always finding someone to stay with her or she would go stay at someone's house. So for her to be alone with her door unlocked on that night is funny to us."

Actually there was no reason for her to worry about crime that night. Remember, everyone on Long Island was at Torrey's that night. Or so it seemed.

# Clark Gillies

*New York Islanders, 1979–80, 1980–81, 1981–82, and 1982–83*

When Clark Gillies watched an ESPN commercial in 2000 featuring Dallas Stars center Joe Nieuwendyk turning the Stanley Cup into a Jell-O mold at a fictional family gathering, it was like a flashback to the New York Islanders' glory years.

No Islander ever turned the Cup into a dessert cup, but Gillies remembers the Stanley Cup being a centerpiece of fun during the New York Islanders' dominance of the NHL in the 1980s.

"I remember the night the Cup was at my house and we were still going strong at 4:30 or 5:00 A.M. and I saw my German shepherd and he was looking kind of forlorn that he wasn't part of the party," Gillies remembered. "So I filled the Cup with Ken-L-Ration and let him eat out of it."

The Islanders may have been the first NHL team to find the proper blend of reverence for the Cup's symbolism and knowledge of its party value. The Islanders would claim the Cup for a couple of weeks and some of the players would get some quality time with it. It definitely toured all of the best restaurants and drinking establishments. Players made sure the Cup got to the Cafe Continental early in the victory march because Bruno the owner always made sure the Islanders had a free Christmas lunch at his establishment.

"The Cup was like a barter device," Gillies remembered. "We would get free meals if we brought the Cup along." Gillies said the "Cup got moved around pretty good" in the early 1980s. "It would end up in someone's trunk and the next morning we would all come back to life and someone would say where is it?" Gillies said. "We would figure out what happened to it, and then we would start again. But we treated it with the respect it deserved. We didn't abuse it. I had heard stories of other teams leaving it all night on their lawn. We never did that."

Clearly the Islanders did respect the Cup's aura because they knew how hard they had worked to get there. In hindsight Gillies believes there were three factors involved in the Islanders' dynasty: First and foremost, this was an exceptionally talented team, with Bryan Trottier and Butch Goring at center ice, Billy Smith in goal, Denis Potvin and Ken Morrow on defense, Mike Bossy, Bob Nystrom, and Garry Howatt on the right wing, and Gillies, John Tonelli, and Bob Bourne on the left wing. Secondly, the Islanders never had any major injuries during their Cup run. Finally, the Islanders were the luckiest team Gillies had ever seen. Other teams seemed to hit crossbars while the Islanders were always finding the net.

In the third Cup year the Islanders were trailing 3–1 with five minutes to go before being eliminated by the Pittsburgh Penguins. They ended up winning that game in overtime.

"I remember thinking then we have something working for us that no one else has," Gillies said.

Remember, fifteen players were on all four Islanders' championship teams; this was a team that was bonded together like brothers. Gillies remembers each celebration as being different, with the first one prominent in his mind.

"That first year had been very emotional for me. Fighting with Terry O'Reilly in the series against Boston and playing Philly in the finals hadn't been easy," Gillies said. "It had been very physical and when finally we won I got my hands on the Cup and just ran around the ice with it over my head. People asked me if the Cup was heavy and I said it wasn't at that time. I was full of emotion. The following year Bryan Trottier did what I had done in our first. He lost it, he went running around with his fist in the air. And he wasn't like that. But winning becomes very emotional. It's just so draining."

Gillies also has vivid memories of the Islanders' parade that went down the Hempstead Turnpike. "It was a little different than riding down Broadway," Gillies said. "But in our own little way it was pretty exciting."

The Islanders rode in Model A automobiles in a procession from Roosevelt Field to Nassau Coliseum. The closer the parade moved to the arena, the more people crowded along the roadside. Near the end, it became difficult for the cars to move and the motorcycle police escorts found it hard not to hit the people. Players escaped to a stage that had been erected on the north side of the arena, but even that plan didn't work well. Planners had put up a snow fence to keep back the thousands of fans who had come to salute the Islanders. Soon that gave way and people fell on top of each other. "It got scary and we were afraid people would get hurt so we got out of there," Gillies remembered. "We went downstairs [in the arena] and drank beer with the motorcycle cops," Gillies says, laughing.

The other fond memory Gillies has of the fourth Cup celebration was Smith's zany acceptance speech for the Conn Smythe Trophy. It was such a funny bit that Gillies now has it on tape. Two bits of knowledge are needed to understand the humor of the moment. First, Smith had a penchant for malapropisms. Figures of speech never came out of his month quite right. For example, Gillies remembers that during one particular snowstorm he turned to one of the clubhouse workers and said, "If you want to get on my good eye, you will come over and shovel my driveway." Of course, he meant to say, "If you want to get on my good *side*." When someone said the wrong thing, it was considered "Smittyness" or a "Smittyism."

During the fourth Stanley Cup run, Smith was embroiled in a handful of physical confrontations with Edmonton Oilers. At one point he slashed Wayne Gretzky in a game at Edmonton and Gretzky went down "like he was shot in the head." He also whacked Glenn Anderson on Long Island. "He was looking like a real villain," Gillies remembered.

In Game 4, Smith obviously schemed to change perception. Anderson did something to him and Smith began rolling around, moaning and groaning, like he had been speared in the throat. Anderson received a major penalty.

After the game, Smith was given the Conn Smythe Trophy as the series MVP with NHL president John Ziegler standing there and *Hockey Night in Canada*'s Dave Hodge conducting the interview.

According to Gillies, while live on the air Smith said during the game Gillies had shown that "two can play at that game," presumably meaning that good acting helped turn the Anderson whack into a major penalty.

"Then he says people all over Canada must be turning over in their graves after that," Gillies said. "It was priceless."

# Maurice Richard

*Montreal Canadiens, 1943–44, 1945–46, 1952–53, 1955–56, 1956–57, 1957–58, 1958–59, and 1959–60*

One major objective of this book was to secure an interview with Maurice "Rocket" Richard. Probably no one in NHL history defined Stanley Cup passion more graphically than did Richard. His piercing green eyes could turn his opponents—most of whom owned well-chiseled physiques—into bags of goo. He possessed a stare that seemed like it could burn through titanium and a competitive zeal that was molten.

On the ice Richard looked angry, mean, like an ornery bear who demanded that all in his territory maintain a respectful distance. Most did because they didn't want to feel the wrath of the Rocket's red glare. What no one understood during Richard's heyday was that his scary demeanor was the byproduct of a highly combustible inner drive. No one pushed the outer edges of his limitations with greater ferocity than Richard. It was his obsession to be the best. To him being the best meant winning the Stanley Cup every year.

That's what I wanted to discuss with him—the special drive that separated him from other superstars. But I never had the opportunity. It was well known that Richard had abdominal cancer. He appeared to be doing as well as could be expected for a while. But when Gordie Howe was interviewed for this book in March 2000, he had seen Richard only a week before and he told me that Richard "wasn't doing very well." He died May 27, 2000, at age seventy-eight.

Richard's life was celebrated in a poignant national funeral with services held at the Notre Dame Basilica in Montreal. The day before he laid in state at the Molson Centre. Thousands paid their respects. Tears puddled in the eyes of the older fans, many of whom viewed him as an icon of French Canadian pride. Perhaps some of the senior citizens remembered the days when Richard would seize control of the puck and fans would rise in unison and say "Envoye, Maurice!" The English slang translation would be "Let's go, Maurice."

Even in death, Maurice brought fans to their feet as they lined the road to pay their final respects to one of the true heroes of hockey.

Although I could no longer interview Richard, how could I ignore a man whose competitiveness seemed burned into his soul? The answer was that I couldn't. At that point, I pondered what Richard might have told me about his Cup experiences had I had the opportunity to interview him. The answer was probably not a lot.

As the years went along Richard's personality seemed to mellow. But he never became verbose. The few times I spoke to him he seemed gentlemanly and classy. But I would never have used the word "open" to describe him. He never seemed like a man who was going to let you analyze his feelings. He was not the kind of person who would have submitted to a Barbara Walters–style interview concerning his innermost thoughts. He certainly wasn't going to go into great detail about why he broke down and cried after he scored a dramatic playoff goal against Boston in 1952. He probably wouldn't have explained—at least not in great detail—what his father had said to soothe him after that famous goal. That didn't seem to be Rocket Richard's style.

Perhaps others tell Richard's story best, anyway.

His playoff numbers scream about his legend. He netted eighteen game-winning goals in just eighty-two playoff games. He boasts the NHL record of six overtime playoff goals. He once scored all five Montreal goals in a playoff game against Toronto—a performance that still places him in the record book with a handful of other great scorers. No one has ever netted six goals in a game.

Richard, who played from 1942 to 1960, played on the "Punch Line" with Elmer Lach and Toe Blake until Blake retired after suffering a broken leg in

1947. He played with Lach until Lach retired in 1954. Regardless of whom Richard played with, however, he would have been a star. He was a powerful skater who charged down the ice more like a skilled, fast fullback in the open field. He used his arms and strength to shield the puck from defenders, much like a running back might use a stiff arm to keep defenders away.

It was that heroic playoff goal in 1952 that will forever symbolize Rocket's competitiveness. Some call it his greatest goal. It came in Game 7 of the semifinals against the Boston Bruins at the Montreal Forum.

Earlier in the period he was bloodied and rendered unconscious by a gash he suffered over his left eyelid. How he was hurt seems have been forgotten over time. What was known was that Richard spent most of the game in the dressing room before coming out in the third period. Legend has it that Richard was so dazed he couldn't read the scoreboard and had to continually ask what the score was and how much time was left.

With four minutes remaining Richard summoned all of his bravado, leaped over the board, claimed the puck as his own, and crackled down the ice like he was lightning rippling across a low horizon. He slipped past Woody Dumart with two powerful strides and swung wide to avoid the Bruins' defense. According to reports of the game, Richard then whipped across the front of the net like he had been propelled by a slingshot. He whistled one of his sidewinders through Bruins' keeper Sugar Jim Henry for the game winner.

A famous photo of the bandaged and still bleeding Richard meeting up with Henry, whose own eyes had been blackened, has frozen the Rocket's dramatic exploit in time. Wrote Elmer Ferguson in the next day's edition of the *Montreal Herald*: "That beautiful bastard scored semiconscious."

Richard had the ego that all great athletes should have—one that needs to be fed with heroics on an almost daily basis. In 1944–45, Richard became the first player to score fifty goals in a season, and he did that in only fifty games. He was very proud of that record. When Gordie Howe reached forty-nine goals with one game to go in the seventy-game 1952–53 season, Richard was clearly glad that Howe would have to face Richard's Canadiens in the final regular-season game.

Coach Dick Irvin would later say that he purposely schemed to keep Richard away from Howe. "The night of that game was the only time I was ever afraid to be a hockey player on the ice," he told *Sports Illustrated* in 1954. "I remember watching Rocket's eyes as we were going across the city in the cab. 'I can't play him tonight,' I said to myself. 'He'll kill somebody.'"

Irvin couldn't keep Richard away from Howe all night; first chance he got he went after Howe. He took a charging penalty. As if fate appreciated Richard's pride, Howe was unable to tie Richard's record that night.

It seemed eerily ironic that Richard should die at the start of the Stanley Cup final, the venue where he often did his best work. All of the players competing for the New Jersey Devils and Dallas Stars knew Richard's legacy. Asking a hockey player about Richard is like asking a baseball player about Ted Williams or Joe DiMaggio. You need not be a history buff to know that Richard was one of the best there ever was.

Some of the former Canadiens and Quebec natives understood best of all. Claude Lemieux told the media that he would always stick around if he heard that Richard was in the building, hoping he would get a chance to shake his hand. "Young French Canadiens view him as a god of hockey and he will always be," said Lemieux, a four-time Stanley Cup champion and ex-Montreal player.

Top scorers have traditionally worn No. 9, but it was Richard who wore it first. He was proud that the Canadiens retired his number.

When the All-Star game was played in Montreal, Canadiens' forward Kirk Muller was assigned to wear No. 9 for the Eastern Conference All-Stars. Richard took note of Muller wearing that number and made a point to speak to him.

"You're a Canadien, don't make a habit of wearing No. 9," Richard reportedly told Muller.

Muller remembers Richard's eyes lasering through him as he spoke his words. "He didn't joke or laugh," Muller said.

Howe says what he remembers most about Richard was the intensity in his eyes. "He could burn a hole through the back of your head with those eyes."

Even though those eyes have closed for the last time, the legend of the Rocket will soar on through eternity.

# Chapter Two

## Watching the Glory:
## Stories from Nonplayers

# Phil Pritchard

*Hockey Hall of Fame Director of Information and Acquisitions*

Phil Pritchard didn't play for the 1974 Stanley Cup champion Philadelphia Flyers, but twenty years later he took bows as if he had.

Serving in his role as one of the Stanley Cup guardians in 1994, Pritchard was pressed into service as a Flyers' stand-in during a parade to honor the twentieth anniversary of Philadelphia's first NHL championship. Short on players to ride on a float, ex-Flyers player Joe Watson drafted Pritchard to play a role.

"Joe said, 'Just get on the float and wave and pretend you are Gary Dornhoefer,'" Pritchard recalled. "There I was with Bernie Parent, Bob Kelly, and Watson going down the street waving at every one."

No fan asked him who he was. Did he feel like a Flyer? "No," he said, chuckling. "I felt like an idiot."

Whether Pritchard enjoyed that particular day or not, his Stanley Cup duty has put him in a variety of roles that most fans can only dream of. He has sat in a sauna with Dallas Stars winger Jere Lehtinen in Finland as part of a Stanley Cup celebration. He went fishing with then–Colorado Avalanche winger Chris Simon and golfing with Patrick Roy in a pro tournament.

Aside from NHL players, no one is more intimate with the Cup's aura and mystique than Pritchard. No matter who wins the championship series, Pritchard is there when the Cup is presented. Other employees now serve as bodyguard/babysitter for the Cup on visits to players' hometowns, but for big events Pritchard is the one wearing the white gloves necessary to handle the world's most famous sports trophy.

It's part of Pritchard's job to assure that the Cup is treated with the respect and dignity befitting its history and tradition. He finds that is the easiest aspect of his job. Despite the public perception that the Stanley Cup is often treated like a giant beer stein, it has been Pritchard's observation that many players treat the Cup like a religious artifact. Players do have fun with the Cup, but that doesn't mean they abuse its symbolism.

"What I've always found is that the players respect it so much," Pritchard said. "The other thing is that the players that you think would have the wildest celebrations are the ones that usually have the quiet celebrations with family."

One of the most memorable moments of Pritchard's Cup tour was being with Lehtinen when he invited all of his childhood hockey buddies to the Stanley Cup sauna party at his cottage on an island off the coast of Finland. Pritchard traveled in an army boat to reach the location.

"But he wouldn't bring the Stanley Cup inside the sauna and close the doors, because he thought the heat might wreck the Cup," Pritchard said. "He just put it right at the entrance. But it was a traditional Finnish scene."

He went fishing with Simon and the Stanley Cup on a lake in the small northern Ontario hamlet of Wawa. Nary a walleye or perch landed in their bucket, and yet it was the best day of fishing Simon and Pritchard can ever remember experiencing.

"Chris put his arm around me at the end of the day and said, 'A lot of people never fulfill their dream. Today I fulfilled two. I had the Cup in my hometown and I went fishing.' He was so emotional," said Pritchard.

Pritchard was struck by Roy's generosity as he played in a pro-am tournament with the Cup in Lake Tahoe, Nevada.

"He was playing the course, but every hole that he finished he came back to meet the people and have photos taken with fans and the Cup," Pritchard said. "It made me proud to be associated with hockey because the other athletes weren't doing this. Only Patrick was. To be in a nontraditional hockey place like Nevada with people lining up to see the Cup, it was amazing. And Patrick was so good with the fans. He was like a god in this nonhockey environment."

> "The players that you think would have the wildest celebrations are the ones that usually have the quiet celebrations with family."
>
> — *Phil Pritchard*

According to Pritchard, players police themselves, particularly with regard to the unwritten rule about nonwinning players lifting the Cup.

The Stanley Cup's unwritten rules were lost in translation on a night in 1998 when some Japanese hockey fans tried to convince then–Vancouver Canucks player Trevor Linden to pose with the Cup in Tokyo.

Attending a party at the Canadian Embassy during the season-opening Anaheim-Vancouver series at the start of the 1998–99 series, Linden struggled to overcome the language barrier and find a polite way to explain why he couldn't touch the Stanley Cup.

"The friendly Japanese people kept telling him to come closer and look at it, and he wouldn't," Pritchard said. "He stayed five feet away and looked at some of the names and he wouldn't go closer. When he left, I tried to explain to them that he wouldn't come closer because he has never won the Cup."

No rule exists that bars a player from hoisting the Cup before he has won it. Yet current and even former players act as if they might face criminal charges if they touch the Cup without having actually won it. That tradition has grown stronger in recent years, with the Cup travelling around the globe. Today, even European players know the NHL's tradition. But that wasn't always the case. "When we took the Cup over to Finland, some Finnish players got their pictures taken with the Cup," Pritchard recalled. "Today you wouldn't see Saku Koivu getting his picture with the Cup if it was in Finland."

Hall of Fame officials have noted that Darryl Sittler, who played fifteen seasons without winning the Cup, won't have his picture taken with it. "He will stand near it, but he won't have his picture taken with it," Pritchard said.

Although the Hall of Fame has never tried to hide it, most fans don't realize that there are actually two Cups. In 1993, the Hall of Fame had a duplicate

Stanley Cup produced at a cost of $75,000. The engraving was copied exactly, although legend now has it that some of the misspelled names of the past were corrected on the duplicate. The only real difference is supposed to be the Hall of Fame seal on the bottom of the true Stanley Cup.

Most fans presume incorrectly that the duplicate Stanley Cup is the one that travels to the players' hometowns.

"That's the most popular question that we get at the Hall of Fame," Pritchard said. "Which Cup goes out to the players."

When the duplicate Cup was created, NHL Commissioner and then–Hall of Fame director Scotty Morrison conducted a meeting at which the issue was discussed at length. It was unanimously agreed upon that NHL players should always have the true Cup at their personal celebrations.

"It's felt that players work so hard to earn this Cup that they deserve nothing but the real one," Pritchard said. "You wouldn't want a guy who works for thirty-five years to win the Cup to get the fake one."

Pritchard said he has never had to step in and say no to a player's idea of what to do with the Stanley Cup.

"[Dallas Stars winger] Blake Sloan said he was going to take it sky diving, but I think he was kidding," Pritchard said.

When it comes to the Stanley Cup, you really can't be too sure.

# Red Fisher

*Hall of Fame Hockey Journalist*

Even Henri Richard's revered record of eleven Stanley Cup championships looks puny compared to Montreal Gazette sportswriter Red Fisher's marathon of Cup experiences.

Fisher, who turned seventy-four in 2000, has covered forty-three of forty-five Stanley Cup finals since 1955. He missed the 1985 final because of illness, and missed the 1999 Stanley Cup to celebrate his fiftieth wedding anniversary.

"I covered seventeen of the Montreal Canadiens' twenty-four Stanley Cups, and some people think I covered all twenty-four," quipped Fisher.

His first NHL assignment for the Montreal Star came March 17, 1955. He knows the exact date because that was the day of the famed Maurice "Rocket" Richard riot. NHL president Clarence Campbell had suspended Richard for the final three games of the regular season and the rest of the playoffs for slugging linesman Cliff Thompson, who was breaking up a fight between Hal Laycoe and Richard. Canadiens' fans were upset. Fisher was assigned to hang out at the Montreal Forum all day. "You could smell the trouble in the air," Fisher recalls.

Fisher was perfect for the role of eyewitness to history because of his uncanny ability to remember incidental details. He recalls decades-old scores, events, and players as if he had written about them the day before instead of forty years ago. This is a man who can remember the score of a preseason game he was covering the night he found that the *Montreal Star* had folded.

What Fisher remembers about that night was the defiant Campbell strolling into the arena midway through the first period. By then, the Rocket-less Canadiens were already losing in the game to the Detroit Red Wings and were being badly outplayed. Montreal fans were in a foul mood, and the sight of Campbell walking up from ice level to his aisle seats ten or twelve rows up must have felt like having an enemy in their midst.

"Everyone in the joint could see him," Fisher said. "He had been asked not to go to the game by Mayor Jean Drapeau," Fisher recalled. "But that was like waving a red flag in front of Mr. Campbell. That's what I called him. That's what everyone called him, except maybe the owners."

Not only were Montreal fans incensed; they were armed. Before the game, Fisher had been hit with an egg.

Fans began hurling various fruits and vegetables at Campbell almost from the moment he sat down, but the night didn't get out of hand until after the first period when a fan approached Campbell and stuck out his hand as if he wanted to shake hands with Campbell. "Campbell was wary, but he stuck out his hand and the fan just slapped him," Fisher remembered.

Retired Detroit Red Wings player Jimmy Orlando was sitting nearby. He was a proven tough guy; everyone in the game from that era remembers a famous photo of a bloody stick fight between Orlando and Gaye Stewart. As a hockey guy, Orlando wasn't going to allow Campbell to be pummeled. He attacked Campbell's assailant. "Teeth were flying out in all directions," Fisher said.

Fisher recalls tear gas being tossed shortly thereafter and yellow smoke rising to the Montreal Forum rafters. "Everyone was coughing, choking, spitting, cursing, and in a matter of seconds they announced the fire department had ordered everyone out of the building," Fisher recalled.

With ticket buyers now joining the others who were already milling about outside, a full-blown riot developed. Seeing rioters setting fires, turning over police cars, and creating mayhem, he dutifully walked to the corner to call his newspaper. When pressed for more details about the rioting fans, Fisher suggested "the silly city editor should come up here and circulate in this crowd."

Perhaps Fisher should have viewed his first NHL game as an omen that his career would be anything but pedestrian. In the years to follow Fisher would become one of the legends of the game. Everyone in hockey knows his name and his status in the game. Famed Guy Lafleur has said that he knew he had made the NHL a couple of years into his career because Fisher started talking to him. Fisher's rule is he doesn't talk to rookies. (Fisher says that story is exaggerated because he did make an exception for Lafleur.)

Another time Fisher listened to former Canadiens player Mark Recchi spew forth a string of clichés after Montreal had claimed a 2–0 series lead in a playoff series against the Rangers and couldn't take it any longer. In front of other media members, Fisher told Recchi he wasn't going to listen to his malarkey any longer and stalked off. Not wanting to be in Fisher's doghouse, Recchi followed after Fisher with one hand holding up his hockey pants.

"What did you want me to say, Red?" he said.

"I wanted you to say the Rangers sucked," Fisher said.

"I can't say that," Recchi said.

"Yes you can," said Fisher. "And you will in tomorrow's paper."

Fisher never followed through on his threat, but he made his point.

Former Montreal player Brian Engblom said being interviewed by Fisher could be as memorable as anything that happened on the ice. He compared talking to Fisher to listening to famed Montreal coach Toe Blake. Both had more interesting stories than he could have ever provided them.

In 1982 the Montreal Canadiens gave rings to the twelve players who had won five consecutive Stanley Cup championships. The team also awarded one to Fisher, and three other members of the media—Jacques Beauchamp, Danny Gallivan, and Rene Lacavalier—who had covered the five championships. He had rejected rings before then.

> "The players didn't see me as being part of it [their championships]. And I never felt that way. They were the guys who did it."
>
> — *Red Fisher*

"The players didn't see me as being part of it [their championships]," Fisher said. "And I never felt that way. They were the guys who did it. That's the way it is. That's the way it should be. The fact I have only one [Montreal] Stanley Cup ring proves that."

Fisher does have one other Stanley Cup championship ring—an Edmonton Oilers' version given to him as a gift by former Oilers' general manager Glen Sather. A former Canadiens' player, Sather is Fisher's long-time close friend.

As one might expect, the championship has a story attached that is probably more meaningful to Fisher than the actual jewelry.

When the World Hockey Association was annexed by the NHL in 1979 and Sather had to begin building the Edmonton Oilers, he immediately called Fisher for his recommendations for the expansion. Remember, at the time Fisher had already been covering the league for almost a quarter of a century, and Sather had been concentrating on the WHA. Fisher gave him a list of players including defenseman Lee Fogolin, who would win two Cups with the Oilers.

Of course Fisher wasn't paid for his scouting insight because it was essentially an act of friendship.

But Sather told Fisher that when the Oilers won their first Stanley Cup he would order him a championship ring.

"I said, 'Slats, it will never happen in my lifetime,'" Fisher recalls, chuckling.

Five years later, Sather was in his office yelling into Fisher's ear with the Oilers' championship celebration in full roar.

"What's your ring size?" Sather screamed.

"What are you are talking about?" Fisher said.

"I promised you a ring, and I'm going to give you one," Sather said.

"Oh, forget about it," Fisher replied. "I forgot about it, the moment you told me about it five years ago."

Sather wouldn't accept Fisher's rejection. "If you don't tell me, I will just phone your wife."

The following season, when Fisher accompanied the Canadiens back to Edmonton, Sather was there to greet him with the ring. But as is always the case with a Fisher-Sather happening, the postscript is juicier than the story.

According to Fisher, the Oilers' ring is quite beautiful. But former Montreal standout Steve Shutt's wife worked for the company that produced Stanley Cup rings, and she confirmed to Fisher that what he thought was a diamond in the ring was actually a zircon worth about $7.50.

"As I mentioned, he has always been a cheap prick," said Fisher, still amused by the story almost two decades after the fact.

The ring story still wasn't over. He kept telling Sather he wouldn't be wearing that cheap ring. One day, he received a special delivery from Sather of a jewelry box with what appeared to be a full, nice-sized diamond in it. Accompanying the gift was a letter from an Edmonton jeweler certifying that the diamond was worth $30,000.

This was an official-looking document on a jewelry company's letterhead. The rock itself was sparkling. Fisher admits he thought it was real. He rushed it upstairs to tell his wife, and had her read the letter.

"So?" she said.

"Did you read it?" Fisher says. "It's worth $30,000."

"Did you read the signature?" his wife retorted.

Fisher looked at the signature. It read I. M. Kidding. The initials underneath were B. S.

Fisher called Sather immediately to tell him that he was a "cheap prick" again.

"He must have laughed for twenty minutes, and it was on my dime of course," Fisher said. "When I call him a prick, I mean it in only the fondest terms."

Fisher means it when he speaks of fondness for Sather. In 1985, when he missed the final between the Sather-coached Oilers and the Philadelphia Flyers, Sather called him before every game, right after his players went on the ice for warm-up.

"Before the fifth game in Edmonton, the Oilers were leading 3–1 at the time, he called me and told me he would be calling me after the game because the series was all over," Fisher said. "The Flyers were switching from Pelle Lindbergh to Bob Froese and the Oilers could hardly wait to get at him."

Sather told Fisher that the Oilers felt like they owned Froese. They ended up winning the game by an 8–3 verdict. True to his word, Sather was on the phone with Fisher immediately afterwards.

"The reason why I tell this story is I don't think there is a coach in any sport who would take the trouble to do what he did when his team was going for the big prize," Fisher said.

Fisher covers the Canadiens as a beat—meaning he is at all home games and plenty of road games. He became a full-time beat writer in 1955–56—that was his condition to accept the *Montreal Star*'s job offer. "That was pretty presumptuous of me," he says, chuckling.

Perhaps it was, but today no one understands the Canadiens' dynasty with greater insight than Fisher. He has written about all of the Montreal heroes from "Rocket" Richard, to Jean Beliveau, to Guy Lafleur, to Patrick Roy. He might understand their strengths and weaknesses better than they do. But his view of the Montreal mystique is far more pragmatic than it is romantic.

"The Montreal mystique was the great players," Fisher said. "There were no ghosts. The Montreal mystique was all the people who came through their system, their great drafts. The mystique was Sam Pollock having the advantage over every other general manager. Why did he win nine Cups? There were no ghosts here, just great players and great management. That's the mystique."

Does he still enjoy the Stanley Cup final the way he did in the 1950s? "I'm here aren't I?" he said during the 2000 Stanley Cup final between the New Jersey Devils and the Dallas Stars.

He has no plans to retire. "I'm going to do this until I get it right."

# Bill Tuele

*Vice President of Public Relations, Edmonton Oilers*

Only a real alien autopsy video could have stunned NHL officials more than the morning in 1990 when the *Edmonton Sun* published a photo of what could only be called a dismembered Stanley Cup.

The controversy began rather innocently when Oilers' general manager Glen Sather, seeing that the Cup looked battered, bruised, and dinged after a couple of weeks in Edmonton, asked Oilers' assistant equipment manager Lyle "Sparky" Kulchisky to tidy it up a little before it was returned to the Hall of Fame. The expectation was that the Cup would only get a coat of polish and a careful straightening.

Kulchisky decided to take the Cup to the West Town Ford automobile dealership and let the body shop boys try to bump it out a bit.

"They dismantled the whole cup to tap out the dents and bruises," Bill Tuele remembers. "Unfortunately, he had given the photographer at the *Edmonton Sun* a heads-up about what he was doing. The photographer was there to capture the Cup in its dismantled state. It had never been seen like that before. And it ended up on the front page of the Sun."

The Cup comes apart, with the rings falling away to show a central shaft, if you pop up the bottom and unscrew it. The bowl comes off and the Cup ends up in nine or ten pieces.

"That was not an amusing time for the league," Tuele said. "They didn't like that."

At the time, NHL officials were aghast, considering the photograph to be almost sacrilegious. But in recent years the story has simply become one of the long string of humorous tales that make up Lord Stanley's legacy.

Few non-players have enjoyed a relationship with the Cup as strong as the bond Tuele has enjoyed. He was the team's public relations boss since the Oilers' joined the league in 1979, and he was one of the key social directors for the Oilers' championship celebrations during their five NHL titles over a seven-season period from 1984 to 1990.

He might have as many Cup stories as any person in hockey. He says he is saving some of them, particularly tales about Wayne Gretzky, for his own book, which he hopes to write someday. But the tales he does share provide evidence that the Oilers were the first franchise to make a concerted effort to turn the Stanley Cup into a people's trophy as well a tribute to a century of hockey tradition. The Canadiens moved the Cup around Montreal during their 1970s dynasty years and the Cup made guest appearances at select homes and restaurants during the Islanders' four-season run from 1980–83. But it was the Oilers who turned the Cup into a hobnobbing celebrity.

"The media literally got tired of it," Tuele said. "It got to the point that it was no longer a story where the Cup was going because it was everywhere."

The Oilers would get the Cup for a few weeks after each championship. "Mark [Messier] was the most social with the Cup, along with Glenn Anderson," Tuele recalled. "They would go from bar to bar to bar. They would go on three-day howls with the Cup." This was before the NHL decreed that all members of the championship team should receive their day with Cup. Yet the Oilers always tried to make sure everyone in the organization got some time with the Cup, even if it was an hour or two. At this point, the Cup didn't have a guard wherever it went.

> "It went everywhere without security, without any concern that we needed to be careful or it might disappear."
>
> — *Bill Tuele*

"What I liked about the Oilers' relationship with the Cup was that we had unbelievable access and we made it unbelievably accessible to Edmontonians," Tuele said. "It went everywhere without security, without any concern that we needed to be careful or it might disappear."

The Cup literally spent a night out on a patio table outside Yannios Psalios' Greek Restaurant on White Avenue, a popular spot with the Oilers. Everyone who came by stopped to look at the Cup. Even police officers would pull up, pop out of their cars, and have their pictures taken with the Cup.

Legend has it that during the Oilers' watch the Cup was also involved in some lewd behavior involving dancers at a local strip club. That story seems to have become exaggerated over time.

According to Tuele, the establishment was the Forum Motor Inn, located directly across from Northlands Coliseum. There were in fact naked dancers in close proximity to the Cup.

"That's true," Tuele said. "The boys called it the ballet. But some have suggested that players were egging on the dancers to get involved in the Cup. That's not true. Players were mindful of the history. When a girl jumped on the table and tried to get in the Cup, she was quickly moved away."

Tuele's memories of his Cup experiences range from the poignant, to the hilarious, to the surreal.

He can't forget how overwhelmingly happy Jaroslav Pouzar was to win the Stanley Cup in 1984. What makes the story so fascinating was that Pouzar didn't even play in the final game. He was watching the final moments of the game on television when Tuele entered the dressing room to prepare for the postgame celebration.

"He was a bull of man, and he picked me up when we won and he refused to put me down," Tuele said. "He carried me around for what seemed like ten minutes. It was probably a minute and a half. He took me back into the player's lounge and out the door. I will never forget that."

His other poignant moment was watching Captain Wayne Gretzky choose to give Oilers' defenseman Steve Smith the Cup to carry around the ice after their 1987 championship. The order in which players carry the Cup around the ice is important to the Cup tradition. Usually, the captain will choose to give the Cup to a long-time veteran. Gretzky chose Smith because Smith had knocked the Oilers out of the playoffs in 1986 by inadvertently knocking the puck into his own net. Smith was devastated by his error, and Gretzky's generous act in 1987 perhaps brought some closure to his suffering.

"None of us knew that was going to happen, but given how much thought Wayne puts into everything you can be sure he had thought about it," Tuele said. "As soon as it happened the crowd knew, the crowd was aware of the symbolism."

One of the best pranks in Stanley Cup history was engineered by the Oilers during the 1987 Stanley Cup final. Knowing Flyers coach Mike Keenan wanted the Cup brought into the visitor's dressing room in Edmonton as motivation for his Flyers, an unnamed member of the Oilers' staff made sure that didn't happen.

When it was time for the Cup to enter the Flyers' room, it turned up missing. Al Wiseman, the NHL's assistant director of security at that time, demanded to know where the Cup was. He accused Sather of stealing the Cup to keep it away from the Flyers.

"The report given to Wiseman was that no one knew where it was and the last time it was seen it was in the back of a pick-up truck leaving the building," Tuele recalled.

Obviously it did show up after the game. "Although it was quite amusing, it did piss off Al," Tuele said. "In fact, he's still not amused about it."

Legend has it that it was Sparky Kulchisky who had "borrowed" the Cup. "I'm not going to say," Tuele said. "And to this day, he denies involvement."

Tuele's surreal moment came as the Oilers won the 1990 championship—the only one of the five Edmonton Cups that wasn't captured at Northland's Coliseum. This one was won at the Boston Garden.

When the game was over, former Bruins player Ace Bailey, then an Oilers' scout, had enough connections in Boston to set up the postgame celebration at the Blackstone Restaurant.

That party went on most of the night, and Tuele remembers that everyone filed out around 5:00 A.M., wanting to get back to hotel to prepare for a 9:00 A.M. charter flight back to Edmonton. To assist in getting the Oilers back to their hotels, off-duty police officers showed up. Tuele's ride came from a motorcycle-riding officer.

"Here I was holding the Cup on the back of a motorcycle with a burly Boston cop wearing a leather jacket tearing through the streets of Boston," Tuele said. "I'm not going to forget that night."

# Murray Gough

*Witness to an Attempted Cup-Napping*

After Montreal resident Ken Kilander was deported for trying to steal the Stanley Cup during the 1962 NHL Semifinal, he didn't seek legal help, or counseling, or the clergy. He saw a retired barber.

He wasn't looking for forgiveness. He was looking for a few bucks to buy a hamburger.

That's how Windsor, Ontario, resident Murray Gough came to own one of the most unique souvenirs in Stanley Cup lore. He possesses the ticket stub that allowed Kilander to enter Chicago Stadium for his attempted heist during Game 3. The torn and tattered $5.25 mezzanine ticket was for section 22A, row H, seat 1. Before reviewing Gough's connection with Kilander, let's review the facts of the case as they were presented by the media's coverage of the event.

Reportedly Kilander was somewhat miffed after watching the Montreal Canadiens win five consecutive Stanley Cup titles from 1956–60, and then seeing the Chicago Black Hawks unseat them with their championship in 1961. That season was the first in which the Canadiens' were dealing with the retirement of Maurice "Rocket" Richard.

It's unknown whether Kilander planned the attempted thievery or whether it was a spontaneous act cooked up while he was watching the game. The Black Hawks were in the midst of a 4–1 whipping of Montreal on April 1, 1962, to take a 2–1 lead in the series, when Kilander descended from the mezzanine to earn himself a place in Stanley Cup lore. Once in the Chicago Stadium lobby, Kilander headed for the Stanley Cup, on display in a glass case. According to media reports, he picked the lock, grabbed the Cup, and was quick stepping toward the exit when an eagle-eyed sixteen-year-old usher named Roy Perell brought him down. He nabbed Kilander by the door and the police were called to arrest Kilander.

Not exactly guilty of a heinous act by any definition, Kilander ended up with a quick deportation.

When the picture of Kilander ran in the Windsor paper, Gough recognized him immediately. Gough, who had managed the barbershop in the Prince Edward Hotel for a number of years, was well acquainted with Kilander. The Prince Edward was the lodging of choice for some of the NHL teams that came to play against the Detroit Red Wings, and Kilander often followed the team down to Windsor and would hang around the hotel with the hope of bumping into some the Montreal players.

"A couple of days [after the attempted Cup grab] we were walking by the tunnel [the Detroit-Windsor Tunnel, the Canada–United States border crossing] and who do we see walking toward us but Kenny," Gough recalled.

Right there on the street, Kilander confessed to his crime. He then moved on to a more pressing topic.

"He says he doesn't have any money and could I lend him some to get a hamburger for lunch," Gough said.

Gough handed over $10. In lieu of normal collateral, Kilander handed over the ticket stub from the game. The presumption was that Kilander would get his stub back when he repaid the $10.

Kilander's attempt to steal the Cup wasn't the first or last effort made to pilfer it. In 1907 the Montreal Wanderers left the Cup at a photographer's home where they had gone for a team picture. A friend of the photographer, or at the very least an acquaintance, absconded with the Cup with the hope of holding it for ransom.

What he quickly discovered was that no one seemed to care much that the Cup was gone, least of all the Wanderers.

Disappointed in the outcome of his crime, the thief returned the Cup to the photographer's house where it served as a flowerpot until the Wanderers thought it might be time to locate its whereabouts.

After the Toronto Maple Leafs won in 1963, the Cup ran out of room for names. The original Stanley Cup collar was then retired and put on permanent display at the Hall of Fame. In January 1970, it was swiped from the Hall of Fame. Security wasn't exactly militaristic in those days. The police weren't able to solve the crime, but anonymous tipster did point them to the collar. They were told to check in the back room of a cleaning store, and there they found the Stanley Cup, wrapped up neatly like a Christmas present.

Over time, many theories have been offered to explain why Kilander wanted to steal the Cup in the first place. It was widely suggested that Kilander couldn't stand to see Chicago with the Cup, and wanted to take it "back to Montreal where it belonged."

It's also been suggested that he tried to steal it to win a $100 bet, and that he had planned to take the Cup back to a hotel and give it to the sportswriters as an April Fool's Day Joke.

"He told us he just did it as a joke," Gough said. "He was a pretty wild guy, but he wasn't a thief."

But he apparently wasn't a man who paid all of his debts. He said he would be back to reclaim his ticket stub. But Gough never saw him again. Says Gough, "The guy still owes me $10."

# Gary Bettman

*NHL Commissioner Since 1993*

Gary Bettman had no idea that his career path would lead to becoming boss of the NHL the first time he saw the Stanley Cup in 1981. But even as a fan, Bettman marveled at the Cup's aura.

Bettman was among the many fans jammed into Nassau Coliseum May 21, 1981, when the New York Islanders downed the Minnesota North Stars 5–1 to claim the second of their four consecutive Stanley Cup championships.

"I could feel the Cup's charisma. It was almost like it was a living being. It had its own aura—its own personality."

— *Gary Bettman*

"I couldn't believe the electricity in the stadium," Bettman recalled. "Not just from the excitement of the fans because the Islanders had won it again. The electricity went up ten notches when the Stanley Cup came into full view. I remember thinking this is nothing short of spectacular."

His fondest Cup moment came in 1993 when he presented the Cup for the first time. He felt particularly honored that his first opportunity came at the Montreal Forum, one of hockey's shrines. All afternoon, he had rehearsed using French to congratulate the Canadiens. "I thought it would be respectful," Bettman said.

Yet what he remembers most about the day was that it was the first time he had the opportunity to examine the Cup closely. It was like being introduced to one of hockey's superstars.

"I asked where the Cup was and I went into the room by myself," Bettman said. "I could feel the Cup's charisma. It was almost like it was a living being. It had its own aura—its own personality. I know that sounds ridiculous because we are talking about an inanimate object. But it's not like an inanimate object. It's full of life, full of stories, full of people who earned it."

# Christine Simpson

*Friend of Lord Stanley's Cup*

CTV Sportsnet TV reporter Christine Simpson can be forgiven for feeling as if Stanley is an adopted member of her family.

Simpson was introduced to the Cup for the first time in 1988 when her brother Craig was a member of the Stanley Cup champion Edmonton Oilers. "What I remember from the Oilers winning the Cup was Mark Messier pouring bottle after bottle of Dom Perignon champagne into the Cup," Simpson said.

She got even closer when she took a job as the marketing manager for the Hockey Hall of Fame, and these days she keeps tabs on the Cup as a member of the electronic media. Few people have enjoyed the proximity to the Cup that Simpson has known.

While employed by the Hall of Fame, her duties sometimes included escorting the Stanley Cup to various functions.

"What you always worry about is that something will happen to it while you have it," Simpson said. "The Cup of course is big and heavy and people

*Edmonton Oiler Craig Simpson (center) surrounded by his family during his Stanley Cup celebration. His dad is to the far left and his brother Dave, a former New York Islanders' draft pick, is next to him. On the right are his sister, Christine, and his mother. Christine has probably spent more time with the Stanley Cup than Craig because she once worked for the Hall of Fame. One of her duties was to occasionally accompany the Stanley Cup on road trips.*

were always trying to help me with it. I appreciated the chivalry, but I had to tell them it was my job and they really weren't supposed to touch the Cup."

Simpson recalls that wherever she lugged the Cup "it created a bit of a stir." The Cup's celebrity status also drew other celebrities. When she took the Cup to the Los Angeles Great Western Forum in 1995 so it could appear in commercials with *Friends* star Matthew Perry and model Kim Alexis, word got out. Among those who used their celebrity status to meet the Stanley Cup was Canadian songwriter David Foster and attorney Robert Shapiro, whose national notoriety had came from representing retired NFL great O. J. Simpson. Shapiro really wanted his then-nine-year-old hockey-playing son to get a peek at the Cup. The Simpson trial wasn't on his mind that day. According to Christine Simpson's recollections, the younger Shapiro asked if he could touch the Cup.

"Someday you will play for the Cup," the elder Shapiro said.

Even as a reporter, Simpson hasn't been able to shake her connection to the Cup. During the 2000 playoffs she did some reporting work that surprised even some veteran NHL officials. According to Simpson's light investigative work, the NHL doesn't even own the Stanley Cup.

"What I found out was the ownership issue isn't quite as simple as you would think," Simpson said.

When Lord Stanley of Preston, then Canada's governor-general, donated the Cup in 1892, he authorized two trustees to make sure that the Cup was awarded to the Canadian amateur champion. He gave the Trustees broad discretionary power to settle Cup disputes. With hockey's national perspective changed by the NHL's arrival, the trustees decided in 1926 to award the Cup to the best team in the National Hockey League. In 1947, a formal agreement was signed by the trustees and NHL officials to establish an official relationship between the NHL and the Stanley Cup. It was presumed that the NHL took over ownership at that point, but historians who have looked at the document told Simpson that they believe all the NHL really received was a "custodianship."

In an interview with Simpson, one of the current trustees, Brian O'Neill, a former NHL official, said, "No question the trustees own the Stanley Cup by tradition. They have never ceded ownership in any agreement, even the agreement with the trustees and the NHL."

Amid the debate about the Cup's ownership, Simpson's report seemed to conclude that more than anything else, the Stanley Cup may belong simply to the people.

# Frank Brown

*NHL Vice President of Public Relations and Former Hockey Writer*

Frank Brown is a goaltender, but not like Patrick Roy is a goaltender. Brown is a weekend goaltender, a spare-time goaltender, a goaltender who plays against thirty-something and fortyish forwards whose best moves came when they were twelve and playing for the Dunkin Donuts Flyers.

But Brown loves the game like Roy loves the game. He loves it with romantic passion. He loves its smell and its feeling. He loves the clang the puck makes when it ricochets off the goal post and the sound of CCMs churning up freshly cleaned ice. Like Roy, Brown loves the game as a hobby, a career, and a lifestyle.

Manhattan native Brown saw his first NHL game in the old Madison Square Garden in 1965. Bob Nevin had twenty-nine goals for the Rangers that season, and future Hall of Famer Eddie Giacomin was a rookie. But what Brown seems to remember most is that the ice was cleaned with an odd contraption that looked like an "oil can on wheels." It had handles on it like a lawn mower. Two Garden workers on skates were stationed on each side and they pushed it around the ice. A big bag was attached to it into which hot water would drip, which would resurface the ice. Everyone who came to the Gardens seemed fascinated with that primitive ice cleaning apparatus.

Whether it was the "oil can on wheels" or the fact that the Rangers hadn't won a championship since 1940, Brown became a life-long hockey devotee. He started writing about hockey for the Associated Press in 1975, covering his first Stanley Cup final between the Philadelphia Flyers and the Buffalo Sabres. He eventually moved to the *New York Daily News* and his hockey career lasted more than two decades before he joined the NHL in his current capacity.

When Brown was approached to do an interview for this book, it was clear that his Stanley Cup wonder and understanding was worthy of special treatment. In lieu of tales about the Cup, he was asked to write up his own thoughts about the Cup. This is his essay:

> *Somewhere, there's a grave I should visit. The headstone probably is powder by now; certainly the person buried under it is. I owe this person millions—a debt of thanks for crafting, in all its spectacularly simple splendor, the gleaming silver bucket that became Lord Stanley's Cup. In the absence of a bouquet (can there be enough roses to offer gratitude this profound?), in the absence of a factual sense of whether this artisan lived as a man or a woman, in the absence of a clue where this important soul lived, laughed, learned, ate, drank, slept, wept, worried, suffered, and died, these humble words of appreciation are, at once, the least I can do and the best I can do.*
>
> *Good Sir or Madam, wherever you are, wherever you were, thank you for the Cup that makes hockey better than any other sport. Men will work all their lives for the privilege of crying over the Cup. They will cry because they won it, they will cry because they didn't. They will spend ten days or two weeks clubbing each other silly, will break each other's bones, will rend each other's flesh, will shed each other's blood (or their own; it couldn't matter less). And still they will shake hands when the series is over because over that period of time they shared, on a frozen field of combat, the gallant honor of striving for the Cup.*

*The winners will bring it to their parents' homes and say, with words or with smiles, the same words just typed here: Thank you. Thanks, Mom and Dad. Thanks for driving me to the rink. Thanks for the skates at Christmas. Thanks for the goal net in the driveway. Thanks for shivering through all those practices. Thanks for everything. Mom, Dad, when this Cup goes to the engraver, your hands will hold the chisel and the hammer as the name you gave me— YOUR name—is immortalized.*

*Others will speak to parents now gone, to brothers or sisters or friends who didn't live to see the day the dream came true. They will close their eyes and speak with their hearts. From their floats on parade day, they will search the skies for a cloud that looks like someone in Heaven who truly would have loved to have been there.*

*Our Cup is for Howe and Richard and Beliveau and Gretzky. And it is for Holik or Lehtinen or Zubov or Leetch. Canadians can win it. Americans can win it. Or Czech Republicans or Russians or Slovaks or Finns or Swedes. It isn't merely a Cup; it is a wondrous melting pot. And that democracy is a marvel. Everybody who helped win it gets to touch it, to carry it above his head, even hold it in the lap of his wheelchair. The scorers who checked, the checkers who scored, the muckers who passed, the passers who mucked, the fighters who held their tempers and skated away from trouble, they touch sweaty fingers to the cold sterling silver and suddenly all the pain leaves them— flies upward with the spirits of the fans who buy the tickets and the T-shirts and the banners and the posters, the ones who paint their faces and wear their jerseys to the rink for the games in May that matter and the games in September that don't.*

*It is incredible what they put themselves through—the players, the fans, the coaches who would sign any deal with any devil if it guaranteed the last line change, the best match-up, another skate save in overtime of Game 7. And then again, it is not incredible at all. You stand in a rink and you see the faithful wave their towels or their shakers, you hear the choir of their voices in a temple of all that is pure about our game, and you know there is no place else to be. You know there are sixteen teams, then eight, then four, then two, then one, and when that one team is yours, all the energy in the universe channels through Stanley into your cells, your molecules, your atoms.*

*And forgive me, if the bowl was a little smaller or a little taller or a little wider, it wouldn't be the Cup of our fathers and our forefathers, the Cup Bower won at forty-two, the Cup Baun won on a broken ankle, the one Pocket Rocket raised eleven times in twenty seasons. It might be some soaped up candy dish, but it wouldn't be Stanley, which some nameless, long-dead silversmith crafted into hockey perfection just over one hundred years ago.*

*Our gratitude is beyond measure.*

# Bryan Lewis

*Referee, Five Stanley Cup Championship Series, Three Clinching Games*

During Bryan Lewis' Stanley Cup final appearances in the early 1980s, a player would occasionally skate past him after a controversial call and yell, "Hey, this is a big game for us."

What players didn't seem to understand was that Lewis viewed it as a very big game for himself as well. Lewis, today the NHL's supervisor of officials, says referees are as proud to reach the championship series as the players are, particularly because a referee earns the right to officiate in the final on the basis of performance-based merit, not seniority. Lewis refereed during the New York Islanders run of four consecutive Stanley Cups (1980–83) and when the Edmonton Oilers' dynasty was beginning (in 1983–84 and 1984–85).

"The games you remember were the ones that were tough and difficult," Lewis said. "I remember [Islanders' goaltender] Billy Smith in his heyday. Any time players got near the net, you really had to pay attention. That wasn't the down part. That was just when you had to be at your best because you knew that if the puck was near the net it was going to be trouble."

He can still vividly remember the area around Smith as a hornet's nest of trouble as Smith aggressively battled forwards who encroached upon his boundaries. It was always hand-to-hand combat in Smith's crease. Smith wouldn't have liked it any other way.

"Things were always happening and they were generally generated by Bill Smith," Lewis said. "Everybody knew it. We just had to be ready to mitigate if need be."

As it is today, referees didn't find out in Lewis' era whether they would work a Stanley Cup final until the last possible moment. "But as soon as you found out you called home," Lewis said. "Certainly there is pride involved."

NHL officials were always thrilled to learn that the Stanley Cup was stored in their dressing room when a team was one win short of clinching. It was stored in a large box and covered in sponges. Referees were known to steal a peek here and there. In fact, it was commonplace for NHL officials (particularly a stand-by official) to bring their family in for Stanley Cup photos before the game. "That was one of the quiet perks that no one knew about," Lewis said.

Referees are required to stay on the ice to assure that the postgame handshake is conducted "without incident," even though no one can remember any incidents involving one of hockey's grandest traditions. But Lewis would linger on the ice to watch the Cup presentation to the winning team.

> "I've been on the ice when the Stanley Cup was presented. Not many people can say that."
>
> — *Bryan Lewis*

"You seize every moment you can to be able to stand there and watch," Lewis said. "I had a better view than members of the press. I had a better view than a lot of people. I've been on the ice when the Stanley Cup was presented. Not many people can say that."

# Rick Minch

*Vice President for Public Relations, New Jersey Devils*

The New Jersey Devils' Cup triumph in 2000 was significant enough to have an impact on Wall Street, if only for a few minutes.

In celebration of the Devils' second championship in five years, captain Scott Stevens, center Scott Gomez, and winger Jay Pandolfo were invited to the New York Stock Exchange to ring the closing bell and display the Cup.

"We walked through the whole place and I had no idea where we were," recalls Devils' public relations director Rick Minch. "They kept walking us and walking us through this sea of people. Every time one of the guys held the Cup up people just stopped working. Their clients had to be losing money right and left because they just quit working. Pictures, autographs . . . people just went wild."

Minch had a front seat to the poignancy surrounding the crowning of the first Stanley Cup championship of the twenty-first century. His treasured memories: Randy McKay putting his months-old son Dawson in the Stanley Cup's bowl on the bench minutes after the Devils had dispatched the Dallas Stars in the clinching game in Dallas; and the four Russian players, Sergei Nemchinov, Vladimir Malakhov, Alexander Mogilny, and Sergei Brylin, as well as assistant coach Slava Fetisov, posing for a picture.

The Devils are often the under-loved step-child in New York area hockey, overshadowed by the New York Rangers' passionate following and perhaps even by the New York Islanders' aura of having won four consecutive Stanley Cups from 1980–83 (although their luster has been dulled in recent years). When the Devils play home games against the New York Rangers, often Rangers' cheers rule New Jersey's home ice.

That's why Minch won't forget when the Devils took the Stanley Cup to Time Square. It was in essence taking it behind enemy lines.

En route to a special dinner at the All-Star Café, the Devils had the bus stop in Times Square, near the Discount Tickets booth, so all the players could take pictures with Times Square's ambience as a backdrop. When they exited the bus, it was quickly forgotten that they were interlopers in Rangers' country. Said Minch, "When we walked the two blocks to the All-Star Café, people were going bananas."

# Dick Irvin Jr.

*Hall of Fame Broadcaster and Son of Famed NHL Coach Dick Irvin Sr.*

Dick Irvin's headlong dive into the hockey world is as easy to fathom as the Kennedys turning politics into the family business.

With his father already legendary, Irvin developed his love of the game naturally. He attended his first Stanley Cup championship game in 1938 and believes he and Reuters hockey writer Norm MacLean are the only two people who were in the building when the New York Rangers won the Stanley Cup in 1940 and 1994.

Irvin's father was coaching the Maple Leafs in 1940 and he allowed his eight-year-old son to attend the game. "I know it was a Saturday night because he would only let me go to the games on a Saturday night," Irvin recalled. "I remember Bryan Hextall winning the game with a goal in overtime."

MacLean's father was a huge Rangers fan; he had traveled from New York with his young son Norm in tow to see the clincher.

"Norm and I used to kid that maybe we would both be around when the Rangers won, and they did in 1994," said Irvin, who broadcast the game for *Hockey Night in Canada.*

Irvin's father holds the NHL record with sixteen trips to the Stanley Cup Final during his twenty-six seasons. He won the Stanley Cup while coaching Toronto in 1931–32, and while behind Montreal's bench in 1943–44, 1945–46, and 1952–53. His teams made the playoffs during twenty-four of those twenty-six seasons.

"I had to laugh at [Dallas Stars coach] Ken Hitchcock during the playoffs," Irvin said. "He talked about how draining the experience was, and how he felt like he had been through the wringer. I told him my dad made the finals sixteen times, and he couldn't believe it."

Irvin's record as a broadcaster is on par with his father's as a coach. He broadcast twenty-one Stanley Cup Final series for Hockey Night in Canada, including fourteen in a row from 1967–1980. In the broadcasting world he has garnered the same measure of respect as his father earned in the coaching fraternity.

Amid a passel of vivid Stanley Cup championship broadcast memories, his favorite championship was the Canadiens' 1971 triumph, because no one had expected the Canadiens to win. Montreal finished third in the Eastern Conference standings that season, twenty-four points behind Boston. The expectation was that the Bruins would oust the Canadiens in the first round.

It has been well documented that the Canadiens lost Game 1 and then fell behind 5–1 in Game 2 in Boston before rallying to win that game and the series. Irvin agrees that Henri Richard's goal at the end of the second period—to cut the lead to three goals—was crucial. But he adds another layer to that story. He remembers vividly that the *Hockey Night in Canada* cameras caught Bruins' players Derek Sanderson and Bobby Orr sharing a laugh before the start of the third period. Who knows what they were talking about—it could have had nothing to do with the game. But it certainly caused raised eyebrows.

"[Famed *Hockey Night in Canada* producer] Ralph Mellanby called me on our intercom system and said, 'These guys better not be laughing because this game may not be over.' He said he had a funny feeling that Montreal would come back, and they did."

The Canadiens scored five unanswered goals in the third period to win 7–5. "This was Jean Beliveau's last hurrah and he just took over," Irvin said. "It was like he turned back the calendar."

Goaltender Ken Dryden, then in his rookie season, won the Conn Smythe Trophy. "With all due respect to Ken Dryden, the Canadiens don't win that Stanley Cup without Frank Mahovlich," Irvin said.

With almost thirty years of postmortems now available, Boston coach Tom Johnson's decision to use Eddie Johnston as his netminder in Game 2 instead of Gerry Cheevers is frequently viewed as a blunder that may have turned the series in Montreal's favor. Cheevers had been in the net during the Bruins' 3–1 triumph in Game 1.

But Irvin offers two arguments in Johnson's defense: First, Cheevers and Johnston had split duties during the regular season (and Johnston actually had the better record and goals-against average). Secondly, most critics fail to point out that Johnson also alternated Cheevers and Johnston when the Bruins won the Stanley Cup in 1972. Nobody viewed his coaching decision as a faulty strategy then.

Irvin also struggles with the notion of calling Montreal's triumph over Boston one of hockey's great upsets. "Red Fisher and I have argued about this," Irvin said. "How can you say it's an upset? More players off that Canadiens team are in the Hall of Fame then off that Bruins' team."

The fact that the Canadiens needed seven games to dispatch the Chicago Black Hawks in the Stanley Cup Final merely adds to the wonder of that championship march. Irvin has two memories of that game: "Chicago had a 1–0 lead in Game 7 and Bobby Hull hit the goal post. Dryden was ten feet out of the net. He hit the puck so hard it ricocheted all the way to the blue line," he says. "If that puck goes in, the Black Hawks probably win. Then, there was Jean Beliveau's last act as captain carrying the Stanley Cup. We didn't know he was retiring then, but it was so fitting."

Irvin was born to appreciate the grandeur of the quest for hockey's Holy Grail; he absorbed hockey knowledge without even knowing that he had been taught. The elder Irvin was 4–12 in the Stanley Cup Final and had experienced every conceivable hardship a coach can be dealt. Coach Dick Irvin started his NHL career with the Chicago Black Hawks in 1930–31 and surprised many by taking his team to the Stanley Cup championship series, where they lost to a Montreal team led by Howie Morenz. They lost Game 5 by a 2–0 count—typical of the kind of luck Irvin Sr. would have in the Final.

The only time Dick Irvin saw one of his father's teams win the championship was in 1953, when the Canadiens downed Boston. The son remembers it well because of his father's bold actions in the semifinal. The Canadiens had lost three consecutive games to fall behind 3-2 in the best-of-seven series against Chicago when Irvin decided to bench three regulars, including goaltender Gerry McNeil. He replaced McNeil with Jacques Plante, a rookie whose previous NHL experience consisted of three NHL regular-season games.

"I remember my dad calling home before that game and saying, 'If we lose tonight, I will lose my job,'" the son recalls.

Clearly, Montreal General Manager Frank Selke wasn't enamoured with his coach's decision to use the unproven Plante in Game 6. Years later Plante would tell Irvin Jr. that his father had approached him in the hotel in Chicago with news and a forecast.

"You are playing and you are going to get a shutout," Dick Irvin Sr. told Plante.

The young Irvin wasn't present in the dressing room before the game, but he was told that the young goaltender's nerves were showing. "He was so nervous that the trainer had to tie his skates," Irvin Jr. says, laughing. "That's great for his teammates to see."

Early in the game Plante thwarted twenty-three-goal scorer Jim McFadden on a breakaway, and Plante quickly looked as comfortable as any veteran in a game. As the elder Irvin had prophesized, Plante earned a shutout. It came on a 3–0 decision. The Canadiens went on to win the title, although Irvin switched back to McNeil in the championship series against Boston.

> "I remember my dad calling home before that game and saying, 'If we lose tonight, I will lose my job."
>
> — *Dick Irvin Jr.*

"I remember players carried my dad on their shoulders while they were on the ice," Irvin said. "Then we just went home. I remember my dad talking to his brother on the phone. There were no big celebrations back then, just the presentation of the Cup and then everyone went home. There wasn't even a parade back then. There was a private dinner for the team and family the next day."

Dick Irvin was fourteen in 1946 when his father's Montreal team defeated Boston in the Final to win his second Stanley Cup crown. Montreal owner Donat Raymond sent him a check for $1,000 as a bonus. "It was amazing to get $1,000 back then," Irvin recalled. "It was a holiday in our house."

What the young Irvin didn't see with his own eyes he heard with his ears, thanks to the many stories his father told him. Remember that his father coached from 1931 to 1956. He gave the hockey world the Punch Line of Toe Blake, Elmer Lach, and Rocket Richard. He coached against Morenz, the Production Line, Terry Sawchuk, and Glenn Hall.

Dick Irvin Sr. may have appreciated his four championships more simply because he knew—better than most—what it felt like to be at the championship's doorstep without getting in. His unenviable NHL coaching record of twelve losses in the Stanley Cup Final isn't likely to ever be erased. "He had some Game

7 losses, the Tony Leswick goal, overtime games," his son said. "He was so close to winning a few more. In 1955 they played the final without Richard and took the Red Wings to seven games."

Montreal's heartbreaking loss to Detroit on Leswick's goal was a difficult loss to accept because it was a fluky overtime tally in a Game 7. The Canadiens had won Games 5 and 6 to tie up the series. Game 7 was knotted 1–1 entering overtime. Leswick apparently fired the puck toward the net right before a line change. The late Hall of Fame defenseman Doug Harvey, who had a habit of using his glove to punch the puck down on the ice when it was in midair, did it for probably the thousandth time in his career. Only this time, instead of dropping down in front of him or out of harm's way, the puck was inadvertently deflected into his own net. Montreal goaltender McNeil would tell Irvin Jr. in later years: "You all call it the Leswick goal. I call it the Harvey goal."

But that was far from Irvin Sr.'s most disheartening loss. That came in his rookie NHL coaching campaign after he coaxed his Black Hawks team to the final game of the 1931 championship series.

"In later years," said the son. "I found out the biggest disappointment of his coaching career was that loss [in the deciding game]. The reason was he found out that a bunch of his players had gone out and got drunk the night before. He could have won in his first season as coach."

Irvin Jr. is convinced that his family background has heightened his awareness of the game's spirit and historical framework. His father died in 1957. He was sixty-four.

"My only regret as a broadcaster was that my father didn't live long enough to see me do it," Irvin said. "But it is amazing that a lot of what I heard from him would come back to me through the years at certain times. A lot of his wisdom is still valid today."

Irvin is retired as a full-time broadcaster; however, he still occasionally appears on television, on pregame shows for instance. Proud of his long history in the game, Irvin made sure he saw a playoff game in 2000. With Montreal out of the playoffs, he drove to Ottawa for a game. That means he has seen a live postseason game in every decade since the 1930s. "Now I don't have to worry about it for another ten years," Irvin says, laughing.

# Jim Matheson

*Hall of Fame Sportswriter*

When hockey writer Jim Matheson recalls the raw emotion and jubilation he witnessed after each of the Edmonton Oilers' five Stanley Cup championships, he doesn't think of Wayne Gretzky, Mark Messier, Grant Fuhr, or Glenn Anderson.

He thinks of Kent Nilsson.

"Nobody was more excited to win a Stanley Cup than Kent," Matheson said. "When he won the Cup, he was like fourteen years old again. He was just so happy."

On March 2, 1987, the Oilers had acquired eight-year veteran Nilsson from the Minnesota North Stars for future considerations. But unfortunately, Nilsson came with baggage.

"For a long time he had a reputation of being a very talented player, but he wasn't a winner," Matheson said. "They called him Magic. He had talent. But the perception was that all he cared about was getting his points."

Legend has it that Messier bullied Nilsson into cranking up his performance level in the 1987 postseason. "The story has always been that Wayne Gretzky always had his arm around Nilsson and Mark Messier always had his hands around Kent's throat," Matheson said. "That was partially true. They worked the good cop, bad cop routine with him."

Whatever the motivation, Nilsson played like a winner in the 1987 playoffs. He played on a line with Messier and Anderson—certainly one of the most speed-laden lines in NHL history—and produced six goals and thirteen assists in twenty-one games. In the post-Cup celebration Nilsson was giddy, as if a heavy burden had been lifted from his psyche. After winning his only NHL championship, Nilsson took his talents back to Europe, where he stayed except for a six-game stint with the Oilers before retiring in 1995.

Matheson remembers Gretzky and Messier as being beloved leaders—the kind of leaders that teammates followed out of friendship and respect. "They were two great players," Matheson said. "But they never lorded that over teammates. They made sure everyone got credit for their contributions."

Having written and reported on the Oilers since they joined the World Hockey Association in 1972, Matheson considers their Stanley Cup years as some of his most memorable moments as a sportswriter. He never felt like he was part of the Oilers' success, and yet he understood that the more success the franchise had the more people were interested in reading what he had to say.

"My buddies in the business used to complain when their teams would go far in the playoffs because it was so much work," Matheson said. "They would say, 'I'm glad my team was out in the first round.' But I felt that's why you write—to have the hope that you will cover a team that's actually good enough to compete for the Stanley Cup. You aren't on the team. But when you go through two months of playoffs, you are wrung out just like they are. But every writer should get a chance to cover one team that was good enough to win the Cup."

As Matheson recalls, the stories didn't stop when the Cup was won because the Oilers carried the Stanley Cup everywhere they went during a championship summer. He recalls that the Cup was left for hours at the corner of Jasper and First Street, and no one fretted about whether it would be stolen.

"Sparky [Lyle "Sparky" Kulchisky, Edmonton's assistant trainer] would say, 'Who would steal the Stanley Cup?'" Matheson said. "It would be like stealing a cop car. Where would you park it? You couldn't park a stolen cop car in front of your house. If you stole the Cup, what would you do with it? Put it in your closet and invite everyone in the neighborhood over for a party?"

Matheson can amplify the story of what happened when unknown members of the Oilers' organization swiped the Cup to prevent then-Flyers coach Mike Keenan from using it for motivational purposes. This was as much strategy as it was a prank.

"Remember, the Oilers were up three games to one in the series," Matheson said. "On the morning of the fifth game, Keenan brought the Cup to the Flyers' dressing room and said, 'This is what we are playing for.' They won Game 5. He did the same thing in Game 6 and Philly won that game. When we got back to Edmonton for Game 7, the Oilers stuck the Cup in a backroom where Keenan couldn't get it."

Matheson remembers that Sparky's version of what happened was more colorful than accurate.

"The circus was in town and Sparky said he saw it on the way to Red Deer [Alberta] and he just happened to notice that the Cup was in the cage with the lions and tigers," Matheson said.

The Cup mysteriously reappeared when it came time for the Oilers to celebrate after they won Game 7. Maybe the circus clowns brought it back.

Matheson, elected to the Hall of Fame in 2000, attended just one Stanley Cup party—the first one at general manager/coach Glen Sather's home. He didn't drink from the Cup, but he did hoist it. "It was a lot heavier than I thought it would be," he says.

> "You aren't on the team. But when you go through two months of playoffs, you are wrung out just like they are."
>
> — *Jim Matheson*

Sather is a powerful figure in Stanley Cup lore, the mastermind of the Oilers' dynasty. He is a well-spoken, stately figure, quick with a joke and never at a loss for offering the right words at the right time. "Slats tried to take it in stride, but he's more emotional than people realize," Matheson said. "He was pretty charged when they won. It was validation for a young talented team that was arrogant and cocky. He said they would win the Cup, and they did. Slats was a great bench coach."

The Oilers won four Stanley Cup championships over five seasons (1983–84 to 1987–88) and most of their top players were still in their prime. But when Gretzky was dealt to the Los Angeles Kings in 1988—in what was considered hockey's trade of the century—Matheson admits that he believed the Oilers' dynasty was over. That verdict was supported by Gretzky's Kings knocking the Oilers out of the playoffs in 1989.

"That's why the Oilers' fifth Cup was the most interesting," Matheson says. "No one figured they would win another. To a lot of the veterans, that one was the most satisfying. Messier, [Jari] Kurri, [Glenn] Anderson were all really good players and I think they wanted to prove they could win without Gretzky."

Matheson always considered it highly unfair when he heard it suggested that the Oilers wouldn't have won multiple titles without Gretzky. "Even without Gretzky that team would have been good enough to beat teams that are winning it today," Matheson says.

Messier, Anderson, Kurri, Randy Gregg, Charlie Huddy, Kevin Lowe, and Grant Fuhr were the only seven players to be on all five Cup-winning Oilers' teams. Messier and Lowe went on to win a sixth Cup as a member of the New York Rangers in 1994.

Matheson laughs. "Six Stanley Cups for one player," he says. "That's like cheating."

# Chapter Three

## Stories, 1983–The Present

# Lanny McDonald

*Calgary Flames, 1988–89*

As the euphoric Calgary Flames were high-fiving and rebel yelling in celebration of their Stanley Cup championship in 1989, Lanny McDonald experienced an overwhelming sense of tranquility that probably seemed foreign for such a raucous occasion. But it was an appropriate feeling for an NHL player who endured a long journey to reach his summit.

"When you have finally won the Cup and realized your dream of holding it up after sixteen years, it was more a feeling of peacefulness than anything else," McDonald said. "I enjoy looking around the room and seeing everyone whooping and hollering. After sixteen years of hard labor, it was peacefulness."

McDonald was thirty-six; he had reached the end of his career when the Flames won the Stanley Cup. In the prime of his career, he was among the NHL's most dangerous scorers. He had scored forty or more goals for three consecutive seasons in the late 1970s and he had totaled sixty-six goals for the Flames in 1982–83. But the grand prize, the Stanley Cup, had eluded him, the price he paid for playing the majority of his career with non-contending teams. In two of his prime years he was playing with the NHL's Colorado Rockies organization that was closer to being a minor-league team than it was to being a real contender.

"I don't think I ever questioned that I was going to win," McDonald says. "The question was whether I was going to have enough time, or whether I was going to run out of time."

It was as if fate had turned sentimental in 1988–89. Although McDonald was slowing down, he managed to net his five hundredth career goal before the end of the regular season. McDonald had been scoreless in the playoffs, and Coach Terry Crisp had chosen not to use McDonald in three of the first five games in the Stanley Cup final against Montreal. Before Game 6, assistant coach Doug Risebrough had summoned McDonald for a private chat. Not knowing whether he would be in or out, McDonald was relieved when Risebrough simply talked to him about what his role would be on the power play. With Calgary up 3–2 in the best-of-seven series, clearly there had been public sentiment for McDonald to be returned to the lineup to assure his chance to be involved in the possible Cup celebration. For Game 6, Crisp had to choose among McDonald, Jim Peplinski, or Tim Hunter for his twelfth forward spot. Whether Crisp chose McDonald for sentimental reasons or for his offensive knack didn't matter because McDonald's presence turned out to provide an offensive lift as much as a sentimental one.

With the game tied 1–1 in the second period, McDonald emerged from the penalty box and joined a 4-on-2 break into the Montreal zone. Joe Nieuwendyk threaded a pass through Chris Chelios to McDonald, who lofted a shot over goaltender Patrick Roy for a 2–1 lead. The Flames went on to win the game 4–2.

McDonald remembers the charter flight home to Calgary from Montreal as one of the highlights of his career. Trainer Jim "Bearcat" Murray, armed with wire cutters, had come to McDonald and Peplinski before the plane was loaded to get their blessing for his plan to liberate the Stanley Cup from its locked case in the cargo hold. (Legend has it that Canadian customs officials assisted Murray in this.)

"He was going to store it in the back washroom," McDonald said. "Of course we thought that was an awesome idea."

When the jet was airborne, the pilot came on the intercom and said, "Jim Murray had brought a special passenger on board."

> "When you have finally won the Cup and realized your dream of holding it up after sixteen years, it was more a feeling of peacefulness than anything else."
>
> — Lanny McDonald

When Murray emerged from the washroom with the Cup, it signaled the beginning of the most joyous four-and-a-half-hour plane ride that McDonald had ever known. "What I remember was that we all shared in that moment," McDonald said. "We had front office, hockey management, players, wives, girlfriends, fiancées, family members. The heart and soul of the organization was all there together."

McDonald remembers looking around and feeling good for someone—defenseman Rob Ramage, who had also known days in Colorado. "Back then you were supposed to be playing to win the Stanley Cup, but after the first week you didn't like your chances," McDonald said.

Then there was Joe Mullen, "who had grown up in Hell's Kitchen, New York, and now his name was going on the Stanley Cup."

He also felt beholden to goaltender Mike Vernon, whose brilliance, particularly in the first round series against Vancouver, had probably been the most crucial element of the Flames' Cup run. "There were so many stories within the story," McDonald said.

Upon returning to Calgary, McDonald waited for his opportunity and then grabbed the Stanley Cup and whisked it away to his home west of the city in Springbrook for a couple of days. It's still unclear under whose authority McDonald invoked claim to this rare privilege.

"I wouldn't call it stealing it," McDonald said. "But it was pretty neat to wake up and see the Cup at the foot of the bed."

The McDonalds had the Cup for two days. "But we only drank milk out of it," he deadpans. Why don't we believe that? "You probably shouldn't," he says, laughing.

Lanny and wife Ardell invited all of their neighbors to come over for coffee with Stanley. He transported the Cup to his children's schools.

"It was just neat to share that experience," McDonald says. "Whether you are five or fifty-five the mystique of the Cup is phenomenal."

His hockey career now capped in ornate style, McDonald went gently into retirement that summer. Before doing so, he and Joey Mullen tried to impart wisdom to the younger players, such as Gary Roberts and Joe Nieuwendyk. Roberts and Nieuwendyk were both twenty-two when the Flames began their 1989 march to the championship.

"We continually kept telling them *this* doesn't just happen every year." McDonald said. "You think you are automatically going back to the final. But you don't get back easily. You have to enjoy it when you are there. Nieuwendyk won last year, but it took him ten years. Roberts still hasn't been back.

# Jacques Demers

*Coach, Montreal Canadiens, 1992–93*

Coach Jacques Demers truly understood the aura of the Stanley Cup the night it helped him gain safe passage through a frenzied mob on the streets of Montreal June 10, 1993.

The moment came after midnight, a couple of hours after Demers' Montreal Canadiens had defeated the Los Angeles Kings 4–1 to win the twenty-fourth NHL championship in the Canadiens' storied history. Unlike most of the previous championships, this crown had been unexpected. The Canadiens owned the NHL's sixth-best record and, going into the playoffs, most pundits presumed the Mario Lemieux–charged Pittsburgh Penguins were the team to beat. No one could have foreseen the Canadiens winning ten consecutive playoff games in overtime and posting a 16–4 playoff mark. The unexpected joy of the occasion is the only explanation for why Montreal was engulfed in a celebratory riot into the wee hours of morning.

Members of the Canadiens' organization were told to stay at the Montreal Forum until the celebration lost some of its steam. But when Demers and his family left a couple of hours later with hope of going to an Italian restaurant, the streets were still a sea of celebrating fans.

Demers was in his brother-in-law's car, a ten-year-old Mercury Cougar, and as the car inched its way through the mob near the corner of Stanley and St. Catherine's Streets, the revelers began shaking the car. Demers was worried that they were going to tip over the automobile. "My daughter [Mylene] started crying and it was very scary," Demers said.

Against his brother-in-law's pleading, Demers exited the car and the crowd immediately recognized him. The crowd acted as if Demers was a deity who had suddenly appeared.

"It was like the parting of the Red Sea," Demers said. "How powerful can one man be for one night? I wasn't afraid to get out of the car. I told my brother-in-law, 'They aren't going to hurt me.' As soon as I got out of the car, everyone started yelling, 'Let the coach go through. Let him through,' and it just opened up. It wasn't me they were letting through; it was the coach of the Stanley Cup champions. Whoever it would have been, they would have let him through."

He remembers going against his wife Debbie's suggestion to leave the phone off the hook when they went to bed that night. He received his first congratulatory call at 6:00 A.M. and the phone never stopped ringing.

Demers is an outgoing, friendly man who likes to talk to everyone. But he remembers that the week after he won the Cup he was uncharacteristically quiet. "People kept asking me if I was all right," Demers recalled.

He remembers he was emotionally tired from the two-month battle to win the Cup, but perhaps his mood also reflected the reverence he felt for having climbed the mountain. He was a native Montreal citizen who understood the importance of the Cup to Canadian culture.

"It was like a big dream," Demers said. "I never played pro hockey. I never even played junior hockey. All of a sudden I win the Cup in Montreal. Remember I had seen Yvon Cournoyer and Serge Savard raise the Cup. Henri Richard. Now I'm doing it. It was like a dream. I would write a book but no one would believe it. I came from nowhere—fired by Detroit, went into radio for a couple of years. I think my career could be over and then Serge Savard gives me a call. I was on a high for the whole summer. This is like winning the Cup in your own backyard."

Emotionally, he was over-extended that summer. "When I started training camp in September, I was tired," he remembers.

His other fond memory of the experience was seeing his name on the Stanley Cup the following season when he visited the Hall of Fame.

"I had lifted the Stanley Cup and taken it to my golf tournament," Demers said. "But until you see your name on the Cup you really don't believe you won it."

# Jacques Lemaire

*Montreal Canadiens, 1967–68, 1968–69, 1970–71, 1972–73, 1975–76,*
*1976–77, 1977–78, and 1978–79*

*Coach, New Jersey Devils, 1994–95*

One of the more memorable goals in NHL playoff history isn't on the list of favorite memories for the man who scored it.

Older Montreal fans can all remember Jacques Lemaire igniting a come-from-behind 3–2 win against the Chicago Black Hawks in Game 7 of the 1971 Stanley Cup final. It was a crisp shot from center ice that Black Hawks goal-tender Tony Esposito whiffed on. The Black Hawks were leading 2–0 and seemed to be in charge until Lemaire unleashed the fateful shot.

"It was a huge goal, but it was a lucky goal," Lemaire said. "It is not all that special to me. I just wanted to get off the ice. I just shot and went directly to the bench. When I was going to the bench I heard some fans yell. I said, 'What happened?' I didn't know. To me the special moment of winning the Cup came in 1976 when we beat the Flyers."

The Flyers had won Stanley Cup titles in 1974 and 1975, and in 1975–76 they had the Campbell Conference's best record of 51–13–16. Montreal had the Wales Conference's best record of 58–11–11. They were favored when they met Lemaire's Canadiens in the 1976 finals.

"I think they were expected to beat us four in a row," Lemaire said. "But we beat them four in a row."

The first three games were one-goal decisions, and the Canadiens completed the sweep when Guy Lafleur and Pete Mahovlich scored third-period goals in a 5–3 win in Game 4.

"I always said that I will never see another group of guys who will stick to a plan the way that we did that year," Lemaire said. "The intensity we had, the way we felt—that's what I remember most."

Even though Lemaire had eight Stanley Cups, he insists he never worked harder to win one than he did when he coached the New Jersey Devils to the 1995 Stanley Cup. "As a player you think only of yourself," Lemaire said. "As a player, I just worried about doing my job. You worry just about performing. I never worried about making mistakes. As a coach you worry about twenty-four guys. Will this guy be OK? Will our system work? You don't want to make a mistake as a coach. You go through every step. You think about the penalty killing, the power play. You must worry about whether there is a certain thing that they could do that would neutralize your team. You must look at everything so carefully. That's why you feel so good when you win as a coach."

> "I will never see another group of guys who will stick to a plan the way that we did that year. The intensity we had, the way we felt—that's what I remember most about winning."
>
> — *Jacques Lemaire*

# Rob Ramage

*Calgary Flames, 1988–89*

*Montreal Canadiens, 1992–93*

While Rob Ramage was waiting for a bus during the 1989 Stanley Cup final, he remembered former NHL player/farmer Bert Olmstead telling him that winning the Stanley Cup meant more to him sitting on his tractor than it did when he was swigging beer in the postgame revelry.

Olmstead won five Stanley Cup championships during his career—four with Montreal and one with Toronto. "Back then, he would celebrate for two days and then he would be back on the farm," Ramage said. "He said that he would be on the tractor and three weeks later it would come to him: 'I won the Stanley Cup.' He told me, 'You will have some euphoria afterwards, but it's not going to hit you until late in the summer what you have really done.' How profound that was."

Ramage remembers that after the parades, parties, champagne drinking and backslapping were over, after the wave of enthusiasm had worn down, his greatest satisfaction came when he was alone with his thoughts. "When you were able to capture a quiet moment, you think: They can't take this away from me. I won the Cup."

Ramage feels somewhat fortunate to have won the Cup because, after all, fourteen months earlier the Cup wasn't even on his radar. He had settled into a good career with the St. Louis Blues and frankly he didn't predict that team would win a Stanley Cup because of their financial outlook. The cash-strapped Blues seemed content to spend just enough to be competitive but not enough to take the franchise to the championship level. At the time Ramage was only twenty-nine, but he seems embarrassed now to admit that he was actually resigned to the fact that he had no hope of winning a Stanley Cup. He was stunned when the Blues traded him and goalkeeper Rick Wamsley to Calgary for Brett Hull and Steve Bozek.

Upon hearing the news on March 7, 1988, Ramage threw his equipment into his Jeep and headed up old Highway 40 toward his suburban St. Louis home.

"I am bouncing along there and we had just played Calgary and I started to go over their lineup," Ramage said. "I suddenly realized: I am going to have a shot at winning. When I got there it was a different culture and a different attitude. This was a very focused, veteran team."

The Flames won the President's Trophy, but they didn't win the Cup in 1988. Ramage remembers that during the following season, Flames' goaltending consultant Glenn Hall, one of the greatest goaltenders in NHL history, was brought in to address the team. He essentially was brought to preach the wonders of devotion to defensive hockey.

"He said. 'You lit it up and scored a lot of goals last season, but defense wins championships. You have to do something about your goals against,'" Ramage recalled. "We knocked off one hundred goals against that season. Our resolve was that we had let something slip through our hands in 1987–88 and we weren't going to do it again."

The closeness of the Flames was one of the team's greatest strengths. Ramage remembers how tough it was on everyone not to have popular Flames veteran Lanny McDonald playing with them. When the Flames flew home from Montreal after Game 4, Lanny's wife, Ardell, was also on the flight. "There was a real somber mood because he was our leader," Ramage said. "This was a very close team. When we got together for a ten-year reunion, we picked up like it was yesterday."

Defeating the Canadiens was not an easy task. Ramage lauds Flames' general manager Cliff Fletcher for his decision to bring Olmstead and Hall along during the Cup march to provide insight about winning the Cup. It also helped that the staff included Doug Risebrough, a four-time Stanley Cup winner in Montreal.

"We were playing the sweater, the tradition, the legend of the Montreal Canadiens," Ramage said. "Risebrough put it best: 'Stop playing the sweater and play the guy inside the sweater. Don't get overwhelmed by the sweater.'"

When the Flames came back to Calgary after winning the Cup in Montreal, Ramage recalls everyone gathering at Mike Vernon's house. Ramage, thirty-one when the Flames won, remembers he crashed early at the party, and some of the young players who awakened him the next day enjoyed teasing him about his early exit. Some had stayed up all night.

"It was the young guys, [Joe Nieuwendyk and Gary Roberts] waking me up," Ramage said. "They said, 'C'mon, Rammer you old-timer, get up and eat some bacon and eggs. That night was a lot of fun.'"

# Craig Simpson

*Edmonton Oilers, 1987–88 and 1989–90*

In the mid-1980s, the doorway into the Edmonton Oilers' dressing room seemed like a magic portal to a better world for those who were stuck on the outside looking in.

Around the NHL, players viewed the Oilers' room with respect, even reverence. It was as if the mysteries and secrets of hockey were revealed to all those who entered. Oilers' players like Wayne Gretzky, Mark Messier, Kevin Lowe, and others were viewed as hockey's high priests, capable of helping others find their way to a wondrous level of performance. As rich as the Oilers were in talent, they also possessed another talent: they knew how to convert others to their beliefs. Ordinary players might go into that room, but champions came out. That's why players viewed a trade to the Oilers as if they had received a higher calling.

"From the minute you walked down the corridor, for me it was November 25, 1987, you honestly felt like you were part of a winner," remembers Craig Simpson. "From the minute you walked into the room, you weren't an outsider. They were going to help you. You were embraced. Success was a collective. It was a "we" success. The reason why people went to the wall for Gretzky and Messier is because they were willing to share the credit." What was unsaid but immediately understood, Simpson remembers, was that "you had to be the best player you could be to help win a championship."

Simpson had come from the Pittsburgh Penguins, a team with no history of success at that time. "Oilers practices were a lot better than our games in Pittsburgh," Simpson said. "You had to bring up your level. It was hard work, but it was fun. The players made it fun."

Walking through the portal seemed to have a special effect on Simpson, who turned out to be a postseason point-scoring machine. In his NHL career, he averaged better than one point per game (thirty-six goals and thirty-two assists for sixty-eight points in sixty-seven postseason games). During the Cup triumphs in 1988 and 1990, Simpson had fifty points in forty-one games. He led all postseason scorers in 1990 with sixteen goals and fifteen assists in twenty-two games.

"What's so special is you don't think of yourself when you win a Stanley Cup," Simpson said. "You think of your parents, teammates, your family. That's what team sports are about—the connection with teammates. It's a huge bond. It's about sharing emotions."

Tales of all-night parties and strip club escapades often captured the headlines, but there was another side of the Oilers' Stanley Cup revelry that went underreported.

"Everyone felt a responsibility to have the Cup make a difference in someone's life," Simpson remembered. "Everyone took it to a school, or to a hospital . . . the healing power of the Cup is special. Everyone on that team knew that the Cup had to be shared with fans. And there was nothing quite like walking to a children's ward in a hospital with the Stanley Cup."

What made Simpson proud was that the Oilers made the Cup "accessible." He remembers all the players gathering at Barry T's, an Edmonton nightspot, setting the Cup on a table, and letting everyone in the bar take a turn holding it. The Oilers essentially ignored the Cup, and let fans have their time with it.

> "The second time, you now realize how difficult it is to get back there."
>
> — *Craig Simpson*

At the time Simpson lived in an Edmonton cul-de-sac that contained about eighteen other homes. He really didn't know his neighbors all that well, but he printed up invitations and invited all of them to his home at 3:00 P.M. one afternoon. He told them they could bring their family and friends. He ended up with more than one hundred people in his backyard. "And honestly I didn't know a lot of them," Simpson said.

But a decade later he still has people come up to him and tell him that they were at his house that day, and how much it meant to them.

Simpson also remembers that his second Stanley Cup was more special for a variety reasons, not the least of which was that he was able to share it with his wife

Christine, who at the time was his girlfriend. "Her grandfather, Glenn Kirkland, was an intriguing, fun-loving guy," Simpson said. "He was an old train conductor. He had lost half his leg, but he was a feisty character. He was such a hockey fan that it was a joy to bring the Cup to his house and share it with him. He died in 1993."

The victory was also sweeter the second time around because he knew from his first experience that the incredible feeling would pass far too quickly. He purposely savored the second Cup, creating a mental scrapbook of his feelings and images.

"The second time," he says, "you now realize how difficult it is to get back there."

In the days after the 1990 victory, friends kept telling him that they never spotted him on television in the euphoric Oilers' dressing room. That's because Simpson stood back and played the role of observer. He wanted a lasting picture to take with him.

In sweat-drenched underwear, he sat back in his cubicle in the cramped Boston Garden's visitors' dressing room and watched as the best team in the world celebrated its championship. Tina Turner's song "Simply the Best" was blaring loudly. Simpson sat swigging from his champagne bottle and thinking that professional sports couldn't get better than this.

"That was crystallized in my mind," Simpson said. "All of my real close friends, Mess, Andy, Kevin Lowe, Craig MacTavish, Steve Smith, Charlie Huddy, were all dancing around, hugging each other. They were enjoying the moment. I was exhilarated, exhausted, and spent. My body was telling me that I had been through a war. But I remember thinking: This is why I spent my life playing the game of hockey. That moment defined why I wanted to play hockey. To be in that room, as exhausted, battered, and bruised as I was, was worth it all."

His other memory of the Oilers' 1990 Cup triumph was sharing a private moment with the incomparable Gordie Howe, who Simpson had gotten to know at charity events. Long after the arena had emptied and the media was busy chronicling the Oilers' championship, Simpson sat in the stands with Howe and listened as Howe regaled him with tales of winning four Stanley Cup championships in the 1950s.

"That was a special moment," Simpson said. "What makes the Stanley Cup the greatest trophy in professional sports is that I was holding the same Cup that Gordie Howe held thirty-five years before."

Simpson works in television today as a reporter and analyst, and it's been his observation that the childlike pleasures of hockey are slipping away. He hopes he's wrong.

"Guys seem more serious, more focused, more concerned about every thing," Simpson says. "Guys have to be focused, because you have to be ready. But part of why the Oilers would go through a wall for each other is that we all had fun together. We were all part of the practical jokes, and going out together."

The Oilers were serious only on the ice. They were loose and relaxed in the dressing room. They didn't sweat the media or fan pressure, and certainly paid no attention to outside distractions. They seemed to approach the game like a bunch of close friends who believed that when they took to the ice together they were simply the best.

"After practice today, players go home and get on the Internet or they play video games," Simpson said. "It's almost like your kids today: you want them to go out and play and they want to play video games. And it's a little like that for the teams as well. You have to have a bit of a kid in you to be great and to be able to go to the wall like we did."

# Ed Olczyk

*New York Rangers, 1993–94*

Pictures are purported not to lie, but one of the most memorable photos in Stanley Cup folklore has an element of exaggerated legend.

Not long after the New York Rangers won the Stanley Cup in 1994, Rangers player and horse enthusiast Ed Olczyk took the trophy to the Meadowlands Race Track and then to Belmont Park. At Belmont, Olczyk was pictured feeding 1994 Kentucky Derby winner Go For Gin out of the Stanley Cup. The photo was picked up by the wire service, and some folks were offended by the shot, even though most people in the hockey world laughed at the thought that another layer of goofy history had been added to Stanley's legacy.

"Actually I never fed him out of it," Olczyk now says. "Everyone just assumed there was food in the Cup. But the photo was just set up to make him look like he was drinking out of the Cup. It was just to be a photo of a Kentucky Derby winner and a Stanley Cup winner."

Olczyk is a one-time forty-two-goal scorer, but he wasn't a crucial performer on the Rangers' championship team. He played just one playoff game that season, but he remembers Rangers' captain Mark Messier making every member of the organization feel like a part of the success.

"You don't realize how difficult it is to win it until you actually succeed," Olczyk said. "It just seems like yesterday. Even though my part in it was minimal, I still feel as if I was part of it. The bottom line was chemistry. We had it on that team. Mess treated everyone the same from himself to the twenty-eighth guy. He kept everyone in line and he made everyone feel important. He knew the foot soldiers were important."

Olczyk grew up in Chicago as a Black Hawks' fan, hoping that the franchise could break its long championship drought. There was a tinge of justice that Olczyk could be a part of the end of the Rangers' fifty-four-year drought. Rangers' fans let loose in the summer of 1994.

Shortly after the Rangers disposed of the Vancouver Canucks in a dramatic Game 7, Messier and eight or nine Rangers went out for dinner in Manhattan. In

*Ed Olczyk shown with 1994 Kentucky Derby winner Go For Gin.*

characteristic fashion, Messier showed up in a limousine with the Cup in tow. Upon exiting, Olczyk remembers Messier parking Stanley on top of the luxury car's roof. An alien starship landing in Time's Square couldn't have created more commotion than the trophy did on that hot summer's evening.

"It stopped traffic," Olczyk said. "Taxi cabs blocked off the intersection. People came out running. The attention the Cup got was surreal. It was like a magnet. People came from everywhere to check it out."

Most of the players in the group just stood and watched in amazement as people flocked to the Cup. "People kept coming up and saying thanks," Olczyk said. "In fact people still thank me for that championship."

# Joe Kocur

*Detroit Red Wings, 1996–97 and 1997–98*

*New York Rangers, 1993–94*

Having hung out with the Stanley Cup in three separate occasions, Joe Kocur looks at the Stanley Cup almost like a very close friend.

Kocur has been tubing with Stanley. He has partied with Stanley. He has sang with Stanley. He has fished with Stanley. He and Stanley took a ride on a wave runner. Like any good friend, Kocur even put Stanley back together after it fell apart after too many days of revelry.

In 1994, when the New York Rangers had won the Cup, the NHL was still one year away from enacting the official plan to allow players to have possession of the Stanley Cup for twenty-four hours. The Rangers had worked out their own travel itinerary for the Cup. Many members of the Rangers' organization were given their opportunity to have Stanley as a houseguest, and somewhere in the process Stanley had literally come unglued. When Kocur received the trophy, the bowl was separated from the main trophy.

That unfortunate event paved the way for Kocur to become one of the legendary figures in Stanley Cup folklore. He was the first player who actually tried to repair the Cup himself. Knowing he and his friends were going to want to lift Stanley and drink from the bowl, Kocur took it to a machine shop and had it soldered back together. Respectful of the Cup's time-honored tradition, he instructed the worker to use sterling silver solder and to tack it only in five places around the rim.

"I was not trying to put a weld on it," Kocur said. "I was just trying to tack it, to hold it in place. From what I understand, it held together for another month or two. The tacks were small enough that you couldn't tell."

Kocur has long believed that the Cup should be shared with fans, and he has endeavored to allow as many fans as possible to enjoy the three-year ride he's had with the Cup.

On one of Stanley's visits to Kocur's lakefront home out near Milford, Michigan, Kocur put a ski jacket on Stanley and secured it in an inner tube. (He tested the Cup's ski jacket–aided floating potential in four feet of water before starting his perhaps questionable journey.) He jumped into another inner tube and had his wife pull Stanley around the lake with him. Stanley needed no introduction to the lake dwellers. As soon as they spotted the trophy, the honking and hollering began.

During his Red Wings' tour, Kocur had several Cup highlights, including an almost all-night bonfire where Stanley's Hall of Fame escort Paul Oke played the guitar and sang into the night.

After partying with Stanley nearly all night, Kocur got up before dawn and he and Stanley went fishing with friends. "We put some lake water in it and that was our live well," Kocur says. "We put the fish right in there."

Kocur was always happy to be part of the tamer team celebrations, but no player ever enjoyed his private moments with Stanley more than Kocur. When one Red Wings' team function broke up at 2:00 A.M., Kocur noted that "the Cup had nowhere to go." He called a friend at Lutteman's tavern in Highland, Michigan, and he kept the bar open all night to accommodate Kocur and Stanley's thirst for some after-hours celebrating.

"We kept it open all night and every time you looked up someone new would come in with their hair all messed up," Kocur remembered. "Everyone there was calling someone. It was four in the morning, but people were getting up to come in and get their picture taken with the Cup."

Kocur was disappointed once to read that some people complained when his former New York Rangers teammate Ed Olczyk fed a Kentucky Derby horse out of the Cup. Kocur felt that the complainants didn't understand what the Cup is about. To Kocur, the Cup is about hockey and its fans.

"Letting a horse eat out of it . . . well, he was a champion too," Kocur said. "When the players get the Cup, they should share it with the fans."

It's impossible for Kocur to understate his feelings about winning a Stanley Cup as a member of the New York Rangers. When the Rangers won in 1994, it ended the organization's fifty-four-year Cup drought. New York was infatuated with the Rangers when they won the Cup.

But Kocur doesn't need much coaxing to admit that winning the Cup in Detroit might have been more special for a variety of reasons. First, he had started his career in Detroit in 1984 and lived in Michigan during the off-season, regardless of where he played. Secondly, his career seemed over when the Red Wings called him out of retirement in late December of 1996. Finally, Kocur was a member of the "Grind Line" and a far more crucial contributor to the Red Wings' success than he had been with the Rangers.

> "To win it in New York was incredible. But I was a bigger part of the team in Detroit. That is my home and I could walk with my head higher after winning it there."
>
> — *Joe Kocur*

Kocur was thirty-two and playing in an over-thirty "beer league" when captain Steve Yzerman, among others, lobbied the Red Wings to bring him back. Playing on a line with Kirk Maltby and Kris Draper, Kocur was a key checking line performer in both 1997 and 1998. In the 1998 playoffs, he had four goals in eighteen games. He had managed six goals in ninety-seven postseason games before that great season.

"To win it in New York was incredible," Kocur said. "But I was a bigger part of the team in Detroit. That is my home and I could walk with my head higher after winning it there."

To go from the beer league to having his name inscribed once again on the Stanley Cup in a span of about five months was significant enough that the Hall of Fame asked for both his beer league jersey and his Stanley Cup Red Wings jersey.

That should tell you that the Hall of Fame wasn't really all that upset that Kocur had tried to repair the Cup without consulting them. Privately, Hall of Fame representatives knew it was just a matter of time before the Cup broke.

Kocur confessed to having the Cup fixed and said that the Cup had been broken when it had been given to him. To this day Kocur won't say what member of the Rangers' organization had the Cup before him. He just says it wasn't a player.

# Joe Murphy

*Edmonton Oilers, 1989–90*

Joe Murphy was the oldest member of the Edmonton Oilers' celebrated "Kid Line" when they defeated the Boston Bruins for the 1990 Stanley Cup championship. He was twenty-two years and nine months old. Adam Graves had just turned twenty-two and Martin Gelinas was the baby at nineteen.

Yet despite Murphy's youthfulness and the whirlwind nature of the Oilers' run toward a fifth Cup, he came away with a veteran's understanding of what it takes to become an NHL champion.

"I equate it to one of the most grueling thing in sports," Murphy says. "It's an ego challenge. There's just so much to it. Every player is key. Every play is so important. It's a different array of events coming together. When we won it, I could see it in everyone's face. We had really accomplished something here."

The play of the "Kid Line" had been essential to the Oilers' success. Murphy had four points in the final, only one less than Messier. "We were really enthusiastic and we stuck up for each other," Murphy said. "We really did our job, and it was a great feeling."

Murphy can pinpoint the moment when he realized the magnitude of their accomplishment. When the team returned to Edmonton, captain Mark Messier invited all the Oilers players to his house for a night of shooting pool and camaraderie.

"He had miniature Stanley Cups, Canada Cup [memorabilia], his Conn Smythe trophy on display," Murphy said. "When you see that in his house, you realize how great a thing it is to be a part of it all. That fueled my engine."

# Aaron Ward

*Detroit Red Wings, 1996–97 and 1997–98*

The euphoria that comes with a Stanley Cup celebration started for defenseman Aaron Ward a few hours before the Red Wings actually finished the four-game sweep against the Philadelphia Flyers in 1997.

Driving down Brush Street near Joe Louis Arena at four o'clock in the afternoon, he could feel the buzz in the air. Banners hung from the buildings and people were hanging out windows. Talk of the Red Wings filled the radio airwaves. Cars were honking. Traffic moved slowly. "It started to hit me that we can win this thing tonight," Ward said. "I really started to absorb what was happening. Then I remember counting down on the ice and throwing stuff in the air and everything seemed to slow down."

Ward said that day was the longest and most exciting of his life. After finishing off the Flyers and partying in the dressing room for what seemed like an eternity, the Red Wings headed off to Big Daddy's restaurant in West Bloomfield. "You completely lose track of time," Ward recalled. "I never saw a party like that, not even in college. People were just so happy seeing each other. Everyone had something in common to celebrate. It was unbelievable."

Leaving the party at 6:00 A.M., Ward remembers listening to radio personality Art Regner on WDFN, who had stayed on the air all night to talk about the Detroit Red Wings' first Stanley Cup championship since 1955. He was hoarse from his marathon radio session and yet he had never lost his enthusiasm. "I remember guys under the influence of alcohol calling up Art at 6:00 A.M.," Ward said. "I can remember Marty Lapointe calling him at 6:30, mocking him, but still excited about winning."

The whole party sequence was a blur to Ward, who had difficulty believing the Red Wings had won. "I grew up a Toronto Maple Leafs fan, and I never saw them win," Ward said. "Just having the wish and hope that my favorite team would win was a dream, let alone me winning the Cup."

When he had his twenty-four hours with the Stanley Cup, Ward rented a limousine to transport it to various locales. Included on his itinerary was a stop at a children's hospital. "We quickly got an understanding of what kids know and don't know," Ward said. "To some kids, the Stanley Cup was just a big, giant, robot-looking thing that scared the living daylights out of them. To others, they absorbed it. I think it was a bigger deal for the employees."

As part of his celebration, Ward rented a wedding hall and held a party for four hundred people. Later he had a private party at his house for some of his closest friends. There really wasn't a need for the Hall of Fame to have a keeper of the Cup in attendance because Ward remembers one of his pals, Brian Niemy, standing guard over the Cup for the better part of eight hours. When people wanted to snap pictures he would move away, but when they were done Niemy would resume hugging the trophy. "We joke how that was the closest he ever came to getting married," Ward said.

Another Ward memory is of how sore his arms were at the end of day from everyone asking him to raise the Cup over his head for pictures. "It weighs thirty-five pounds, you are so sore you just want to say, no you lift it up and I'll take the picture," Ward says, laughing.

Ward said the highlight of his celebrations was being able to share his championship with his parents, Keith and Wendy, and his wife Kelly.

"Your wife endures a lot for you to win the Stanley Cup," Ward said. "Maybe you aren't quarantined, but you are put away at a hotel even at home. She doesn't see much of you. Your life is put on hold. She must do everything. As hard as you have worked to achieve this, she has been the backbone in support."

Upon winning, he thought of his parents getting up at 4:00 A.M. to make sure he was transported forty-five minutes away to Russell, Ontario, to get to practice on time.

"Being Canadian, my parents had so much respect for the Cup. They know how hard you have to work to get it." Ward said. "My dad wouldn't come near it. Finally, I said, 'Go ahead and touch it. You have to go near it to get our picture taken with it.'"

# Dave Lewis

*Associate Coach, Detroit Red Wings, 1996–97 and 1997–98*

In early March 1980, New York Islanders defenseman Dave Lewis could have been forgiven for thinking that a date with the Stanley Cup was in his future. He was a vital contributor to an Islanders team that appeared to be primed for a strong run at multiple NHL championships.

What Lewis didn't know at the time was that he would get his name on the Cup, but it would be sixteen years later than he had anticipated.

What he also didn't know at the time was that he would help the Islanders win that Cup by being one of two players general manager Bill Torrey would ship to the Los Angeles Kings for Butch Goring. As it turned out, Goring was the final live wire in the Islanders' championship schematic. The Islanders won four consecutive championships, while Lewis was serving as a fixture on the Kings' blue line.

That scenario sheds some insight into the satisfaction Lewis felt when he was one of coach Scott Bowman's associate coaches during the Red Wings' Stanley Cup triumphs in 1997 and 1998.

> "I don't think the horse realized the importance of the Stanley Cup. But everyone else around there did."
>
> — *Dave Lewis*

"I don't know if I can say that I got more satisfaction out of winning [because he had missed out on the Islanders' runs], but I got tremendous satisfaction out of winning it," Lewis said. "It was something that I really wanted."

Had he felt cheated out of the Cup until that point? "Yeah, I did miss out," Lewis admitted. "It had been very close. We were a very close team, and everyone pulled for one another on that team. Unfortunately, Billy Harris and I were plucked out of there. But they got Butch Goring and he was the difference. He was the center to play behind Bryan Trottier."

Lewis got close to the Cup again in 1995 when he was an assistant coach on the Detroit Red Wings team that reached the Stanley Cup final. But the New Jersey Devils ruined the opportunity, sweeping the Red Wings.

When the Red Wings finally won in 1997 and Lewis was given his day with the Cup, he and his son Ryan went tooling down Detroit area highways and byways in a Dodge Viper with Ryan holding Stanley out of the sun roof.

"People followed us and yelled 'Is that the real Stanley Cup?'" Lewis said, chuckling. "We kept saying 'No, we are just carrying a fake around in a Dodge Viper.'"

He then took the Cup for a reception at a local stable where the Lewis' family horse, McLain, is kept. With seventy or eighty people gathered about, Lewis filled the Cup's bowl with cereal and allowed McLain to enjoy his lunch out of one of professional sports' most storied trophies.

"I don't think the horse realized the importance of the Stanley Cup," Lewis said. "But everyone else around there did."

The importance of winning was known to Lewis as he watched the Islanders win the four Cups almost two decades before. He had played sixty-two games for the Islanders that season to help them get in position for their title march.

"I was very excited for them when they won the Cup," Lewis said. "I was at home and I got a call from the locker room right after they won. Bob Bourne, Clark Gillies, Lorne Henning, and some of the other guys talked to me. It made me feel good."

Did he get a share of the championship money? Lewis laughs. "No, that's what I have to remember to ask those guys. Where is my money?"

# Darren McCarty

*Detroit Red Wings, 1996–97 and 1997–98*

Players often save mementos from their Stanley Cup championships. Jerseys autographed by every member of the team are a favorite, along with signed sticks and the replica Stanley Cups given to them by the NHL.

McCarty's favorite memento is a photograph of him scoring the Stanley Cup–clinching goal against the Flyers in 1997. The fact that a fan in the first row snapped the picture makes it even more special.

"It's right where I scored on [Ron] Hextall," McCarty says. "It's awesome. It's right where I cut around him. It's got [Philadelphia defenseman Janne] Niinimaa diving and Hextall. You see me blowing snow and you see people in the background getting ready to jump. That's great personal memorabilia."

He had the picture blown up to sixteen by twenty inches, and it's framed on a wall in his basement.

Like any avid collector, McCarty had to wheel and deal to obtain another one of his favorite collectibles from the Stanley Cup championship. He kept the stick that delivered that winning goal, but he had to trade for the puck.

"[Referee] Bill McCreary originally had the puck," McCarty said. "He got the puck for his kid. He asked me if I'd like to have it. I gave his son a jersey. It's cool because it goes with the stick."

McCarty's other treasured memento from his two Stanley Cups is his collection of videotapes from each game. "It still gives me chills to watch them," McCarty says.

# Kris Draper

*Detroit Red Wings, 1996–97 and 1997–98*

Many of the players on Stanley Cup winning teams can recite the order of hoisting the Cup as if it was the batting order of a World Series championship team.

Detroit's Kris Draper, the speedy, feisty center on Detroit's key checking line on back-to-back champion teams, remembers that he followed Joe Kocur as the Cup was passed from player to play during the postgame, on-ice revelry at Joe Louis Arena in 1997.

"Joey Kocur skated up to me and said take her for a spin around the rink," Draper remembered.

His other favorite Stanley Cup memory occurred when he had his twenty-four hours with the Cup in his hometown of Toronto. For a Detroit player to take a Cup to championship-starved Toronto is akin to waving red in a bull's face. Draper relished being able to showcase the Cup on a ride down Danforth Avenue in Toronto.

"There was this guy in a Wendel Clark jersey who yelled 'Wings suck' as we drove by," Draper said, smiling at the memory.

# Slava Fetisov

*Detroit Red Wings, 1996–97 and 1997–98*

Many in the baby boomer generation grew up wondering and worrying about whether America would some day drop bombs on Moscow's Red Square.

The cold war made the Kremlin seem like the center of the "Evil Empire." That's why even though the Communist regime has been toppled for the better part of a decade, it was still a psychological bombshell for many hockey fans when Slava Fetisov, Igor Larionov, and Slava Kozlov decided to take the Stanley Cup to Moscow's Red Square after the Detroit Red Wings won in 1997.

"If someone had told me even ten years before that we would be taking the Stanley Cup to Moscow I would not have believed them," Fetisov said. "But it was the right thing to do. I had helped to fight to open the doors for Russian players to play in the NHL and now I was bringing the Cup home."

It needs to be remembered that Fetisov is to Russian hockey what Bobby Orr was to the NHL. He is the most revered defenseman in Russian hockey history. When the Soviets were dominating international hockey, Fetisov was on the blue line along with Alexei Kasatonov. Up front was the famed KLM Line with Vladimir Krutov, Igor Larionov, and Sergei Makarov.

The bond between hockey and Russian culture isn't as strong as the tie that exists between the sport and Canadian culture, but the sport is important to the Russian people. They are keenly aware of what Russian players are accomplishing in the NHL, particularly historic figures like Larionov and Fetisov. The players were cheered loudly when they brought the Cup to Luzhniki Stadium. Russian president Boris Yeltsin was among those who paid homage to their accomplishments.

Regardless of what continent Stanley is on, sooner or later the famed trophy ends up in a bar for post midnight revelry. In Moscow, the Russian Red Wings showed up at 2:00 A.M. at a Moscow pub named the Hungry Duck. A Canadian who just happened to be a Red Wings fan as well as a thriving capitalist owns it. They were given a standing ovation.

"I have lots of friends in Moscow and many people who rooted for me. They follow the playoffs. With an eight hour difference, they would call me in the middle of the night to get a score," Fetisov said. "I thought it would be nice to share the Cup with them."

One of the highlights of the trip for Fetisov was taking a picture with his wife and daughter, the Cup, and his three Olympic medals (two gold and a silver earned when the United States pulled off the "Miracle on Ice" in 1980). The snapshot came in front of Lenin's Tomb.

In another time, under another system of government, victorious Olympic athletes would come to Lenin's tomb and salute him.

But neither Fetisov or Larionov entered Lenin's tomb. The site was chosen because the Russian players wanted to show "that the system has changed."

"There is more freedom," Fetisov said that day. "You can feel it."

Fetisov and particularly Larionov had rebelled against the totalitarian Communist regime, particularly with regard to the treatment of their athletes. But Fetisov still has tremendous pride in his country's hockey history. That's another reason why Fetisov wanted to take the Stanley Cup to his native land.

"Soviet hockey school plays a big role in the NHL success right now," Fetisov said. "And not just because of the Russian-born players. Hockey isn't that old in Russia. It started after World War II. Mr. [Anatoli] Tarasov developed his own hockey school. He had no one to learn the game from, and yet others wanted to learn from him."

Fetisov witnessed that first hand when he was playing for the Soviets in the 1970s and 1980s.

"All the specialists from Sweden, Switzerland, Finland, Germany, Czech Republic—they all followed us," Fetisov remembered. "They took the video of our practices and they always invited specialists from Russia to their country. Soviet hockey played a big role in Europe."

He thinks the 1972 Summit Series—won by the Canadians on Paul Henderson's dramatic goal in the eighth game of the series—was the turning point of hockey. "[Canadians] saw a different system," Fetisov said. "We took the best from both systems to get the game we have now."

To reach the NHL in 1989 Fetisov had to fight against the Central Red Army coach Viktor Tikhonov and the Soviet system itself.

"We were fighting for human rights back then," Fetisov said during his Moscow Cup trip. "I was born without chances in my life. Now kids have a chance to reach their goals. They can win the Stanley Cup if they wish."

By bringing the Cup to Russian soil, in a sense Fetisov was trying to unify in his own mind the two hockey cultures that have been so important to his life. Presumably he had aspects of both stages of his career that he liked and disliked, but he feels that each is deserving of respect.

He thought it was important for the youngsters at the Red Army Hockey School "to touch and feel the Cup."

The Red Wings Stanley Cup triumph in 1997 had an importance for Russian players even beyond what it meant for Fetisov, Larionov, Kozlov, Vladimir Konstantinov, and Sergei Fedorov, all of whom played significant roles in Detroit's first Stanley Cup championship since 1955.

The performance of the Russian Five destroyed the final remnants of the outdated hockey belief that Russian players didn't crave the Stanley Cup as much as their North American counterparts. Even into the early 1990s, it was said behind closed doors that the Russians, because of their upbringing, viewed the Olympics with greater reverence than the Stanley Cup.

No member of the Red Wings' doubted the commitment the Russians had toward winning the Cup. The team's feelings about the Russian players were made public after captain Steve Yzerman was given the Stanley Cup in 1997. After he completed the first lap, he immediately looked for Fetisov and Larionov because he had made up his mind that they deserved the next lap.

What even Yzerman didn't know was that shortly before the clock ticked down for the clinching victory against Philadelphia, Fetisov had turned to Larionov and said, "When our turn comes to carry the Cup, can we do it together?"

As Fetisov and Larionov skated together at Joe Louis Arena with the Cup raised between them, the bridge between the past and present was finally bonded together. Tears flowed as freely as the champagne that night.

# Igor Larionov

*Detroit Red Wings, 1996–97 and 1997–98*

When Slava Fetisov speaks of Igor Larionov's courage and spirit, it has nothing to do with Larionov's status as the Wayne Gretzky of Soviet hockey.

Everyone knows that Larionov was a puck handling wizard of the famed "KLM Line," but few seem to know about what kind of human being Larionov has been. Fetisov hasn't forgotten. He gets misty when he talks about how Larionov fought the system on behalf of Russian players. He rebelled against famed Soviet coach Viktor Tikhonov, a man who history has judged to be far more of a bully than he was a great hockey coach. Larionov's playing style is a salute to beauty and grace; off the ice he's been a fighter.

Larionov, a smallish athlete nicknamed "The Professor" because of his scholarly look, refused to follow the Soviet way of doing what he was told without complaint or questioning. When Larionov saw injustice, he said so. Perhaps he came by it naturally; his grandfather spent fourteen years in the gulag prison network for criticizing the tyranny of Joseph Stalin, the Soviet dictator who probably contributed to the deaths of more Soviet citizens than the Germans did in World War II.

Seeing that athletes were treated more like indentured servants than human beings, Larionov demanded freedom. When top Soviet players were denied the opportunity to play in the NHL in the late 1980s, he wrote critical letters to *Sovietski Sport*, a magazine connected to the Communist Party. Tikhonov wouldn't let Larionov travel abroad, even though he was a vital member of the Soviet National Team. When Fetisov was booted off the team for voicing his own criticism of Tikhonov, Larionov organized a player revolt. It was Tikhonov who blinked, and Fetisov came back with an understanding that they would be joining the NHL shortly thereafter. Larionov was allowed to join the Vancouver Canucks in 1989, the same season Fetisov joined the New Jersey Devils. They opened the doors to the flood of Russians that now highlight rosters in North America. It's predicted that one of every five NHL players could be Russian in this decade.

When Larionov and his Detroit teammates planned their trip to Russia, Larionov made sure that the Cup had a stop in his hometown of Voskresensk so it could be displayed at Khimik Arena.

> "The Russian kids grew up dreaming to play for the national team, to play for their country in World Championships and Olympics. Now it's starting to change. The main goal for the [Russian] kids is to try to make it to the NHL and win the biggest trophy—the Stanley Cup."
>
> — *Igor Larionov*

"I wanted to share the Stanley Cup with the people of Russia," Larionov said. "When we played for the national team, we were expected to win. We did. But there was no joy, like there is in winning a Stanley Cup. The attitude was: 'Let's go back to work.'"

Voskresensk is a hockey hotbed, producing other NHL champions like Valeri Kamensky (Colorado in 1996), Valeri Zelepukin (New Jersey in 1995), and Slava Kozlov (Detroit in 1997 and 1998).

When Larionov won his first Stanley Cup he called it the happiest moment of his life. He meant it. "This is the most difficult trophy to win because you have to play at a high level of hockey for two months." Larionov said.

He had always laughed at the notion that Russian players put more emphasis on international competition. "For us, the main goal is to win the Stanley Cup," Larionov says.

"There's no doubt about that. Nobody was thinking about winning the World Championships when we're in the [Stanley Cup] final."

Larionov sees the quest for a Cup and Olympic gold as completely different. He loves the run for the Cup "because it's a marathon from the start of training camp."

He says the attitude of young Russian players is different. "For seventy years, North American kids were brought up to win the Stanley Cup," Larionov said. "The Russian kids grew up dreaming to play for the national team, to play for their country in World Championships and Olympics. Now it's starting to change. The main goal for the [Russian] kids is to try to make it to the NHL and win the biggest trophy—the Stanley Cup."

To no one's surprise, Tikhonov left the Red Army Hockey School an hour before Larionov and Fetisov showed up with the Cup. It didn't matter to Larionov, who hadn't seen Tikhonov in years. He hadn't been looking to resolve anything. He certainly hadn't brought the Cup to Russia to see him. "Like Slava said, we brought it for the kids," said Larionov.

# Vladimir Konstantinov

*Detroit Red Wings, 1996–97*

When the Detroit Red Wings gathered for a post–Stanley Cup golf outing in the summer of 1997, they thought they were acting in an intelligent and cautious manner by hiring limousines to transport players back to their homes after a day of revelry.

To this day, it still haunts the Red Wings that star defenseman Vladimir Konstantinov and popular team masseur Sergei Mnatsakanov suffered permanent career-ending and life-changing injuries at one of the happiest times of their lives. The limousine driver, who served jail time because of the accident, allegedly fell asleep at the wheel. Both Konstantinov and Mnatsakanov suffered brain injuries in the ensuing accident. Mnatsakanov is now confined to a wheel chair and Konstantinov struggles with his short-term memory to this day. He will never play hockey again.

"It just makes no sense," says Detroit vice president Jim Devallano. "This didn't happen on some dark highway late at night. He was in a limousine on Woodward Avenue at 9:15 in the evening. It just should not have happened."

What gnaws at their former teammates is that the two were hurt while acting responsibly.

"It's just so senseless that it happened," says Red Wings left wing Darren McCarty. "The toughest thing is that you think you do everything right, you think, you plan, and then this happens."

He adds, "Sometimes pro athletes and those in the entertainment field are put on a pedestal. They are considered untouchable. But the only difference between us and everyone else is what we do for a living. We are just as susceptible to fate as everyone else. Stuff like this happens all the time, and when it happens to John Doe, it isn't any less significant to his family than it is for us because it's Vladie."

Konstantinov had become a Norris Trophy finalist that season and was generally considered one of the NHL's top defensemen.

Devellano remembers the first time he met Konstantinov, the then twenty-two-year-old captain of the Central Red Army hockey team, in Detroit for an exhibition game in 1992. Devellano arranged for Konstantinov to sneak out of his hotel room and meet him at 1:00 A.M. at Joe Louis Arena. Armed with an appealing five-year contract, Devellano tried to persuade Konstantinov to defect, as Sergei Fedorov had the summer before. "But he told me he had a wife and family back in Russia and he would worry about them if he joined the Red Wings," Devellano says.

It was impressive family dedication for a player so young, Devellano thought to himself. "If he was single, I would have pressured him to sign," Devellano says. "But when he told me he had a family, I backed off."

Konstantinov always played hockey like a commando soldier on an assault mission.

Some say he was a dirty player, but others argue he played the game with the same razor-sharp edge as Mark Messier, Doug Gilmour, or Chris Chelios, all of whom are exalted for their playing style.

Off the ice, Konstantinov was a very different character: quiet, soft-spoken, quick to smile, appreciative of a funny line. He was nicknamed the Vladinator by fans; at each game, the scoreboard showed a collection of his greatest hits, followed by Konstantinov, wearing sunglasses and saying, "Hasta la vista, baby."

Devellano said that Konstantinov ranked only behind Denis Potvin in terms of the most-talented defensemen who played on his teams. "Vladie probably would have played another seven or eight years, and I think he probably would have made the Hall of Fame," Devellano says.

In the limousine that night with Konstantinov and Mnatsakanov was Slava Fetisov. He suffered a lung injury, but was able to recover quickly. Three years later he still feels sadness about the events, and the fact that Konstantinov was unable to make the trip to Russia after their Cup.

The night the Red Wings won the Stanley Cup in 1997 Konstantinov reveled in the victory, calling it the "best night of my career."

Konstantinov hadn't been back to Russia since he left and, before the accident, he had bubbled about the proposed Stanley Cup trip to his homeland.

"All I can remember is how excited he was," Fetisov said. "There was sadness to be over there without him."

# Ken Holland

*General Manager, Detroit Red Wings, 1996–97 and 1997–98*

Ken Holland was part of Stanley Cup championship revelries in Detroit in both 1997 and 1998, yet his favorite celebration moment didn't involve the frenzied on-ice celebrations or any of the team parties.

"It came when I got to take the Stanley Cup home to Vernon, British Columbia, and put it on my mom and dad's kitchen table," Holland said.

Holland said he wanted to do that because he remembered his days in youth hockey when Rienie and Lee Holland would arise before 5:00 A.M. to transport their son to practice. When Holland left home to play junior hockey in Medicine Hat, Alberta, Holland's mom, Lee, told him that his father would play with the radio dials endlessly trying to tune in a low frequency Medicine Hat radio station. He was trying desperately to find a play-by-play broadcast of his son's games. "It would be all garbled, but he would just try to get the score," Holland said. "Hockey was a major, major part of our family life when I was growing up. By bringing the Cup home it was my way of saying thanks."

When Holland took the Cup home, Rienie Holland was already suffering from Parkinson's disease. Ken Holland is glad his father was able to share and feel the Cup's aura before he died in March 1999. What had his father said when Holland brought the Cup home?

"He was a man of few words," Holland remembered. "He didn't say much, but I know he was tremendously proud."

# Scott Niedermayer

*New Jersey Devils, 1994–95, 1999–2000*

Cranbrook, British Columbia, is a city of only seventeen thousand citizens, and yet it has produced three Stanley Cup champions from 1995 to 1999. New Jersey Devils' defenseman Scott Niedermayer won it in 1995, followed by Colorado Avalanche defenseman Jon Klemm in 1996, and then forward Brad Lukowich helped the Dallas Stars claim the Cup in 1999.

"Maybe they are getting bored with it," jokes Niedermayer even though he knows that isn't likely.

What he remembers most about his own day with the Stanley Cup was just having it there in his childhood home. "To have it, sitting on the floor as we had breakfast and lunch in the house where I grew up, was special," Niedermayer recalled. "I used to play street hockey right out front, and now the Stanley Cup is in my house."

Niedermayer was the Canadian dream played out. Although Niedermayer didn't participate, he believes Lukowich, on his day with the Cup, actually put together a street hockey game in downtown Cranbrook. The winning team of course was presented the Cup.

Also attending Niedermayer's victory celebration was his younger brother, Rob Niedermayer, who plays for the Florida Panthers. Rob hasn't won the Cup, although the Panthers did reach the Stanley Cup final in 1996. A number of brother combinations appear on the honor roll of Stanley Cup winners—Maurice and Henri Richard, Frank and Peter Mahovlich, Lionel and Charlie Conacher, Phil and Tony Esposito, just to name a few. But there are other examples of brothers whose careers are marked by the fact that one brother has experienced a championship and the other brother has not. Geoff Courtnall, for example, won a title with the Edmonton Oilers, and Russ Courtnall hasn't won. Six Sutter brothers landed in the NHL, but only Brent and Duane managed to become Cup winners.

"It was a little weird," Scott Niedermayer recalls. "A lot of hockey players are superstitious. I think my brother took some pictures with us but I don't think he handled it."

# Brett Hull

*Dallas Stars, 1998–99*

To appreciate how Brett Hull felt when he scored the dramatic triple-overtime goal against Buffalo to give the Dallas Stars the Stanley Cup championship, it must be remembered that Hull wakes up every day "scared to death" that he won't score another goal.

It wasn't satisfaction he felt, as much as it was an overwhelming sense of relief.

"I can't say winning the Cup changed my life, but it added a piece to my career that everyone else seemed to think was missing," he says with the usual Hull candor. "It was punctuation."

Winning the Cup was also more like validation for a player who has looked for validation each morning he plays the game. Throughout his career he has been plagued by self-doubt, a bizarre, unfounded fear that he is going to be discovered as a fraud, a player that really isn't quite as dominant as he has always appeared to be. Never mind that he is one of the top scorers in NHL history and that the quickness of his shot release intimidates even Hall of Fame–bound goalkeepers.

It's difficult to know whether Hull's fear of failure is real or just his subconscious using psychological chicanery to give him added motivation. However, whatever the basis for Hull's self doubt, it seems to have given him the push he needs to seize the moment in big games. Hull fought through a gruesome collection of medical woes to add another chapter to his legend with the controversial goal in Buffalo.

After playing with a torn groin muscle and a blown collateral knee ligament without a whimper, Brett Hull could be excused for grimacing over a few words of praise.

After Stars coach Ken Hitchcock compared Hull's performance in Game 6 to Bobby Baun scoring a 1964 finals overtime goal on a broken leg, Hull scrunched up his face. "I'm no Bobby Baun—that's for sure," he said.

Hitchcock was less sure of that after watching Hull use his hobbled skating style to get to the front of the net to score the game winner in the second-longest game in finals' history.

"When the dust settles, Brett Hull is going to be an incredible story," Hitchcock said. "What this man did to go on the ice and what we had to do to him between periods to get him back on the ice was incredible."

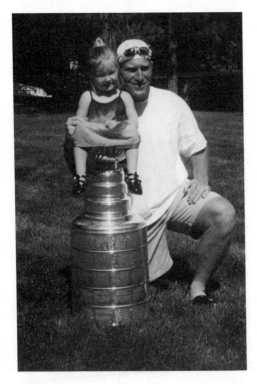

*Dallas Stars winger Brett Hull poses with the Cup and his daughter, Jayde.*

Hull hurt his knee on an open-ice hit by Buffalo defenseman Alexei Zhitnik earlier in the series. The Stars revealed only Hull's groin injury. "I was kind of numb on half of one leg and the other one was all buggered up," he said. "You just go out and do the best you can."

His injuries were retaped between every period, and heat was applied. To make matters worse, he aggravated the groin injury with seventeen seconds left in the first overtime.

"He limped around the ice," Hitchcock remembered. "The goal he scored, if you watch the shift, he limped into the corner, he limped in front of the net."

Limping or not, he battled for position and swatted the puck past goalie Dominik Hasek for the controversial goal. Replays showed that Hull was in the crease, and yet for some reason the video replay judge did not overturn the goal. That fact caused a firestorm of protest in Buffalo. Somehow it was fitting that Hull had played a role in the controversy because his outspokenness has always put him in harm's way when it comes to controversy.

No player understands living on the edge of a deep fryer more than Hull. He has always seemed to be just one topple away from getting scalded by all the heat directed toward him. His entertaining mouth always gets him in trouble. It's also a heavy burden to have your team counting on you to score big goals in every big game. When he came to Dallas he was viewed as the final piece in the Stars' puzzle.

> "I can't say winning the Cup changed my life, but it added a piece to my career that everyone else seemed to think was missing. It was punctuation."
>
> — *Brett Hull*

What makes the Hull story more dramatic is that Dallas signed Hull hoping he could help the team climb the final rung.

"Do you know how much pressure that is?" Hull said.

That was why he felt such relief after he had delivered a championship to the Stars. "It is the most unbelievable feeling just to shut up all the naysayers," Hull said.

Despite producing Hall of Fame numbers in St. Louis, he left without a championship.

"I don't have to answer to anyone any more," Hull said. "And neither does Eddie [Belfour], Joe [Nieuwendyk] or Mike Modano. Joe has a cadaver ligament in his knee. That's fabulous. Mike Modano. He's the biggest competitor I've seen."

He had added incentive to make sure the Stars won in six. "I don't think I could have played a Game 7," Hull said. "I really don't think I could have."

His only regret about 1999 is that the championship feeling came and went before he could actually savor the moment. That summer he took the Stanley Cup to Duluth, Minnesota, where he had first been discovered as a college standout. That's where he makes his summer home today. "You are just too emotionally spent to absorb the experience," Hull said.

But he had one epiphany regarding winning his Stanley Cup. "If I hadn't won," he said, "I don't think I would have gone to my grave thinking something was missing."

# Craig Ludwig

*Montreal Canadiens, 1985–86*

*Dallas Stars, 1998–99*

Defenseman Craig Ludwig would have had no reason to feel like a fossil in his final NHL season if not for the fact that his dressing room stall became a museum.

A teammate or member of the media was always stopping by to view the shin pads that had protected Ludwig's legs since the 1970s. He got them from trainer Dave Cameron when he was a college freshman at North Dakota and wore them through his final NHL campaign in 1998–99. Ludwig was never sure how old the pads were, but in his last year he was sure the pads were older than twenty-one-year-old teammate Jon Sim. "They were old when I got them," Ludwig says. "When you are a rookie like I was, you don't get the new stuff."

In the male tradition, Ludwig has kept the pads in working order with improvised repairs and a healthy dose of duct tape.

> "It was surreal.
> Me, the cops, and
> the Stanley Cup at
> 3:00 A.M."
>
> — *Craig Ludwig*

"I just don't like new equipment," he says with a shrug. "I see guys now that go through five pairs of skates in one season."

He used the same pair of skates through his final three seasons in Dallas. He estimated he had about "two weeks left in them" in 1999 when the Stars wrapped up their first Stanley Cup championship in franchise history.

Having won his only other Cup in 1986, Ludwig established a new league mark of thirteen seasons between Stanley Cup titles. The previous mark of twelve had been held by Terry Sawchuk, who captured the Stanley Cup in 1952, 1954, 1955, and not again until he shared goaltending duties with Johnny Bower when the Maple Leafs won in 1967.

When given his time with the Cup he opted to hold a party in his hometown of Elk River, Wisconsin, over the Fourth of July weekend. After picking up the Cup and its escort at the airport, Ludwig had to struggle to return to his house because so many cars were lining his street. More than three hundred folks were at his house, including three PeeWee hockey teams that just happened to be in town for a tournament.

"They came because they just figured they might not ever get a chance to see the Cup again," Ludwig said. "But I swear there were a ton of people there that I had never seen in my life."

At approximately 2:00 A.M., the police showed up at the door asking for "Mr. Ludwig."

Ludwig figured people had complained about the party, but much to his surprise he was asked if he would be willing to bring the Cup down to the police and fire stations so the officers and firemen on the night shift could get a look at Lord Stanley's prize. "It was surreal," Ludwig told members of the Dallas media. "Me, the cops, and the Stanley Cup at 3:00 A.M."

Ludwig also put the Cup on display in the local Fourth of July parade. "It's like traveling with Elvis," Ludwig said. "The Cup is really a celebrity and you don't know what people are going to do when they meet it."

Having won a second Cup at age thirty-eight, Ludwig felt no need to continue his career, particularly when it became clear that the Stars had decided not to bring him back. He was content to move more aggressively into his other passion—big-time, national caliber softball.

In the end, his equipment was probably more tired than he was. While many hockey players are superstitious, that played no role in Ludwig's love of vintage equipment. "It is a comfort thing," he says. What's even more remarkable about the ragged nature of Ludwig's pads is that he was one of the league's premier shot blockers. That means he was constantly trying to throw those pads toward shots coming at him at eighty-five miles an hour or more. His well being relied on the duct tape holding up.

His shin pads are so legendary in the sport that the Hockey Hall of Fame has requested he donate them for display after his career is over. "I got two letters saying they wanted to put them in the Hall," Ludwig says. "I said no thanks. If you take them, you have to take me, and I never got a letter again."

Ludwig's plan was to display the pads in his bar in Wausau, Wisconsin. Presumably if they are there on the wall, they are attached by duct tape.

# Claude Lemieux

*Montreal Canadiens, 1985–86*

*New Jersey Devils, 1994–95 and 1999–2000*

*Colorado Avalanche, 1995–96*

Opponents have always sworn *at* Claude Lemieux's playing style. But teams trying to win the Stanley Cup have sworn *by* his playing style.

His nails-down-the-chalkboard on-ice behavior style has forever made him public enemy No. 1 around the NHL. Detroit Red Wings winger Darren

McCarty still won't shake hands with Lemieux because of his hit against Kris Draper in 1996. He is irritating, like a barking hound dog or a wasp at a company picnic. He is lippy, chippy, and not averse to applying lumber to the back of your leg. He's also one of the most proven winners in NHL history. He is among eight players in NHL history to win Stanley Cup championships with three different teams, joining Frank Foyston, Jack Walker, and Hap Holmes (who each played for Cup winners in Toronto, Seattle and Victoria all before 1925), plus Mike Keane (Montreal, Colorado, and Dallas), Larry Hillman (Detroit, Toronto, and Montreal), Al Arbour (Chicago, Detroit, and Toronto as a player and New York Islanders as a coach) and Gordon Pettinger (New York Rangers, Boston, and Detroit) on that exclusive list. Jack Marshall is the only player to earn a Stanley Cup championship with four different teams (1901 Winnipeg Vics, the 1902 Montreal AAA, 1910 Montreal Wanderers, and 1914 Toronto Blueshirts).

Lemieux is the only player on that list to have won the Conn Smythe Trophy as playoff MVP. He did that in 1995 when he netted thirteen goals in twenty games to help the New Jersey Devils win the first Stanley Cup in that franchise's history.

"It's just incredible that my name is on that," Lemieux commented. "To be the most hated man in hockey and have your name on the Conn Smythe is really special."

Lemieux's fierce championship pride was nurtured in Montreal where winning was intertwined with the dressing room culture. He was a twenty-year-old rookie in 1986 when he netted ten postseason goals to help the Canadiens win the twenty-third Stanley Cup in franchise history. He says the experience he earned on the ice wasn't quite as valuable as what he learned in the dressing room. The Montreal organization was a like a village in which the secrets of winning were passed down from generation to generation.

"When I was twenty years old and in my first year I looked up to Larry Robinson and Bob Gainey and looked up to all the guys to see how they reacted," Lemieux said. "I remember how Gainey hardly showed any emotion or excitement until the moment, until it was done. He was never too high or too low. You learn from these guys. Then you pass it along. It isn't something you invent. It's something that is handed down to you. It's taught to you. You have to pass it down."

Lemieux believes that former Montreal players take their winning tradition wherever they go. "The fans in Montreal don't just expect you to play," Lemieux said. "They expect you to win."

That's why Lemieux plays the way he does—on the border between shameless violence and championship caliber grit. His playoff resume shows nineteen game-winning goals, only five short of Wayne Gretzky's NHL record. Brett Hull (with twenty-one) is the only other player between them.

The only way Lemieux knows how to play is with bayonet fixed. "You can call it old school," Lemieux said. "But I think it's the only way to play the game. It's the way it was played twenty or thirty years ago. The game really hasn't changed. Look at the success of [coach] Scotty Bowman. That's the Montreal way of playing the game. The players have changed. You may call the drills by a different name or the forechecking may be called a different kind of system. But it's still the same game."

Lemieux insists that each Cup victory has a unique identity of its own that is difficult to describe. "But the first one is probably the one you remember most, especially with me having grown up in Montreal," Lemieux said. "You have to put that one in first place. "

In Lemieux's view, very few professional championship scenarios could match the grandeur associated with a Montreal fan growing up to become a member of a Canadiens' championship team.

"I would compare it to maybe growing up a baseball fan and a Yankee fan, playing the game from the time your are five or six," Lemieux said. "Then you are twenty, and all of a sudden you are with the Yankees and you win the World Series. You are involved, chipping in, making a contribution. That is what it was like for me as a Montreal player. It was the ultimate. It doesn't get any better than that."

In 1986 the league wasn't involved in making sure each player got the Cup. But Lemieux was given his time with it and he took it home. He remembers a parade and picture taking but, to be truthful, he says, it was mostly a blur. But he does believe that possessing the Cup without a chaperone for a day or two back then meant more to him than his next possessions when the Cup came with its babysitter.

"Back then you were just trusted to go get the Cup and then bring it back," Lemieux says, smiling. "I guess they had some adventures back then and now they take better care of it. They make sure it's supervised. But back then we could do whatever we wanted to do."

Lemieux's favorite moments with the Stanley Cup came on the ice and in the dressing room, not in the subsequent victory celebrations around town. "When you win the first one, you don't remember much," Lemieux insists. "You win. It's over. When you have won the Cup before, you savor the moment more the second time. You watch the other guys a lot more. You understand what it means to all the young players who have never won before. Afterward, the Cup is for the fans, your family, and your kids. Afterward, it's about picture taking."

His satisfaction came on the ice. "When you have the Cup and you are carrying it around, that's the best feeling in the world," Lemieux said. "It means the most when you are lifting it above your head on the ice."

However, winning his fourth Cup in 2000 was important to him for family reasons. "I have four kids, and one lacked a Stanley Cup victory," Lemieux said. "So the fourth is for my little girl. They are all blessed now."

Lemieux is proud of his reputation of being a player that coaches want around when the march for the Stanley Cup begins.

"You can never get tired of winning," says Lemieux. "Once you get a taste of it you want to do it every year."

# Mike Keane

*Montreal Canadiens, 1992–93*

*Colorado Avalanche, 1995–96*

*Dallas Stars, 1998–99*

One of the regrets Mike Keane had about the Dallas Stars' failure to win the Stanley Cup in 2000 was that he didn't get to share the first Stanley Cup triumph of the twenty-first century with a dear lady who was born at the end of the nineteenth century.

His grandmother, Georgie, was turning one hundred and one—and Keane was hoping to once again take the Stanley Cup back to her Winnipeg nursing home.

"The last time I won the Cup [in 1999] my grandmother turned one hundred and it was special for me to take it to her home," Keane said. "She wasn't the oldest person there. There was another person who was 104."

Keane says his centenarian grandmother is still sharp—very aware of the Stars' progress and the role her feisty grandson plays in the Dallas attack. She watches his games whenever possible. "She is still going strong," he says. Does she have the Keane wit? "She will tell you to [screw] off every once in a while," Keane joked.

That may not necessarily sound like a witticism. "In the Keane household it is," he says, laughing.

# Patrick Roy

*Montreal Canadiens, 1985–86 and 1992–93*

*Colorado Avalanche, 1995–96*

Nothing defines Patrick Roy's career more than his quest for the Stanley Cup. He pursues it the way a renowned artist pursues the inspiration for yet another masterpiece. The Cup is almost like an intoxicant to Roy. "As soon as you win a Stanley Cup, you want to win it again," he says.

No one who has seen his name engraved on the Stanley Cup has appreciated it more than Roy has. As he makes history in the postseason, he has also been studying it. He views the record book with reverence and feels honored to have his name immortalized alongside other heroes of the game. He is a millionaire who collects old hockey and baseball cards. He's a superstar who is also a fan of the game.

"Even when he was a young goaltender he knew all of the stats," said Colorado General Manager Pierre Lacroix, who was Roy's agent back then. "He has always been very interested in the history of the game. Actually, I think he would have made a good sportswriter."

Each of Roy's Stanley Cup triumphs reads like a novel, complete with plot twists, antagonists, and a good guy winning in the end.

At twenty years old in 1985–86, he helped the Montreal Canadiens win. He posted a 1.92 goals-against average and won the Conn Smythe Trophy. "Starting the playoffs, I was the question mark of the team," Roy said. "People didn't know whether I could do the job. Then we beat Hartford and I will remember the [4–3 overtime win in] Game 3 against the New York Rangers forever. Then beating Calgary in the Final. It was like a dream."

In 1992–93, he overcame a trying regular season to help the Canadiens win again. A clever promotional arrangement between Roy and Upper Deck trading cards backfired when the Canadiens didn't play well coming out of the gate. Upper Deck launched a "Trade Roy" campaign, which was meant to inspire collectors to trade his hockey cards to one another. But the "Trade Roy" billboards were turned into a rallying cry for those who really wanted him gone. Radio shows conducted polls asking whether Roy should be traded, and the majority said he should be dealt. That was quickly forgotten when Roy won ten overtime games en route to his second Conn Smythe Trophy. "The season was tough and to win the Stanley Cup after that was very rewarding," Roy said. "That Upper Deck [campaign] had really turned against me."

> "Starting the playoffs, I was the question mark of the team. People didn't know whether I could do the job."
>
> — *Patrick Roy*

In 1995–96, he spearheaded the Colorado Avalanche's successful campaign for the Stanley Cup. This was after he had vowed that he would never play for Montreal again because Coach Mario Tremblay embarrassed him by leaving him in a game in which he was being shellacked by the Detroit Red Wings. His spirit reinvigorated by a move to Colorado, Roy posted a 2.10 goals-against average in the postseason. "After all the commotion in Montreal, to be able to turn around my season with Colorado was important," Roy said. "I wanted to show a lot of pride that season, to show that I could still reach that ultimate goal."

Roy is a charming, friendly people person, often lionized by the media because of his outgoing, "Technicolor" personality and well-oiled wit. Remember that this is a character who once said he didn't hear opponent Jeremy Roenick's yapping during a playoff game because he had his Stanley Cup rings inserted as earplugs. His passion shows up each time he plays, whether it's through a wink at his opponent, a bold declaration, a glib comment, or his reverence for hockey's history.

Roy has more playoff wins than any goaltender in NHL history and is scheduled to surpass Terry Sawchuk's regular-season NHL record of 447 wins in 2000–01.

It comes as no surprise that this Colorado Avalanche netminder devoured the 1998 David Dupuis' Sawchuk biography, and that he knows the minutia of Sawchuk's career as well as he knows his own. He seems fascinated by Sawchuk's mental toughness—affording it the same level of respect that a modern rocker might give the Beatles or Elvis Presley.

"How often would a goaltender win three Stanley Cups in four years and then lose his job?" Roy says, his voice unable to mask his incredulity about Sawchuk's career. "With only six teams back then, a goaltender had to play knowing he might lose his job at any time to a guy like Glenn Hall or Roger Crozier. Sawchuk wins in 1955 and then he's traded away to Boston."

The statistical comparison between Sawchuk and Roy shows Sawchuk with four Stanley Cup championships and three Vezina trophies, while Roy had three Stanley Cup championships and three Vezina trophies. Sawchuk's career goals-against average is 2.52 and Roy's was 2.63 going into the 2000–01 season. But Roy won't venture into a debate about whether his postseason accomplishments—including his three Stanley Cup championships—were accomplished under harsher conditions. All of Sawchuk's titles came in the Original Six Era. Roy is now competing in a thirty-team NHL.

"It's just so hard to compare eras," Roy says. "They were playing with no masks, or little masks. Today we have outstanding protection. It's just too hard to compare. The last thing we want to do is to [diminish] how a player performed in his own time."

Roy was thirty-five when he entered the 2000–01 season, and there was a sense that he was driven to win one more Stanley Cup victory. Some of his friends believe that if he wins that fourth Cup he'll retire—punctuating his Hall of Fame career with a Michael Jordan–style grand exit. That would be befitting of Roy's extreme reverence for hockey's history and spirit. He would love it if the fans' final picture of him was the image of his last trip around the ice with the Cup.

Roy doesn't even hesitate when asked to list his favorite Stanley Cup memories. One is obvious: the 1992–93 season when he turned the Stanley Cup playoffs into his own private playground, winning ten overtime games in the Canadiens' improbable romp to the Stanley Cup crown. "I especially remember the second game in overtime, when Eric Desjardins scored to win it for us," he recalls.

Another memory is subtler. He remembers the feeling he had in 1986 when the Canadiens beat the New York Rangers in the Conference Finals. "It was a huge game for us," Roy said. "And I remember facing the media afterward. I could barely speak English. So I made sure someone was beside me to make sure that I didn't say the wrong thing."

Even at the age of twenty, Roy's respect for the Cup was so acute that he worried about dishonoring himself or the game with the wrong words.

With all due respect to Roy's reverence for the game, don't think he hasn't howled into the night with Stanley by his side. Let it be known that Lord Stanley's chalice was baptized in St. Patrick's pool in Montreal in 1993. Roy's impishness takes over when he tells the tale about how the Cup accidentally ended up in his pool a few dozen times during the course of the evening.

"Everyone kept getting pushed in the pool and the Stanley Cup just ended up in there with them," he says.

And what about reports that some Canadiens took the Cup apart?

"Oh no," he says, laughing. "The bottom just fell off and only then did we start trying to put our names inside the Cup."

# Guy Carbonneau

*Montreal Canadiens, 1985–86 and 1992–93*

*Dallas Stars, 1998–99*

Guy Carbonneau believes he was framed with regard to the "Cup Caper" of 1999. Evidence suggests that he was.

Drummer Vinnie Paul fingered Carbonneau as the culprit in the denting of the Stanley Cup during a wild celebration at Paul's home. Carbonneau was charged with an errant throw of the Stanley Cup into a pool.

Eyewitnesses say that never actually happened. Upon further review of replays, Hall of Fame Cup guru Phil Pritchard says that the Cup was probably dented in the celebration in the dressing room in Buffalo. He says that video shows that there was already a dent in the Cup when goaltender Ed Belfour showed off the Cup to fans when the Stars landed at Dallas airport the day after the Cup clinching.

*The Wall Street Journal* "broke" the story with Paul's allegations and several newspapers actually pursued it as if a crime had been committed. The truth is that the Stanley Cup dents quite easily, and the Hall of Fame, although it would never admit it publicly, expects the Cup to come back dented. Precautions are taken to keep damage to a minimum, but the denting of the Cup is as inevitable as old age. It's going to happen. It's just a question as to when.

Theories abounded in Dallas that summer on how the Cup actually became dented. One story had the Cup bouncing out of the back of a pickup truck as the Stars were caravanning to the Big Apple Café, a favorite Stars' watering hole.

Although the truth is hardly important at this juncture, it probably did get dinged up in the visitor's dressing room in Buffalo. It got passed around quite a bit that night, and champagne-influenced reflexes probably weren't what they should be.

Whatever happened to the Cup, Carbonneau shouldn't have been treated like a perp. This is a guy who learned Stanley Cup reverence in Montreal. That's like studying Catholicism in the Vatican. Carbonneau believed in the Canadiens' mystique, and he took a piece of that with him.

"Everyone talks about the pressure of playing in Montreal," Carbonneau said. "I always say that even though players in the 1990s don't like it, it does make them better players."

Carbonneau's comments came at the 2000 Stanley Cup final where the Dallas Stars, with ex-Canadiens star Bob Gainey as general manager, faced the New Jersey Devils, with ex-Canadians star Larry Robinson as coach. Former Canadiens captains Carbonneau, Mike Keane, and Kirk Muller played on one Dallas line. Former Cup hero Claude Lemieux played for New Jersey. That's no coincidence, says Carbonneau.

"When you are a Canadien it makes you perform every game," he insists. "It makes you understand what it is to be a winning team. Everybody who left Montreal brought that with him."

In the misguided exposure of the Cup Caper, what Carbonneau really did with the Cup was nationally overlooked. His father died during the playoffs, and Carbonneau took the Cup to his grave. "It was very emotional," he said.

# Joe Nieuwendyk

*Calgary Flames, 1988–89*

*Dallas Stars, 1998–99*

In 1989, when Lanny McDonald and Joe Mullen were preaching about what it means to win the Cup late in your career, Joe Nieuwendyk was listening. He wasn't really hearing. But he was definitely listening.

It wasn't until a decade later that he understood completely. During the 1999 Stanley Cup final against Buffalo, Nieuwendyk talked about wanting to savor every moment of being there. He sounded almost as if it were the first time, even though he had won the Stanley Cup with McDonald, Mullen, and the Calgary Flames in 1989. In that series, the Flames won the Stanley Cup and Nieuwendyk was named the Conn Smythe Trophy winner with eleven goals and twenty-one points in twenty-three games.

Nieuwendyk seemed like a man on a mission in 1999. He boasted six game-winners in the Stars' sixteen wins. He was twenty-two when he won his first Cup and thirty-two when he won his second.

"I was a little naive the first time I won the Cup," Nieuwendyk said. "I thought we had such a great team that we would be back. It took me ten years to get back. That's when you realize what a battle it is to get to the Final. Then you have to win it. All the adversity, all of the injuries—it's just one battle after another."

The time interlude between Cups allowed Nieuwendyk to develop a greater sense of enjoyment about winning. When it came time for the Cup to be brought to a site of his choosing. Nieuwendyk talked the powers that be into letting him have the Cup in two different sites, squeezing an extra half-day into his celebration. He wanted to take it to his hometown of Whitby, Ontario, and his summer home in Ithaca, New York. In Whitby he took it to his local hockey arena. He also hosted a private party for 275 guests.

"To me it's the people's Cup," Nieuwendyk said. "I just get pleasure out of watching everyone's reaction to the Cup. I just enjoyed having a good time with it . . . my brother Gill and Rick in the back of the Chevy Tahoe going to downtown Whitby hanging out of the back of the Tahoe with the Cup."

In Ithaca, his favorite Cup moment was less flamboyant and more poignant. While at Cornell, his favorite professor was Dan Sisler, who is blind.

"I had a lot of respect for him," Nieuwendyk said. "I had a reception for some people at Cornell and he was there. It was a neat feeling to see him scan the Cup with his hands. Everyone stopped what they were doing to see him going over the Cup. It was awesome."

During the 2000 Stanley Cup playoffs, Nieuwendyk was featured on ESPN in a comical commercial picturing him using the Stanley Cup as a Jell-O mold at a family gathering.

Of course, that never happened.

But Nieuwendyk reportedly did use the Stanley Cup as a serving bowl for the Canadian specialty of gravy and french fries.

> "I was a little naive the first time I won the Cup . . . It took me ten years to get back. That's when you realize what a battle it is to get to the Final."
>
> — *Joe Nieuwendyk*

Growing up in Whitby, Nieuwendyk always enjoyed his dining experiences, not to mention the hamburgers and fries at North End Burgers. If he won again, he said, he would take the Cup there. True to his word, Nieuwendyk showed up there with the Cup in the summer of 1999. A bowl of gravy was set inside the Cup and Nieuwendyk and his friends began dipping their fries. Maybe the name should be changed to Lord Stanley's gravy bowl.

# Ed Belfour

*Dallas Stars, 1998–99*

The fact that Belfour needed a Lear jet to accommodate his Stanley Cup party itinerary wasn't all that shocking to those who know him.

This is a guy who rented Maple Leaf Gardens a couple of years ago so he could play an after-hours pick-up hockey game with friends from Michigan,

Chicago, North Dakota, and Manitoba. It was Eddie the Eagle's way of saying goodbye to one of hockey's great arenas. Belfour played forward, not goaltender, and by all accounts had a grand time.

One story that made the rumor circuit was that Belfour dented the Cup as he brought it off the plane. But it didn't take much investigation to uncover that Belfour put only miles on the Cup, not dents.

In a span of forty-eight hours, he transported the Cup to his hometown of Carman, Manitoba, population 2,500, where he was greeted like a conquering hero. In North Dakota, he brought the Cup to accent the groundbreaking of an ice arena. Belfour played his college hockey at North Dakota.

Then it was off to Chicago where he hosted a gathering at the Palmer House Hotel. Belfour, a man of few words, said only that it was all that he had dreamed it would be.

# Dave Reid

*Dallas Stars, 1998–99*

Dave Reid was thirty-five when he won his Stanley Cup in 1999 and he figures that saved plenty of wear and tear on the Cup's bodyguard.

"They like guys who are married," Reid joked. "Some of the single guys get in a little trouble with it. But the guy who brought it to my house got a lot of sleep."

Of all the stops he made, one highlight was simply taking the Cup around to his father's business associates in downtown Toronto. With parking a major headache, Reid found it easier just to walk up and down Yonge and Bloor Streets with the Cup on his shoulder.

"We were moving at a pretty good clip so it wasn't like people were coming out of the buildings to see it," Reid said. "But people would pass you and say, 'Hey is that the Stanley Cup?'"

The funny part was that some people didn't believe Reid when he told them that it was indeed the Cup. "They would say, 'That's not the Cup,'" Reid recalled.

What he remembers most about his Cup possession was spending the whole day taking pictures. "I always had one arm around the Cup and the other around whoever was next to the Cup."

One treasure for Reid was his championship ring. But that had to go on hiatus during the playoffs. After the Cup, Reid moved over to the Colorado Avalanche; he didn't feel right about wearing a Stars' ring in that dressing room, especially given that they played them in the Western Conference Championship round.

# Pat Verbeek

*Dallas Stars, 1998–99*

The Stanley Cup has always been called hockey's Holy Grail, but that description took on a new meaning the day Pat Verbeek received the Cup in 1999.

Through the years, Stanley has seen its fair share of debauchery. Too many lost nights to accurately count. Way too much alcohol poured into its bowl. Stanley has seen the inside of strip joints and countless taverns and gin mills. So it seemed only right that Verbeek should introduce Stanley to his church and religion.

On July 3, 1999, Verbeek brought Stanley to the 5:30 P.M. Saturday Mass at Christ the King Catholic Church. The congregation broke out in sustained applause when Verbeek entered the church with Cup in hand. Verbeek, his wife, Dianne, and their five children had belonged to the parish since Verbeek joined the Dallas Stars in 1996. Verbeek's youngest child had been baptized there.

One reason why Verbeek brought the Cup to church is that he wanted his pastor, Monsignor Donald Zimmerman, to bless it. The parish arranged for a photographer to be present while the Cup was in the church, and after mass Verbeek obliged those who wanted to pose with him for pictures.

In his homily, pastor Zimmerman talked about hockey and jokingly offered his own prayer that the Stars' future Cup clinchings would last only one overtime instead of three.

Verbeek, raised on a farm in Petrolia, Ontario, has always had a deep Catholic faith. He has always mixed his faith with his hockey. He has had a lasting friendship with Sister Eileen Marie Hunter, a nun who taught him at St. Patrick's High School in Sarnia, Ontario. Throughout Verbeek's career, he has made a habit of leaving Sister Eileen tickets when he plays in Detroit. It has been even easier for Sister Eileen to attend the games since she accepted a new assignment as coordinator for the Sisters of Saint Joseph Holy Rosary Convent in Windsor, Ontario, right across the river from the Red Wings' Joe Louis Arena. On one of the Stars' visits in 1998–99, Sister Eileen pointed out that she had never seen Verbeek play in a winning game against the Red Wings. He told her not to worry because he wasn't superstitious, even though the Stars had won only once in twenty games at Joe Louis Arena.

> "I thought it would be a good way of showing that I am thankful to God, and bringing the Cup to church was a way of showing him respect."
>
> — *Pat Verbeek*

Verbeek jokingly suggested he should bring in Sister Eileen to perform "an exorcism" to remove the demons who haunted the Stars on their trips to Joe Louis Arena. Sister Eileen joked back that she would "leave the exorcisms to the priests." But she told Verbeek that before every game she prayed that he wouldn't be hurt, nor would any of his teammates or his opponents. For this game, she said, she was going to add an extra prayer for the Stars. The Stars ended up defeating the Red Wings 5–1.

Having once had his thumb reattached after a farming accident early in his NHL career, Verbeek has always been thankful to God for the longevity of his career. That's why he felt strongly about bringing the Stanley Cup to Mass after the Stars won the championship in 1999.

"My parents instilled the Catholic faith in me and I've held onto it," Verbeek said. "God has always been a guide in my decisions in life. I thought it would be a good way of showing that I am thankful to God, and bringing the Cup to church was a way of showing him respect."

# Derek Plante

*Dallas Stars, 1998–99*

In the well-oiled Dallas Stars' championship machinery, Derek Plante was a spare part. He had been acquired from the Buffalo Sabres on March 23, 1999, as insurance against injury. He played in just six games during the playoffs, contributing one goal.

But when players were gathered in the Buffalo visitors' dressing room a couple of hours after winning the title, Plante had had an impact on the play. He spoke from the heart and touched everyone with his simple explanation of how much it meant to him to share in the championship experience.

"Even though I didn't play, I said it had been an honor for me to play with the Dallas Stars," Plante said. "It was an honor to be on the same team with those guys. The reason I didn't get to play was that this was a great team. And if I didn't play, it was fine with me as long as we won. I still felt like I was a part of it. And the guys had made me feel like I was part of it."

In retrospect, Plante said the Stars' celebration "was a blur." The highlight for him was bringing the Cup to his hometown of Cloquet, Minnesota. He slept with the Cup in his bed that night. Stars' winger Jamie Langenbrunner is from the same place. They took the Cup to the local hockey arena, and about five thousand people showed up during the day to view it. A Duluth television station asked Plante to bring the Cup to the studio for a live appearance and he happily obliged.

One of Plante's favorite moments came when the flight brought the Stars back to Dallas the next morning after they had captured the Cup on Buffalo ice. As they came down off the plane to the tarmac, Eddie Belfour had the Stanley Cup. A huge crowd was at the cheering.

"He was carrying the Cup like a sack of potatoes," Plante remembered. "He took the Cup over to the fans, and everyone was touching it and high-fiving. It was funny to see Eddie so excited. The people were excited. I never saw Eddie happier than that."

# Mike Modano

*Dallas Stars, 1998–99*

Immediately after Brett Hull scored the Cup-winning goal for the Dallas Stars in 1999, it was almost as if Mike Modano's career flashed before his eyes.

Tears fell from his eyes, and his composure took a short leave of absence. He was overwhelmed by an indescribable blend of relief and jubilation. He had joined the Stars' organization as a potentially high scoring No. 1 draft choice in 1988 and had endured a long climb to the summit. In the beginning, he had been a flashy, open ice player who looked as if he had the potential to win a scoring championship. By the time he reached his championship moment, he had been transformed into a different player. Somewhere in the process Modano had been transformed into a warrior.

"Being with one organization the whole eleven years of my career maybe made it more special," Modano says. "All the trials and tribulations that I went through . . . and then being able to finish what I started, to have a say in the outcome . . . it's really hard to explain."

On the off day before the final game, Modano said he purposely spent some time by himself. "You visualize [winning the Cup]," Modano said. "When it comes it feels like relief. The two months that we went through were probably the most physically and emotionally draining thing I've ever been a part of. I think that's why you see the emotion kind of pour through. When you have been pushed to the edge like that and then come out on top it makes it that much more."

Modano said his Cup celebrations were tame in comparison to the excitement of the night when the Stars defeated the Sabres for the title in the triple-overtime thriller. He did get to take the Cup on Craig Kilborn's *Late Late Show* and host a family party at his home in Irving, Texas. He says his best moment was taking the Cup to the Children's Medical Center.

> "When it comes it feels like relief. The two months that we went through were probably the most physically and emotionally draining thing I've ever been a part of."
>
> — *Mike Modano*

"There is no trophy like this trophy," Modano said. "You bring it in and the kids just light up."

His strangest Cup moment? "All the women kept flashing us [during the parade]," he said, laughing. "That's Dallas."

# Ken Hitchcock

*Coach, Dallas Stars, 1998–99*

Coach Ken Hitchcock's favorite moment from the night the Dallas Stars won the 1999 Stanley Cup championship came long after the champagne flow had been reduced to a trickle.

It was past 4:00 A.M. The media had finished milking the players for all the emotion and tales of jubilation that they could muster. Wives, girlfriends, and family members had cleared the visitors' dressing room in Buffalo, leaving the players by themselves for the first time since Brett Hull had changed the course of franchise history by scoring the Cup-clinching goal against the Sabres.

"All of a sudden it just got quiet," Hitchcock remembered. "All that was left was us. Just players, coaches, other members of the organization."

Hitchcock believes it was general manager Bob Gainey who spoke first. Gainey is a soft-spoken, classy man who had won five Stanley Cup championships as a member of the Montreal Canadiens. Hitchcock remembers Gainey speaking eloquently about what the Stars had accomplished.

"It is a special feeling when you're basically in first place from start to finish," Hitchcock said. "It's special when you come out of the gate and play so well for so long and come out of it with the Stanley Cup championship."

That was Gainey's message, and then one by one players said their peace about what the Stanley Cup meant to them. Some had plenty to say and some said very little. "But I can remember what people said that night almost verbatim," Hitchcock said. "The guy that broke me down was Derek Plante."

Plante was a spare player on the Stars; Hitchcock had only used him in six games during the playoffs. He hadn't played in the Stanley Cup final.

"He just talked about how much it meant to him to be part of the championship," Hitchcock said. "It was very emotional."

The other special moment for Hitchcock came when he took the Stanley Cup to Kalamazoo, Mich. Hitchcock had previously coached in the International Hockey League for the Kalamazoo Wings, and his wife and her children were from there. About 70–80 friends were there, and Hitchcock felt as if he was carrying the Holy Grail as he opened up the box and took out the Stanley Cup from his truck.

"There was total silence," Hitchcock said. "This thing has such a special appeal that it invoked silence."

# Roman Turek

*Dallas Stars, 1998–99*

One indication of the NHL's popularity in the Czech Republic is the fact that when Roman Turek took the Stanley Cup to Ceske Budejovice he had difficulty trying to find time to drink even one beer out of the Cup.

More than ten thousand people showed up in the city square with the hope of glimpsing Turek with the Cup. Turek was the sixth Czech-born player to win the Cup, but the first to bring the Cup to Czech soil. A flight snafu caused a five-hour delay in the Cup's arrival and forced cancellation of the official public ceremony. Hall of Fame officials arrived in the Czech Republic, but the Stanley Cup didn't make the connection in Frankfort, Germany. Turek was amused as the Cup handlers sweated out the arrival of thirty-five pounds of metal that is insured for $75,000. "They were nervous," Turek said. "They kept looking out the window and asking if it had arrived yet."

When the Cup finally arrived a multitude of Czech hockey enthusiasts were still on hand and everyone got their chance to be up close and personal with the Stanley Cup. Turek put it on display at the local hockey arena.

"I can't tell you how many photographs were taken," Turek said, "but it seemed like a thousand or more."

Turek would lift the thirty-five-pound Cup on demand, and by the end of the day he felt as if he had put in some hard work as a laborer. Several hundred residents of Turek's hometown of Strankonice gathered at their city hall to chant Turek's name and catch a glimpse of the world's most famous sports trophy and their hometown hero.

"Hockey is very big in the Czech Republic," Turek said. "People know what the Stanley Cup is."

Satellite dishes have brought the NHL into Czech living rooms with regularity, but it is the Czech players that really have turned this nation of ten million into a hockey-crazed society. Dominik Hasek and Jaromir Jagr are national heroes, and the Czech Republic's triumph at the 1998 Olympic Games has pushed hockey to a higher point of reverence.

Many would have expected, maybe even hoped, that it would be Hasek that brought the Cup to the Czech Republic. Turek was honored to bring the Cup to his homeland, proud of his position as one of the world's top goaltenders. But perhaps there was a tinge of guilt to be celebrating a championship because he felt his contributions were limited. It had been Ed Belfour, not Turek, who had bested Hasek's Buffalo Sabres in the 1999 Stanley Cup final. Although Turek lost only three of twenty-two decisions in the 1998–99 regular season, Belfour played every minute in the playoffs. There was no reason to switch because Belfour had a 1.67 goals-against average.

"Of course I was happy we won the Cup, but it is very different when you watch from the bench," Turek said. "I didn't feel like I did much for us to win.

Guys on the team told me not to think like that because I had won games in the regular season and worked hard. But I didn't play in the playoffs and I didn't make any big saves."

Turek's words came after he had been traded to the St. Louis Blues and had led that team to the President's Trophy in 1999–2000. He had been outstanding in the regular season, but he longed for a chance to take the Cup back to the Czech Republic under even better circumstances. Turek is a proud athlete, a player who once politely declined to appear on television after a game because he had given up three goals and didn't believe he had played well enough to warrant being interviewed.

Even as a backup on a championship team, Turek was so mobbed by fans that he remembered just having only one beer all day as he dealt with the demands of the fans. If he ever comes back to the Czech Republic as the star of a championship team, he probably won't have time to drink at all.

# Larry Robinson

*Montreal Canadiens, 1972–73, 1975–76, 1976–77, 1977–78, 1978–79, and 1985–86*

*Assistant Coach, New Jersey Devils, 1994–95*

*Coach, New Jersey Devils, 1999–2000*

One of the tenets of modern sports philosophy is that great professional players often struggle to become great professional coaches.

The theory is that great players become frustrated watching average players make mistakes they would never have made. As much as Ted Williams loved baseball, he couldn't make managing work for him. Some of Magic Johnson's dunks lasted longer than his NBA coaching career. You could almost see the pain on Larry Bird's face as he watched his Indiana Pacers perform. Most NFL quarterbacks are smart enough to scramble into the broadcast booth rather than walk the sideline as a football coach. Hall of Famers like Bob Griese and Len Dawson enjoyed more longevity on television than they would have found in the coaching profession.

That's why Larry Robinson's attitude about winning the Stanley Cup as a coach vs. winning as it a player is so intriguing.

He insists it was a "lot more" satisfying to win it as the New Jersey Devils' head coach in 2000 than it was any of his six times as a player.

"It was great as a player because you were banged up and you had been playing for so long that you said, "Oh, jeez, it's finally over—my bruises can go away," Robinson said. "But as a coach, it's great seeing guys that have never been there before. The euphoria they are feeling—you understand because you were there before. It's great to see the guys jumping around like a little kid. It's a super feeling for a coach."

It's difficult to argue against the notion that coaching is far more emotionally demanding than playing. Top players approach thirty minutes of ice time, while a coach sweats and grinds for every tick of every contest. An inbred frustration is built in because you can't personally make the play on the ice. You can offer a plan. You can diagram it with a magic marker on your coach's board. But you cannot make the play. You are at the mercy of your players.

> "It's great to see the guys jumping around like a little kid. It's a super feeling for a coach."
>
> — *Larry Robinson*

"The toughest thing about being a coach is that you have to prepare twenty to twenty-four guys as opposed to just preparing yourself," Robinson said. "You are always thinking of what you can do to prepare them and what you can say and when is the best time."

Until the 2000 glory season with the Devils, Robinson often seemed like a reluctant coach. He had been the Devils' coach Jacques Lemaire's assistant when he won the Stanley Cup in 1995, and then moved to Los Angeles to become the head coach. He coached there for four seasons and often seemed frustrated by his experience. Rightly or wrongly, his tenure was marked by constant rumors that he was fed up with coaching.

When Robinson was let go by Los Angeles, New Jersey general manager Lou Lamoriello invited him to return to New Jersey to be one of Robbie Ftorek's assistants. He agreed to come but he made it clear that he wasn't coming as a head coach-in-waiting. In fact, Robinson was initially eager to move from behind the bench when Lamoriello fired Ftorek with eight games to go in the regular season.

No team has ever won a Stanley Cup after switching coaches so late in the season. The only historical basis for Devils' optimism was that the 1970–71 Montreal Canadiens had switched from Claude Ruel to Al MacNeil with twenty-three games remaining and then won the Stanley Cup. But that certainly wasn't a smooth ride. Remember, that was the season Henri Richard called McNeil the worst coach he had ever encountered. Lamoriello's instincts told him that the Devils weren't going to be able to win with Ftorek in charge. He believed Robinson's style was perfect for the Devils. His instincts proved to be beyond reproach.

During the Stanley Cup final, key center Bobby Holik said that the Devils couldn't have gotten that far if Ftorek had remained as coach. What he didn't say, but what insiders were saying, is that veterans just weren't buying what Ftorek was selling.

Nobody questioned Robinson's ideas, and they appreciated his candor. It's widely held that the turning point of the championship season was Robinson's tongue lashing when they fell behind 3–1 to the Philadelphia Flyers. It was a cross between a temper tantrum and an old-fashioned ass whuppin'. At no point

*Then-Montreal Canadien defenseman Larry Robinson kisses the Stanley Cup with teammate Jacques Lemaire waiting his turn. Both would later win the Cup as head coach of the New Jersey Devils, Lemaire in 1995 and Robinson in 2000.*

during his presentation would the players have been stunned to see a lightning bolt shoot out of his mouth. They were living in the eye of a Robinson storm.

Robinson has tried to downplay what happened, saying he was simply doing what all coaches do. But when the Devils came back from that 3–1 series, "the speech" became part of Stanley Cup folklore.

Robinson is the fourteenth person to win a Stanley Cup as both a player and a coach. The list includes Toe Blake, who was Rocket Richard's linemate and famed coach of the Montreal Canadiens, plus Al Arbour, who gained notoriety as a bespectacled dependable defenseman long before he coached the New York Islanders to four Cups in a row. Jacques Lemaire was also a Hall of Famer for the Montreal Canadiens before he coached the Devils to the crown.

But an argument can be made that Robinson is the best player to ever become a Stanley Cup coach. In addition to his six Stanley Cup championships, Robinson won the Norris Trophy twice as the league's best defenseman, the Conn Smythe Trophy in 1978, and played in the All-Star game ten times.

When he was coaching the Devils in the Stanley Cup, the media tried repeatedly to prompt Robinson to discuss his playing career and how it related to his success as a coach. Robinson wouldn't bite that apple.

"I don't look back on my career as it was too damn long ago," Robinson said. "I don't see how it has any bearing on what is happening now. I try to keep my focus on the here and now."

Perhaps that explains why Robinson was able to exorcise the demons that often haunt superstars that venture into coaching. Maybe he has learned not to measure players' reactions to what he was able to do. That's a theory, nothing more.

When it was over, Robinson's jubilation seemed as fresh as if he had never won a Cup before. Patrik Elias insisted that Petr Sykora's jersey be brought on the ice for the celebration because he had been carried off the ice on a stretcher early in the game after being walloped by Dallas defenseman Derian Hatcher's crushing hit. Sykora, Elias, and center Jason Arnott had been the Devils' top line throughout the playoffs. It was Robinson who put on Sykora's jersey to honor the injured Devils warrior.

When the Devils had finished off the Stars in Game 6, Robinson struggled to find the right words to sum up how he felt about the experience.

"I wish I could describe it," he said. "It is an unbelievable feeling. I've had these feelings as a player and I've had them as an assistant. But what went through me in the 2000 playoffs was a fairytale."

# Brad Bombardir

*New Jersey Devils, 1999–2000*

A couple of minutes after the Devils had won the 2000 Stanley and bedlam surrounded him on the ice, Devils coach Larry Robinson was rattling off the names of New Jersey players during a live ABC interview.

He wasn't mentioning key players like Martin Brodeur, Jason Arnott or Scott Stevens. He named Steve Kelly, Kenny Sutton, Brad Bombardir, and others who hadn't played a minute in the Stanley Cup Final. It was Robinson's acknowledgement that the triumph was aided by those in the background.

Bombardir had played thirty-two games in the regular season and he wasn't in the postseason plans. But no one seemed to cherish the Stanley Cup experience more than he did.

In the champagne-drenched Devils' dressing room, Bombardir was truly enjoying the moment.

"What do you do on a Saturday night?" Bombardir kept saying, even if no one was listening. "I drink from the Stanley Cup."

Not long after the event, he was one of the few Devils who already had an itinerary planned for his day with the Cup.

"Gotta somehow have it where people can come see it, touch it, get pictures with it, kiss it if that's what they choose to do," Bombardir told Kara Yorio of the Asbury Park, New Jersey, Press. "I'm going to take it out to my cabin where I grew up when I was a kid. They had a raft out in the water that we always played on. I want to take it out there with the sunset in the back."

# Martin Brodeur

*New Jersey Devils, 1994–95 and 1999–2000*

The Surgeon General should put a label on the Stanley Cup to suggest that it's bad for Martin Brodeur's health.

When he won his first Stanley Cup in 1995, he brought his first cigar to the podium for the Stanley Cup postgame press conference. When he arrived at the podium after winning the 2000 Stanley Cup, he had a cigar—different cigar, but same euphoria.

"I think you only realize how hard it is to win the Stanley Cup after you win it the second time," Brodeur says. "You just realize it took us five years to get back there. It's a great, great feeling to win."

One of the symbols of the Devils' arduous journey to the Cup should be a picture of Brodeur sitting next to his wife after Game 6 with a cigar in one hand and an empty champagne bottle in the other. He looked as exhausted, content, and happy as one person could possibly look.

*Martin Brodeur with the Stanley Cup in a photograph taken by his father, Denis Brodeur, former goaltender for the bronze medal–winning Canadian Olympic team.*

Recovery came quickly for Brodeur. Two days later he took the Stanley Cup on the *Live! With Regis and Kathie Lee* television show on ABC.

He also made big personal plans. First, he planned to barter for an extra day with the Cup so he could have a day with it in both New Jersey and Montreal. In New Jersey it would be shared with friends. In Montreal it would be shared with friends and family. The family includes father Denis Brodeur, a former goaltender for the bronze medal–winning Canadian Olympic team of 1956. The elder Brodeur is more known as a highly respected professional sports photographer for the Montreal Canadiens and Expos. Two of his photos of Paul Henderson's famed goal at the 1972 Summit Series were shown on Canadian postage stamps. A hockey bond exists between the Brodeur father and son that goes beyond the conventional parental relationship.

Brodeur had another humorous reason for wanting to take the Cup back to Montreal: revenge.

In 1995, during his Cup sojourn in Montreal, he organized a street hockey game with buddies. A chance to dance with the Cup was the prize. Brodeur's team lost. "I'm 2–0 on the ice, but 0–1 on the street," he told reporters.

# Barry Smith

*Assistant/Associate Coach, Pittsburgh Penguins, 1990–91 and 1991–92*

*Detroit Red Wings, 1996–97 and 1997–98*

When Barry Smith thinks of the highlights of his NHL career, he instantly recalls the feeling he had sinking to the bottom of Mario Lemieux's pool after the Pittsburgh Penguins won the Cup in 1991.

"I just remember going over backwards with the Cup in my hand and looking up at the surface of the water," Smith said. "We had so many laughs that night. People were getting drenched. There was water everywhere. I got tossed into the pool right off the hop. Just being at Mario's house was special."

Smith has been on the coaching staff of two of the most talent-laden teams in the 1990s. He was part of two championship teams in Pittsburgh and two more in Detroit. The Buffalo Sabres have never won the Stanley Cup, but thanks to Smith and fellow Buffalo area resident Scott Bowman, the city has hosted the Cup several times. Each time Smith has won, he has brought the Cup to his home on the beach. Part of Smith's celebration is to put the Cup on the back of his boat and tool along the beachfront. "Immediately people start yelling and hollering," Smith says.

Of all four of Smith's Cup associations, the one that he seems to feel best about was the Penguins' win in 1991. That was late coach Bob Johnson's team, and Smith can't help feeling that the championship was predestined based on the events that followed.

Johnson was one of hockey's most likeable people, a gregarious man who never seemed to have a day that wasn't the best day of his life. When the Penguins had a bad practice, Smith would be upset and Johnson would find a reason to exonerate his players.

"Barry," he would say. "It was just bad ice out there."

Smith smiles at the memories. "It was funny how that worked," Smith said. "It would only be bad ice on the right side, but not the left side."

No coach was ever more enthusiastic about the trappings of the game than Johnson. He would hold impromptu power play meetings wherever he could find open spaces. He even held one once in a public bathroom. Sometimes during a meeting he would get people out of their chairs and then move the chairs around to demonstrate how he wanted players to move. He had coached college hockey at Wisconsin, and he was a teacher in his heart. But what made him a valuable pro coach was that he could also deal with the superstar player.

"When Mario came in to see Bob Johnson for the first time, Mario seemed nervous to see Bob Johnson, not the other way around," Smith said.

"Badger Bob," as he was known, was a gifted storyteller who often used his tales to get a point across to his players. When Lemieux was experiencing back difficulties, Johnson said to the media: "Did you ever go to the zoo? The lion is the king of the beasts and every day he gets up and he stretches. We can learn from watching the animals."

Johnson also wasn't shy about praising his stars, and he publicly doted on his players like a proud father dotes upon his sons.

"He would walk through the room and say, 'Hey Barry, look, Mario is getting that massage. He's got tired muscles from working so hard. He's going to be re-energized tonight,'" Smith recalled, smiling.

Johnson coached the Calgary Flames from 1982–83 to 1986–87; he had exceptional teams, but he couldn't break free from the Edmonton dominance. He reached the Stanley Cup final in 1986, but the Canadiens and Patrick Roy denied him the prize he wanted. He left the Flames in 1987 to become executive director of USA Hockey, a job he expected to hold until his retirement. But the Penguins came calling and Johnson decided he really hadn't lost his desire to coach.

"It was like he was getting one last kick of the can," Smith said. "It was really just a storybook ending to his life."

The Penguins swept the North Stars in the final, and yet Smith can remember that Johnson sweated out the final minutes of the game even though the Penguins had a 6–0 lead going into the third period.

"We kept telling everyone to stay back, and Bob kept looking at the clock as if something was going to happen," Smith said.

After the Penguins won, the usually vocal Johnson was unusually silent. "He was so exuberant," Smith said. "He didn't have words to say."

Two months later, as Johnson prepared to coach Team USA in the World Cup, he was diagnosed with brain cancer. He died a few months later.

"He was such a special man," Smith said. "Winning the Cup was a storybook ending."

# Mario Lemieux

*Pittsburgh Penguins, 1990–91 and 1991–92*

It was fitting that the Stanley Cup would end up in Mario Lemieux's pool because the Penguins' ability to win that Cup had been in his hands almost from the second he entered the league as a skinny eighteen-year-old French Canadian in 1984.

If anyone deserved to bathe in the Cup's aura, it was Lemieux. His arrival saved hockey in Pittsburgh; people began coming to the Civic Center to see him dominate like no other forward had except Wayne Gretzky. No one could have anticipated that less than a decade later a thirty-four-year-old Lemieux would save hockey in Pittsburgh again by putting together an ownership group to buy the Penguins and pull the franchise out of bankruptcy.

In 1991 Lemieux helped the Penguins win the Stanley Cup despite over-whelming hardship. His back problems were so severe that he played only twenty-six regular-season games. In the playoffs he was unable even to tie his own skates. Dressing room assistant Tracy Luppe would dutifully lace up his boots before every game. No one understood how much pain Lemieux had endured to win that Cup. Yet he had forty-four points in twenty-three playoff games and won the Conn Smythe Trophy as playoff MVP.

In 1992 he played only three-quarters of the regular season and could play only fifteen of the team's twenty-one postseason games; yet he managed to net thirty-four points and won his second consecutive Stanley Cup and his second consecutive Conn Smythe Trophy.

He was not the kind of man to scale a waterfall or baptize the Cup in chlorine-filled water. But he did share in the celebration that night.

"The party was calm until [Phil] Bourque went up on the waterfall," Lemieux says, laughing. "Then it was a free-for-all."

> "The party was calm until [Phil] Bourque went up on the waterfall. Then it was a free-for-all."
>
> — *Mario Lemieux*

The Cup spent so much time in the pool that the chlorine tarnished the silver. Legend has it that Lemieux had the Cup cleaned before the parade the next day. Not true, Lemieux says.

"It wasn't clean," Lemieux said. "We just showed the silver side during the day. We just had to be careful."

If you look carefully at the parade and celebration video, it's easy to see that the Penguins seemed to be holding the Cup rather gingerly all day. The truth is that the bowl had actually come loose from the body of the trophy when the team attempted to get it out of the bottom of the pool. "It was a little crooked," Lemieux says, laughing. "We gave it back to them that way."

Having started with the NHL's last place team in 1984, it might have meant even more to Lemieux to be swimming in success. He says he never doubted his ability to win.

"You work all your life to get to the final," Lemieux said. "It was a great challenge to start with the worst team and turn it into a championship team. To lift that Cup at center ice, there is a lot of looking back, feeling the emotions. You can't express it. You just feel it. It's the best feeling in the world."

# Craig Patrick

*General Manager, Pittsburgh Penguins, 1990–91 and 1991–92*

Craig Patrick may not have been born to win the Stanley Cup, but genetics were on his side in his pursuit of hockey's Holy Grail.

Many NHL players have grown up reading about hockey's legends. Patrick grew up with hockey's legends frequently sitting at the dining room table. He is the grandson of Lester Patrick, one of the most storied figures in NHL history. In 1928, then forty-four-year-old New York Rangers coach Lester Patrick was forced to play goal in the Stanley Cup final when Lorne Chabot was injured. "I've heard many versions of that story, but the version I know from my family is that the New York players suggested that Lester go in the goal," Craig Patrick says.

In those days, the Stanley Cup was merely the silver bowl that now serves as the head of the trophy. Lester Patrick actually took the trophy to his house one summer, and it was stored in his basement. Craig was told that his father, Lynn, and uncle, Muzz, played with the trophy like young boys are apt to do. "My dad and uncle scratched their names inside the bowl," Craig said. "On the under side they put their initials."

Certainly the youngsters never realized that they would someday win the Stanley Cup when they were playing for the New York Rangers in 1940. Their father, Lester, was manager of that team. As they defaced the Stanley Cup in 1928 they also couldn't have imagined they would grow up to have a son who would win the Cup as a general manager.

Although the Patrick name was synonymous with hockey for the better part of the twentieth century, it was not planned, or even encouraged, for each generation of Patricks to follow a hockey course. "It wasn't preordained. All the kids were steered away from hockey," Patrick said. "My dad's parents told him to go be a dentist. That's what my parents told me: Go do something else. They wouldn't drive me to practices or games. I had to get rides—my brother [Glenn] and I."

But all of Craig Patrick's friends and teachers could see that hockey was his passion. By simply introducing hockey to their kids, the Patrick elders had fostered an addiction.

"My elementary teachers would send home notes or call home and say, 'Can you get this kid to do something else but draw hockey rinks?'" Craig remembers. "Hockey has been in my blood from the beginning."

Patrick played college hockey at the University of Denver with the idea of becoming a pro player. He made it, toiling in the NHL as a journeyman player for parts of eight seasons. He ended up playing in St. Louis in 1974-75 where his father, Lynn, was general manager. Lynn Patrick didn't like that very much, and the decision to trade for Craig came from Lynn's bosses.

"My dad always said he would never have any of his kids play for him because of what he went through in New York [playing for Lester]," Craig said. "The Blues traded for me against his wishes, and I knew it wouldn't last long."

He played forty-three games for the Blues before his father dealt him to the Kansas City Scouts.

In 1991 and 1992, Patrick had done as much to bring a Cup to Pittsburgh as any of the players. He was a bold trader, acquiring Ron Francis and Ulf Samuelsson from Hartford in 1991 as the missing pieces. In 1992, he added Rick Tocchet, who was the team's leading scorer in the 1992 final.

No one was prouder to have won a Cup than Patrick.

"You start playing the game at a young age and you fall in love with it," Craig says. "As early as I can remember this has been my life. That's what I wanted to be, a player, a coach, and then into management. I'm living a dream. I feel like the luckiest person."

# Phil Bourque

*Pittsburgh Penguins, 1990–91 and 1991–92*

By all accounts the Pittsburgh Penguins' Stanley Cup party at Mario Lemieux's Mt. Lebanon, Pennsylvania, house in 1992 was a tame affair until valuable role player Phil Bourque, attired only in his skivvies, climbed the waterfall sometime after 3:00 A.M.

The Penguins had reason to let their hair down after winning their second consecutive Stanley Cup. For much of that season it looked as if the Penguins' Cup victories would be limited to one. After winning the Cup in 1991, the Penguins had only finished third in their division in 1991–92, and they weren't even sure of making the playoffs until they got hot late in the season.

"There was a big meeting three-quarters of the way through the season in Calgary," Bourque remembered. "Craig Patrick came in and explained to us what Scotty Bowman is about. That really put us over the top."

The much-heralded Bowman had replaced the late Bob Johnson as head coach at the start of the 1991–92 season after Johnson was diagnosed with brain cancer. The difference between the two coaching styles was pronounced: Johnson was a rah-rah coach who had optimism spilling out of every pore of his being. He was enthusiastic, chatty—a true people person. Bowman was more accomplished than Johnson in terms of NHL success. Before moving behind the Pittsburgh bench, he had already won five Stanley Cup championships with the Montreal Canadiens. But Bowman was far less communicative than Johnson; he was old school in his approach about who played and who didn't. He didn't feel a need to explain his actions. Complicating the situation was the fact that the Penguins boasted many veteran players who were also set in their ways.

"We didn't know how to take Scotty's personality," Bourque remembered. "And he certainly didn't know how to adapt to our team. We had a lot of unique characters."

Patrick's talk helped immeasurably. "He let us understand how Scotty operates," Bourque said. "That was a major hurdle for us. He changed a bit, and we changed a bit. We started to play better. I really don't know if we would have even made the playoffs without that meeting."

Lemieux was clearly the most crucial player because he was simply a dominant offensive player. He could take over a hockey game like Michael Jordan could take over a basketball game or Tiger Woods can command a golf tournament. He inspired the Penguins through his on-ice dominance and his willingness to play through pain. It was difficult not to play with heart and purpose when you saw how much pain Lemieux had to endure just to get on the ice. But Lemieux was a reserved man in the dressing room. "He wouldn't say boo," Bourque remembered. "So when he did speak and you were lacing up your skates or whatever you were doing you stopped," Bourque said. "You directed your attention to him because if he was speaking you knew it was important."

In addition to Lemieux, Bourque recalls, there were also "three or four other guys who were the glue in the room."

He remembers Ulfie Samuelsson and Bob Errey keeping things light with their humor. He remembers Ron Francis as the team's composure monitor. "He had a calming effect on the team when things got scrambly or even if there was an issue with Scotty," Bourque said. "He didn't say a lot of words, but his choice of words was always on the money."

Next to Lemieux, the most important player on the team was probably Kevin Stevens. "He was the go-between for every guy on the team," Bourque said. "On every team you have your millionaires club and then you have the guys swimming in the bottom. Kevin was the guy in the middle keeping us all together."

Stevens was as close to the role players and the clubhouse attendants as he was to Mario. He was very democratic in spreading around his time and friendships. He made it his business to make sure that everyone felt comfortable. According to Bourque, the role players on the Penguins were afforded the same amount of respect as the stars. "That's what balanced our team," Bourque recalled. "The role players took pride in their contributions, and we all got along. There was no place for an ego on this team. It didn't matter whether you were Mario Lemieux or [tough guy] Jay Caufield who wasn't playing. You didn't get away with anything in that room. It didn't matter how much money you had or how many goals you scored. If you weren't cutting the mustard, you were hearing about it from someone."

Bourque's job was primarily as a checker. He was supposed to use his speed to be an effective defensive player. But in the final against Chicago, he scored what seems now to have been an important goal. The Black Hawks had taken a 3–0 lead in Game 1 and then Bourque scored to make it 3–1 and suddenly the Penguins believed they had a shot. They ended up winning that game 5–4 and then swept the series.

In celebration, Lemieux invited everyone to his home for a team party. He had never before held a team function at his house, and when all of the coaches, teammates, and families arrived that night the sense of accomplishment was heavy in the air.

Bourque recalls Lemieux's house as "a palace." One highlight was a regulation in-ground pool, with an adjacent four-layered waterfall that sloped down to the decking. Neon lights had been installed at each level, providing a festive background for the party. Goaltender Tom Barrasso was the first to take the Cup to the summit of the waterfall, leading to a picture-taking frenzy.

At about 3:00 A.M., Bourque was sitting in the hot tub "enjoying a cocktail" and marveling at how awe-inspiring the Cup looked with the waterfall backdrop when he was moved to act in a manner that would forever make him a legend in Stanley Cup lore.

If ever a man was born to march to the beat of a different percussionist, it was Bourque. He was a proud American, a Chelmsford, Massachusetts, native, who went against New England tradition by electing to play Canadian junior hockey rather than college hockey. Not gifted enough to play alongside the elite players of the game, Bourque carved his own path to the NHL with a blue collar work ethic and a Tasmanian devil playing style that always endeared him to fans and coaches. Pittsburghers loved Bourque. He may not have been a native but he seemed to embody the city's spirit as much as Iron City beer and a lunch pail. In Pittsburgh, you must work for what you have; Bourque seemed like a poster boy for that kind of thinking. He once aspired to host his own hockey commentary television show, much like Don Cherry has in Canada. He's always had a flair for the unexpected. Once, much to the chagrin of Coach Johnson, Bourque found himself on a breakaway and decided to push the blade of his stick nose-down and pinned the puck to the ice. He carried the puck down the ice in that manner. He didn't score, but he made every highlight show in North America. That indeed had been his goal. Bourque was a spirited player on and off the ice. That is the simple explanation of why he did what he did.

> "It didn't matter how much money you had or how many goals you scored. If you weren't cutting the mustard, you were hearing about it from someone."
>
> — *Phil Bourque*

"It hit me that this Cup needs to go in the water," Bourque remembered. "I hiked up there and grabbed the Cup."

As the underwear-clad Bourque stood up and held the Stanley Cup above his head he struck a pose that was ever so close to King Kong standing on the top of the Empire State Building.

It's unclear whether people really thought Bourque would throw the Cup, but when he heaved it over his head it was if the party started anew. The Cup filled with water and sank to the bottom. It took five or six players to dive in and pull it out. Some say it was more like seven or eight players. People were stunned at how heavy the Cup was after it had been filled with water.

Asked whether Lemieux was a member of the Cup rescue team, Bourque laughed. "I think Mario was just trying to hold down the fort. This was a multi-million-dollar mansion and there was water all over and food everywhere. He had his hands full. And, truthfully it is hard to picture him stripped down to his skivvies and jumping in the water."

Once the Cup had taken its first belly flop into the water, a new round of picture taking began. The Cup stayed in the pool for the rest of the night. "As soon as the Cup made contact with the water, it got wild after that," Bourque said. "Before then, the party was going all right, but it wasn't really jumping. I remember thinking we've got to get a little crazy."

Originally the Penguins were guarded about the evening's events, thinking they would be submerged in trouble for their shenanigans. "We weren't being disrespectful," Bourque said. "We were just letting loose."

Only through the years did the Penguins come to understand that they weren't the first, nor would they be the last Stanley Cup winners to swim with the Stanley Cup. The Hall of Fame now expects the Stanley Cup to be baptized in chlorine on a yearly basis. The removal of the Cup's tarnish is a fall ritual at the Hall of Fame. Engravers know immediately how much pool time the Cup has received simply by the look of the Cup.

Instead of getting himself and the Penguins in trouble, Bourque made himself a Stanley Cup legend that starry night in Mount Lebanon.

He would touch the Cup again before it was returned to the Hall of Fame. After the second consecutive championship, the Cup was passed among the players more than it was after the first title. Through a quirk in the informal scheduling, he picked up the Cup from team president Paul Martha on a Thursday. Today's formalized Cup sharing allows for each player to have it only for twenty-four hours, but when Bourque received it in 1992 he was told that the Cup's next appearance wasn't scheduled until Paul Coffey got it at a Toronto golf tournament. That meant Bourque had possession for four days.

He loaded up the Cup in the back of his Ford Bronco and immediately headed off to see a friend at the Baltimore shore where he set up shop in a bar. Plenty of friends and acquaintances drank out of Lord Stanley's mug that weekend.

"But what was really neat was going down the highway with the Cup bouncing around in the Bronco.

"The look on everyone's faces as they looked inside," Bourque said, laughing. "They were trying to figure out if that was the real Cup."

But the legend of Bourque's Cup escapade doesn't end with the dunking in Mario's pool or the drive to Baltimore. When he returned home, he discovered a rattling in the Cup. A quick investigation showed him that the nonmetal base was held together only by four bolts. Although he confesses that he isn't mechanically inclined, he thought he might be able to take the Cup apart and determine the cause of the rattle. He put a pen light in his mouth, stuck his whole head in the Cup, and quickly determined that one nut holding on the bowl at the top had become loose. He quickly solved that problem. But while his noggin was up there he saw that those who had repaired the Cup before him had engraved their names. There were three names and dates showing. An idea began brewing in Bourque's head.

He found a screwdriver and, near the names of the formal engravers, he began chiseling in his own inscription. It took him three hours. When it was done it read: "Enjoy it . . . Phil "Bubba" Bourque."

Proud of his work, Bourque presumed that he would forever be the only player who has his name engraved both on the front of the Cup and inside. Already a legend for his Cup toss, Bourque didn't feel obliged to share his secret engraver's life with the rest of the world. His only fear was that the Hall of Fame, during its annual summer cleaning of the Cup, might discover his handiwork. If someone did uncover his secret, he wondered whether his crude effort would be buffed out. But that thought certainly didn't consume the rest of his summer. Having earned a reputation as a strong role player and coming off a twenty-goal season, he was able to get a good free agent contract from the New York Rangers that following summer.

He actually forgot about his Cup caper until he was on the National Hockey League boat cruise in the summer of 1993. Fans pay to take a cruise with NHL players; Bourque signed on for the journey.

Defenseman J. J. Daigneault, a member of the Montreal Canadiens' 1993 championship team, was also on the NHL cruise. At one point on the trip he came up to Bourque and started laughing before words finally emerged from his month: "I saw what you did!"

Bourque looked at him in a quizzical manner; he had no idea what Daigneault was talking about.

"I saw your name inside the Cup," Daigneault said. Bourque was stunned. "How did you see it?"

Daigneault just grinned. "Because I put my name there too."

# Stanley Cup Timeline

# Stanley Cup Timeline

**1892:** Lord Stanley, governor-general of Canada, announces he will donate a trophy to designate Canada's national champion.

**1893:** Montreal AAA becomes the first winner of the Cup.

**1907:** The Montreal Wanderers become the first team to engrave the names of all of their players, in addition to the team name, in the Cup. Prior to this season, only team names were engraved on the Cup's bowl.

**1907:** An unidentified man absconds with the Stanley Cup and holds it for ransom. However, the champion Montreal Wanderers had no interest in paying any amount for its return. The Cup was returned without payment.

**1908:** The Wanderers become the first team not to engrave their championship on the bowl.

**1925:** The Stanley Cup unofficially becomes the NHL championship trophy.

**1948:** The NHL remodels the Stanley Cup into a two-piece trophy with a wider base.

**1949:** The NHL and the Stanley Cup trustee sign an agreement giving the league jurisdiction over the awarding of the Cup (but not ownership).

**1955:** Detroit Red Wings captain Ted Lindsay holds up the Cup for fans to see and then skates over along the boards so fans can get a closer look.

**1958:** The modern one-piece Stanley Cup is introduced.

**1969:** The original Stanley Cup bowl is retired to the Hall of Fame. This means that there are actually three Stanley Cup bowls (see 1992 entry).

**1973:** The Montreal Canadiens win the Stanley Cup, and Henri Richard establishes the new NHL record of having his name engraved in the cup eleven times as a player.

**1971:** After Montreal wins the Stanley Cup at Chicago Stadium, Canadiens' captain Jean Beliveau skates around the ice with the Cup over his head. The Canadiens follow him. This was the start of the traditional victory lap.

**1977:** A Hall of Fame employee thwarts an elaborate plan to steal the Cup. Seven men with tools fled the scene, but police discover plans and photos of the Hall in a car parked nearby.

**1979:** Montreal Canadiens star Guy Lafleur "steals" the Stanley Cup and takes it to Thurso, Quebec where he entertains family and friends.

**1992:** A duplicate Stanley Cup is produced at a cost of $75,000. In a meeting of the NHL, the Hall of Fame, and the Stanley Cup trustees it's agreed that the players should always receive the original as a tribute to the work they put in to earn it.

**1995:** NHL commissioner Gary Bettman decrees that every player, trainer, coach, and member of management from the Stanley Cup championship team should get at least a day with the Cup. Players had been able to spend some time with the Cup unofficially before; however, at this point the passing of the Cup became organized, assuring that no one would be left out. Part of the agreement is that a member of the Hall of Fame must accompany the Cup on its many stops.

**1996:** Colorado's Peter Forsberg becomes the first player to take the Stanley Cup to Europe. He takes it to his native Sweden. The Cup had gone to Finland and Germany in 1994, but not with a player.

**1996:** Avalanche player Adam Deadmarsh becomes the first NHL player to have his name corrected on the Cup. The engraver had inadvertently listed him as "Deadmarch."

**1997:** The Cup goes to Russia for the first time. Detroit Red Wings Slava Fetisov, Slava Kozlov, and Igor Larionov take it to Red Square, among other stops in Moscow.

**1998:** The Red Wings win the Stanley Cup, giving Coach Bowman his eighth Stanley Cup championship as a coach. This ties him with Tow Blake for the NHL record.

**2005:** In this year the Cup's engraving space will be used up and another band will have to be retired.

# Stanley Cup Winners

# List of Stanley Cup Winners through 2000

This is a list of the players who have earned the right to have their names engraved on the Stanley Cup. In theory, players need to have played forty games in the regular-season or to have played at least one game in the championship in order to qualify to be included on the Cup roster. However, exceptions have been made in recent years.

## A

Abel, Clarence "Taffy"—New York Rangers 1928; Chicago 1934
Abel, Sid—Detroit 1943, 1950, 1952
Acton, Keith—Edmonton 1988
Adams, Jack—Toronto 1918; Ottawa 1927
Aikenhead, Andy—New York Rangers 1933
Albelin, Tommy—New Jersey 1995
Allen, "Bones" —Ottawa 1905
Allen, Keith—Detroit 1954
Anderson, Doug—Montreal 1953
Anderson, Glenn—Edmonton 1984, 1985, 1987, 1988, 1990;
    New York Rangers 1994
Anderson, Jocko—Victoria 1925
Andrews, Lloyd—Toronto 1922
Apps Sr., Syl—Toronto 1942, 1947, 1948
Arbour, Al—Detroit 1954; Chicago 1961; Toronto 1962, 1964
Arbour, Amos—Montreal 1916
Armitage, Jack—Winnipeg Vics 1896
Armstrong, George—Toronto 1962, 1963, 1964, 1967
Arnold, Josh—Montreal Wanderers 1906
Arnott, Jason—New Jersey 2000
Ashbee, Barry—Philadelphia 1974
Asmundson, Ossie—New York Rangers 1933
Aurie, Larry—Detroit 1936, 1937
Awrey, Don—Boston 1970, 1972

# B

Babando, Pete—Detroit 1950
Backor, Peter—Toronto 1945
Backstrom, Ralph—Montreal 1959, 1960, 1965, 1966, 1968, 1969
Bailey, Garnet "Ace"—Boston 1972
Bailey, Irvine "Ace"—Toronto 1932
Bain, Dan—Winnipeg Vics 1896, 1901
Balfour, Earl—Chicago 1961
Balfour, Murray—Chicago 1961
Balon, Dave—Montreal 1965, 1966
Barber, Bill—Philadelphia 1974, 1975
Barilko, Bill—Toronto 1947, 1948, 1949, 1951
Barlow, Billy—Montreal AAA 1893, 1894
Barrasso, Tom—Pittsburgh 1991, 1992
Barry, Marty—Detroit 1936, 1937
Bathgate, Andy—Toronto 1964
Bauer, Bobby—Boston 1939, 1941
Baun, Bob—Toronto 1962, 1963, 1964, 1967
Beaudro, Roxy—Kenora 1907
Belfour, Ed—Dallas 1999
Beliveau, Jean—Montreal 1956, 1957, 1958, 1959, 1960, 1965, 1966,
    1968, 1969, 1971
Bell, Billy—Montreal 1924
Bellingham, Billy—Montreal AAA 1902
Bellows, Brian—Montreal 1993
Benedict, Clint—Ottawa 1920, 1921, 1923; Montreal Maroons 1926
Benoit, Joe—Montreal 1946
Bentley, Max—Toronto 1948, 1949, 1951
Berenson, Gordon "Red"—Montreal 1965, 1966
Berlinquette, Louis—Montreal 1916
Beukeboom, Jeff—Edmonton 1987, 1988, 1990; New York Rangers 1994
Blachford, Cecil—Montreal Wanderers 1906, 1907, 1908, 1910
Black, Steve—Detroit 1950
Bladon, Tom—Philadelphia 1974, 1975
Blair, Andy—Toronto 1932
Blake, Hector "Toe"—Montreal Maroons 1935; Montreal 1944, 1946
Blinco, Russ—Montreal Maroons 1935
Bodnar, Gus—Toronto 1945, 1947
Boesch, Garth—Toronto 1947, 1948, 1949
Boisvert, Serge—Montreal 1986
Bombardir, Brad—New Jersey 2000
Bonin, Marcel—Detroit 1955; Montreal 1958, 1959, 1960

Boon, Dick—Montreal AAA 1902
Bordeleau, Christian—Montreal 1969
Bossy, Mike—New York Islanders 1980, 1981, 1982, 1983
Bouchard, Emile "Butch"—Montreal 1944, 1946, 1953, 1956
Bouchard, Pierre—Montreal 1971, 1973, 1976, 1977, 1978
Boucher, Billy—Montreal 1924
Boucher, Bobby—Montreal 1924
Boucher, Frank—New York Rangers 1928, 1933
Boucher, George—Ottawa 1920, 1921, 1923, 1927
Bourgeault, Leo—New York Rangers 1928
Bourne, Bob—New York Islanders 1980, 1981, 1982, 1983
Bourque, Phil—Pittsburgh 1991, 1992
Boutilier, Paul—New York Islanders 1983
Bower, Johnny—Toronto 1962, 1963, 1964, 1967
Bowman, Ralph "Scotty"—Detroit 1936, 1937
Boyd, Bill—New York Rangers 1928
Brannen, Jack—Montreal Shamrocks 1899, 1900
Brennan, Doug—New York Rangers 1933
Brewer, Carl—Toronto 1962, 1963, 1964
Brimsek, Frank—Boston 1939, 1941
Brisebois, Patrice—Montreal 1993
Broadbent, Harry "Punch"—Ottawa 1920, 1921, 1923; Montreal Maroons 1926
Broda, Walter "Turk"—Toronto 1942, 1947, 1948, 1949, 1951
Broden, Connie—Montreal 1957, 1958
Brodeur, Martin—New Jersey 1995, 2000
Brophy, Bernie—Montreal Maroons 1926
Broten, Neal—New Jersey 1995
Brown, Adam—Detroit 1943
Brown, Art—Winnipeg Vics 1901
Brown, Dave—Edmonton 1990
Brown, Doug—Detroit 1997, 1998
Brown, Gerry—Detroit 1943
Bruce, Morley—Ottawa 1920, 1921
Brunet, Benoit—Montreal 1993
Bruneteau, Moderre "Mud"—Detroit 1936, 1937, 1943
Brylin, Sergei—New Jersey 1995, 2000
Buchberger, Kelly—Edmonton 1987, 1990
Bucyk, Johnny—Boston 1970, 1972
Burke, Marty—Montreal 1930, 1931

# C

Cain, Herb—Montreal Maroons 1935; Boston 1941
Callender, Jock—Pittsburgh 1995
Callighen, Patsy—New York Rangers 1928
Cameron, Allan—Montreal AAA 1893, 1894
Cameron, Billy—Montreal 1924
Cameron, Harry—Toronto 1914, 1918, 1922
Campbell, C.J.—Winnipeg Vics 1896
Carbonneau, Guy—Montreal 1986, 1993; Dallas 1999
Carleton, Wayne—Boston 1970
Carpenter, Bob—New Jersey 1995
Carpenter, Ed—Seattle 1917
Carr, Lorne—Toronto 1942, 1945
Carroll, Billy—New York Islanders 1981, 1982, 1983; Edmonton 1985
Carson, Bill—Boston 1929
Carson, Frank—Montreal Maroons 1926
Carson, Gerald—Montreal 1930
Carveth, Joe—Detroit 1943, 1950
Cashman, Wayne—Boston 1970, 1972
Caufield, Jay—Pittsburgh 1991, 1992
Chabot, Lorne—New York Rangers 1928; Toronto 1932
Chamberlain, Erwin "Murph"—Montreal 1944, 1946
Chambers, Shawn—New Jersey 1995; Dallas 1999
Chartraw, Rick—Montreal 1976, 1977, 1978, 1979
Cheevers, Gerry—Boston 1970, 1972
Chelios, Chris—Montreal 1986
Chorske, Tom—New Jersey 1995
Chychrun, Jeff—Pittsburgh 1992
Clancy, Frank "King"—Ottawa 1923, 1927; Toronto 1932
Clapper, Aubrey "Dit"—Boston 1929, 1939, 1941
Clarke, Bobby—Philadelphia 1974, 1975
Cleghorn, Odie—Montreal 1924
Cleghorn, Sprague—Ottawa 1920, 1921; Montreal 1924
Clement, Bill—Philadelphia 1974, 1975
Coffey, Paul—Edmonton 1984, 1985, 1987; Pittsburgh 1991
Cole, Danton—New Jersey 1995
Collins, Herb—Montreal AAA 1894
Colville, Mac—New York Rangers 1940
Colville, Neil—New York Rangers 1940
Conacher, Brian—Toronto 1967
Conacher, Charlie—Toronto 1932
Conacher, Lionel—Chicago 1934; Montreal Maroons 1935
Conacher, Pat—Edmonton 1984

Conacher, Roy—Boston 1939, 1941
Connell, Alex—Ottawa 1927; Montreal Maroons 1935
Connolly, Bert—Chicago 1938
Connor, Cam—Montreal 1979
Cook, Bill—New York Rangers 1928, 1933
Cook, Fred "Bun"—New York Rangers 1928, 1933
Cook, Lloyd—Vancouver 1915
Cook, Tom—Chicago 1934
Corbeau, Bert—Montreal 1916
Corbeau, Con—Toronto 1914
Corbet, Rene—Colorado 1996
Costello, Les—Toronto 1948
Cotton, Harold "Baldy"—Toronto 1932
Coughlin, Jack—Toronto 1918
Coulter, Art—Chicago 1934; New York Rangers 1940
Cournoyer, Yvan—Montreal 1965, 1966, 1968, 1969, 1971, 1973, 1976,
    1977, 1978, 1979
Courtnall, Geoff—Edmonton 1988
Coutu, Billy—Montreal 1924
Couture, Gerald "Doc"—Detroit 1950
Couture, Rosario "Lola"—Chicago 1934
Cowick, Bruce—Philadelphia 1974
Cowley, Bill—Boston 1939, 1941
Crawford, Jack—Boston 1939, 1941
Crawford, "Rusty"—Quebec 1913; Toronto 1918
Creighton, Billy—Quebec 1913
Crisp, Terry—Philadelphia 1974, 1975
Currie, Alex—Ottawa 1911
Curry, Floyd—Montreal 1953, 1956, 1957, 1958

# D

Dahlin, Kjell—Montreal 1986
Dahlstrom, "Cully"—Chicago 1938
Daigneault, J.J.—Montreal 1993
Damphousse, Vincent—Montreal 1993
Dandenault, Mathieu—Detroit 1997, 1998
Daneyko, Ken—New Jersey 1995, 2000
Daniels, Jeff—Pittsburgh 1992
Darragh, Harold—Toronto 1932
Darragh, Jack—Ottawa 1911, 1920, 1921, 1923
Davidson, Bob—Toronto 1942, 1945
Davidson, Cam—Montreal Victorias 1896, 1897, 1898

Davidson, Shirley—Montreal Victorias 1895, 1896, 1897
Davis, Lorne—Montreal 1953
Dawes, Robert—Toronto 1949
Day, "Hap"—Toronto 1932
Deadmarsh, Adam—Colorado 1996
Dean, Kevin—New Jersey 1995
DeBlois, Lucien—Montreal 1986
Delvecchio, Alex—Detroit 1952, 1954, 1955
Denneny, Corb—Toronto 1918, 1922
Denneny, Cy—Ottawa 1920, 1921, 1923, 1927; Boston 1929
Desjardins, Eric—Montreal 1993
Dewsbury, Al—Detroit 1950
Dey, Edgar—Ottawa 1909
Dickens, Ernie—Toronto 1942
Dillon, Cecil—New York Rangers 1933
Dineen, Bill—Detroit 1954, 1955
Dinsmore, Chuck "Dinny"—Montreal Maroons 1926
Dionne, Gilbert—Montreal 1993
DiPietro, Paul—Montreal 1993
Doak, Gary—Boston 1970
Dobby, John—Montreal Shamrocks 1899
Dornhoefer, Gary—Philadelphia 1974, 1975
Douglas, Kent—Toronto 1963
Douglas, Les—Detroit 1943
Dowd, Jim—New Jersey 1995
Draper, Kris—Detroit 1997, 1998
Drillon, Gordie—Toronto 1942
Drinkwater, Graham—Montreal Victorias 1895, 1896, 1897, 1898
Driver, Bruce—New Jersey 1995
Dryden, Ken—Montreal 1971, 1973, 1976, 1978, 1979
Dube, Gilles—Detroit 1954
Dufresne, Donald—Montreal 1993
Duff, Dick—Toronto 1962, 1963; Montreal 1965, 1966, 1968, 1969
Dumart, Woody—Boston 1939, 1941
Dupont, Andre "Moose"—Philadelphia 1974, 1975
Durnan, Bill—Montreal 1944, 1946
Dye, Cecil "Babe"—Toronto 1922

# E

Eddolls, Frank—Montreal 1946
Ehman, Gerry—Toronto 1964
Elias, Patrik—New Jersey 2000

Elliot, Roland—Montreal Victorias 1895; Montreal AAA 1902
Ellis, Ron—Toronto 1967
Elmer, Wally—Victoria 1925
Engblom, Brian—Montreal 1977, 1978, 1979
Erikson, Aut—Toronto 1967
Eriksson, Anders—Detroit 1998
Errey, Bob—Pittsburgh 1991, 1992
Esposito, Phil—Boston 1970, 1972
Esposito, Tony—Montreal 1969
Evans, Jack—Chicago 1961
Evans, Stewart—Montreal Maroons 1935
Ewen, Todd—Montreal 1993
Ewing, Jack—Montreal Victorias 1897, 1898
Ezinicki, Bill—Toronto 1947, 1948, 1949

# F

Farrell, Art—Montreal Shamrocks 1899, 1900
Fedorov, Sergei—Detroit 1997, 1998
Fenwick, Art—Montreal Victorias 1895
Ferguson, John—Montreal 1965, 1966, 1968, 1969, 1971
Fetisov, Viacheslav—Detroit 1997, 1998
Fillion, Bob—Montreal 1944, 1946
Finnie, Dave—Ottawa 1905
Finnigan, Frank—Ottawa 1927; Toronto 1932
Fiset, Stephane—Colorado 1996
Fisher, Joe—Detroit 1943
Flaman, Fern—Toronto 1951
Fleming, Reg—Chicago 1961
Flett, Bill—Philadelphia 1974
Flett, Magnus—Winnipeg Vics 1901
Flett, Rod—Winnipeg Vics 1896, 1901
Fleury, Theoren—Calgary 1989
Fogolin, Jr., Lee—Edmonton 1984, 1985
Fogolin, Sr., Lee—Detroit 1950
Foote, Adam—Colorado 1996
Forsberg, Peter—Colorado 1996
Fortier, Charles—Montreal 1924
Fournier, Jack—Montreal 1916
Foyston, Frank—Toronto 1914; Seattle 1917; Victoria 1925
Francis, Ron—Pittsburgh 1991, 1992
Franks, Jim—Detroit 1937

Fraser, A.A.—Ottawa 1903
Fraser, Gordon—Victoria 1925
Fredrickson, Frank—Victoria 1925; Boston 1929
Fuhr, Grant—Edmonton 1984, 1985, 1987, 1988, 1990

# G

Gagnon, Johnny—Montreal 1931
Gainey, Bob—Montreal 1976, 1977, 1978, 1979, 1986
Gainor, Norman "Dutch"—Boston 1929; Montreal Maroons 1935
Galbraith, Percy "Perk"—Boston 1929
Gallagher, John—Detroit 1937
Gamble, Bruce—Toronto 1967
Gamble, Dick—Montreal 1953, 1956
Gardiner, Chuck—Chicago 1934
Gardner, Cal—Toronto 1949, 1951
Gardner, Jimmy—Montreal AAA 1902; Montreal Wanderers 1910
Gaul, Horace—Ottawa 1905, 1911
Gauthier, Jean—Montreal 1965
Gee, George—Detroit 1950
Gelinas, Martin—Edmonton 1990
Geoffrion, Bernie—Montreal 1953, 1956, 1957, 1958, 1959, 1960
Gerard, Eddie—Ottawa 1920, 1921, 1923; Toronto 1922
Geroux, Eddie—Kenora 1907
Getliffe, Ray—Boston 1939; Montreal 1944
Gilbert, Greg—New York Islanders 1982, 1983; New York Rangers 1994
Gilchrist, Brent—Detroit 1998
Gillelan, David—Montreal Victorias 1896, 1897
Gillies, Clark—New York Islanders 1980, 1981, 1982, 1983
Gilhen, Randy—Pittsburgh 1991
Gilmour, Billy—Ottawa 1903, 1904, 1905, 1909
Gilmour, Dave—Ottawa 1903
Gilmour, Doug—Calgary 1989
Gilmour, Larry—Montreal Wanderers 1908
Gilmour, Suddy—Ottawa 1903, 1904
Gingras, Gaston—Montreal 1986
Gingras, Tony—Winnipeg Vics 1901
Glass, Frank "Pud"—Montreal Wanderers 1906, 1907, 1908, 1910
Golham, Bob—Toronto 1942, 1947; Detroit 1952, 1954, 1955
Goldsworthy, Leroy—Chicago 1934
Goldup, Hank—Toronto 1942
Gomez, Scott—New Jersey 2000
Goodenough, Larry—Philadelphia 1975

Goodfellow, Ebbie—Detroit 1936, 1937, 1943
Goodman, Paul—Chicago 1938
Goring, Butch—New York Islanders 1980, 1981, 1982, 1983
Gorman, Ed—Ottawa 1927
Gottselig, Johnny—Chicago 1934, 1938
Goyette, Phil—Montreal 1957, 1958, 1959, 1960
Gracie, Bob—Toronto 1932; Montreal Maroons 1935
Graham, Leth—Ottawa 1921
Grant, Danny—Montreal 1968
Grant, Mike—Montreal Victorias 1895, 1896, 1897, 1898
Graves, Adam—Edmonton 1990; New York Rangers 1994
Gray, Alex—New York Rangers 1928
Green, Red—Boston 1929
Green, Rick—Montreal 1986
Green, Ted—Boston 1972
Gregg, Randy—Edmonton 1984, 1985, 1987, 1988, 1990
Grenier, Lucien—Montreal 1969
Gretzky, Wayne—Edmonton 1984, 1985, 1987, 1988
Griffis, Si—Kenora 1907; Vancouver 1915
Grosso, Don—Detroit 1943
Guerin, Bill—New Jersey 1995
Gusarov, Alexei—Colorado 1996

# H

Haidy, Gordon—Detroit 1950
Hainsworth, George—Montreal 1930, 1931
Halderson, Harold "Slim"—Victoria 1925
Hall, Glenn—Chicago 1961
Hall, Joe—Quebec 1912, 1913
Haller, Kevin—Montreal 1993
Halliday, Milt—Ottawa 1927
Hallin, Mats—New York Islanders 1983
Hamill, Robert " Red"—Boston 1939
Hamilton, Reg—Toronto 1942, 1945
Hannan, Dave—Edmonton 1988; Colorado 1996
Harmon, Glen—Montreal 1944, 1946
Harper, Terry—Montreal 1965, 1966, 1968, 1969, 1971
Harris, Billy—Toronto 1962, 1963, 1964
Harris, Ted—Montreal 1965, 1966, 1968, 1969; Philadelphia 1975
Harriston—Toronto 1914
Hart, Harold "Gizzy"—Victoria 1925
Hartman, Mike—New York Rangers 1994

Harvey, Doug—Montreal 1953, 1956, 1957, 1958, 1959, 1960
Hatcher, Derian—Dallas 1999
Hay, Jim—Detroit 1955
Hay, Bill—Chicago 1961
Hayes, Chris—Boston 1972
Healy, Glenn—New York Rangers 1994
Hebert, Sammy—Toronto 1918
Heffernan, Gerry—Montreal 1944
Heller, Ott—New York Rangers 1993, 1940
Helman, Harry—Ottawa 1923
Henderson, Harold—Montreal Vics 1895, 1896, 1897
Henning, Lorne—New York Islanders 1980, 1981
Hern, Riley—Montreal Wanderers 1907, 1908, 1910
Hextall, Sr., Bryan—New York Rangers 1940
Hicke, Bill—Montreal 1959, 1960
Hicks, Wayne—Chicago 1961
Higginbotham, Fred—Winnipeg Vics 1896
Hill, Mel—Boston 1939, 1941; Toronto 1945
Hill, Sean—Montreal 1993
Hiller, Wilbert "Dutch"—New York Rangers 1940; Montreal 1946
Hillier, Randy—Pittsburgh 1991
Hillman, Larry—Detroit 1955; Toronto 1964, 1967; Montreal 1969
Hillman, Wayne—Chicago 1961
Hitchman, Lionel—Ottawa 1923; Boston 1929
Hodge, Charlie—Montreal 1959, 1960, 1965, 1966
Hodge, Ken—Boston 1970, 1972
Hodge, Tom—Montreal AAA 1902
Hodgson, Archie—Montreal AAA 1893, 1894
Hodson, Kevin—Detroit 1997, 1998
Hoerner, Charles—Montreal Shamrocks 1899
Hogue, Benoit—Dallas 1999
Holik, Bobby—New Jersey 1995, 2000
Hollett, Bill "Flash"—Boston 1939, 1941
Holmes, Harry—Toronto 1914, 1918; Seattle 1917; Victoria 1925
Holmstrom, Tomas—Detroit 1997, 1998
Holway, Albert "Toots"—Montreal Maroons 1926
Hooper, Art—Montreal AAA 1902
Hooper, Tom—Kenora 1907; Montreal Wanderers 1908
Horne, George "Shorty"—Montreal Maroons 1926
Horner, Reginald "Red"—Toronto 1932
Horton, Tim—Toronto 1962, 1963, 1964, 1967
Houle, Rejean—Montreal 1971, 1973, 1977, 1978, 1979
Howard, H.—Winnipeg Vics 1896
Howatt, Garry—New York Islanders 1980, 1981

Howe, Gordie—Detroit 1950, 1952, 1954, 1955
Howe, Syd—Detroit 1936, 1937, 1943
Hrkac, Tony—Dallas 1999
Hrdina, Jiri—Calgary 1989; Pittsburgh 1991, 1992
Huddy, Charlie—Edmonton 1984, 1985, 1987, 1988, 1990
Hudson, Mike—New York Rangers 1994
Hughes, Pat—Montreal 1979; Edmonton 1984, 1985
Hull, Bobby—Chicago 1961
Hull, Brett—Dallas 1999
Hunter, Dave—Edmonton 1984, 1985, 1987
Hunter, Mark—Calgary 1989
Hunter, Tim—Calgary 1989
Hutton, Bouse—Ottawa 1903, 1904
Hyland, Harry—Montreal Wanderers 1910

# I

Irving, Alex—Montreal AAA 1893, 1894

# J

Jackson, Art—Boston 1941; Toronto 1945
Jackson, Don—Edmonton 1984, 1985
Jackson, Harold—Chicago 1938; Detroit 1943
Jackson, Harvey "Busher"—Toronto 1932
Jackson, Stan—Toronto 1922
Jagr, Jaromir—Pittsburgh 1991, 1992
James, George—Montreal AAA 1894
Jarvis, Doug—Montreal 1976, 1977, 1978, 1979
Jeffrey, Larry—Toronto 1967
Jenkins, Roger—Chicago 1934, 1938
Jennings, Grant—Pittsburgh 1991, 1992
Johnson, Ernie "Moose"—Montreal Wanderers 1906, 1907, 1908, 1910
Johnson, Ivan "Ching"—New York Rangers 1928, 1933
Johnson, Tom —Montreal 1953, 1956, 1957, 1958, 1959, 1960
Johnson, Virgil—Chicago 1938
Johnston, Ed—Boston 1970, 1972
Johnstone, Charles—Winnipeg Vics 1896, 1901
Johnstone, Ross—Toronto 1945
Joliat, Aurel—Montreal 1924, 1930, 1931

Jones, Robert—Montreal Victorias 1895, 1896
Jonsson, Tomas—New York Islanders 1982, 1983
Juzda, Bill—Toronto 1951

# K

Kallur, Anders—New York Islanders 1980, 1981, 1982, 1983
Kamensky, Valeri—Colorado 1996
Kampman, Rudolph "Bingo"—Toronto 1942
Karakas, Mike—Chicago 1938
Karpovtsev, Alexander—New York Rangers 1994
Keane, Mike—Montreal 1993; Colorado 1996; Dallas 1999
Keeling, Mel "Butch"—New York Rangers 1933
Kelly, Bob—Philadelphia 1974, 1975
Kelly, Leonard "Red"—Detroit 1950, 1952, 1954, 1955; Toronto 1962, 1963, 1964, 1967
Kelly, Pete—Detroit 1936, 1937
Kendall, Bill—Chicago 1934
Kennedy, Rod—Montreal Wanderers 1906, 1907
Kennedy, Ted "Teeder"—Toronto 1945, 1947, 1948, 1949, 1951
Keon, Dave—Toronto 1962, 1963, 1964, 1967
Kerr, Albert "Dubbie"—Ottawa 1909, 1911
Kerr, Dave—New York Rangers 1940
Kilrea, Hec—Ottawa 1927; Detroit 1936, 1937
Kindrachuk, Orest—Philadelphia 1974, 1975
Kingan, A.B.—Montreal AAA 1893, 1894
Kitchen, Chapman "Hobey"—Montreal Maroons 1926
Klein, Lloyd "Dede"—Boston 1929
Klemm, Jon—Colorado 1996
Klima, Petr—Edmonton 1990
Klukay, Joe—Toronto 1947, 1948, 1949, 1951
Knuble, Michael—Detroit 1998
Kocur, Joe—New York Rangers 1994; Detroit 1997, 1998
Konstantinov, Vladimir—Detroit 1997
Kordic, John—Montreal 1986
Kovalev, Alexei—New York Rangers 1994
Kozlov, Vyacheslav—Detroit 1997, 1998
Krupp, Uwe—Colorado 1996
Krushelnyski, Mike—Edmonton 1985, 1987, 1988
Kurri, Jari—Edmonton 1984, 1985, 1987, 1988, 1990
Kurvers, Tom—Montreal 1986
Kypreos, Nick—New York Rangers 1994

# L

Lach, Elmer—Montreal 1944, 1946, 1953
Lacombe, Normand—Edmonton 1988
Lafleur, Guy—Montreal 1973, 1976, 1977, 1978, 1979
Lake, Fred—Ottawa 1909, 1911
Lalonde, Edouard "Newsy"—Montreal 1916
Lalor, Mike—Montreal 1986
Lamb, Mark—Edmonton 1990
Lambert, Yvon—Montreal 1976, 1977, 1978, 1979
Lamoureux, Leo—Montreal 1944, 1946
Lane, Gord—New York Islanders 1980, 1981, 1982, 1983
Lane, Myles—Boston 1929
Langelle, Pete—Toronto 1942
Langenbrunner, Jamie—Dallas 1999
Langevin, Dave—New York Islanders 1980, 1981, 1982, 1983
Langlois, Al—Montreal 1958, 1959, 1960
Langway, Rod—Montreal 1979
Laperriere, Jacques—Montreal 1965, 1966, 1968, 1969, 1971, 1973
Lapointe, Guy—Montreal 1971, 1973, 1976, 1977, 1978, 1979
Lapointe, Martin—Detroit 1997, 1998
Larionov, Igor—Detroit 1997, 1998
Larmer, Steve—New York Rangers 1994
Larochelle, Wildor—Montreal 1930, 1931
Larocque, Michel "Bunny"—Montreal 1976, 1977, 1978, 1979
Larose, Claude—Montreal 1965, 1966, 1968, 1971, 1973
Larouche, Pierre—Montreal 1978, 1979
Laviolette, Jack—Montreal 1916
Leach, Jamie—Pittsburgh 1992
Leach, Reg—Philadelphia 1975
Lebeau, Stephan—Montreal 1993
LeClair, Jack—Montreal 1956
LeClair, John—Montreal 1993
Leduc, Albert "Battleship"—Montreal 1930, 1931
Leetch, Brian—New York Rangers 1994
Leeman, Gary—Montreal 1993
Lefebvre, Sylvain—Colorado 1996
Lehtinen, Jere—Dallas 1999
Lefley, Chuck—Montreal 1971, 1973
Lehman, Hugh—Vancouver 1915
Lemaire, Jacques—Montreal 1968, 1969, 1971, 1973, 1976, 1977, 1978, 1979
Lemay, Moe—Edmonton 1987
Lemieux, Claude—Montreal 1986; New Jersey 1995, 2000; Colorado 1996

Lemieux, Mario—Pittsburgh 1991, 1992
Leonard, George—Quebec 1912
Lepine, Alfred "Pit"—Montreal 1930, 1931
Leschyshyn, Curtis—Colorado 1996
Lesieur, Art—Montreal 1931
LeSueur, Percy—Ottawa 1909, 1911
Lesuk, Bill—Boston 1970
Leswick, Jack—Chicago 1934
Leswick, Tony—Detroit 1952, 1954, 1955
Levinsky, Alex—Toronto 1932; Chicago 1938
Lewicki, Dan—Toronto 1951
Lewis, Gordon—Montreal Victorias 1896, 1897, 1898
Lewis, Herbie—Detroit 1936, 1937
Lidster, Doug—New York Rangers 1994
Liffiton, Charles—Montreal AAA 1902; Montreal Wanderers 1908
Lindsay, Ted—Detroit 1950, 1952, 1954, 1955
Lidstrom, Nicklas—Detroit 1997, 1998
Lindstrom, Willy—Edmonton 1984, 1985
Linseman, Ken—Edmonton 1984
Liscombe, Carl—Detroit 1943
Litzenberger, Eddie—Chicago 1961; Toronto 1962, 1963, 1964
Loney, Troy—Pittsburgh 1991, 1992
Lonsberry, Ross—Philadelphia 1974, 1975
Loob, Hakan—Calgary 1989
Lorentz, Jim—Boston 1970
Lorimer, Bob—New York Islanders 1980, 1981
Loughlin, Clem—Victoria 1925
Lowe, Jim—Montreal AAA 1893
Lowe, Kevin—Edmonton 1984, 1985, 1987, 1988, 1990;
  New York Rangers 1994
Lowery, Fred "Frock"—Montreal Maroons 1926
Ludwig, Craig—Montreal 1986; Dallas 1999
Lumley, Dave—Edmonton 1984, 1985
Lumley, Harry—Detroit 1950
Lupien, Gilles—Montreal 1978, 1979
Lynn, Vic—Toronto 1947, 1948, 1949

# M

MacAdam, Al—Philadelphia 1974
MacDonald, Kilby—New York Rangers 1940
MacInnis, Al—Calgary 1989
MacKay, Calum "Baldy"—Montreal 1953

MacKay, Duncan "Mickey"—Vancouver 1915; Boston 1929
MacKenzie, Bill—Chicago 1938
Mackie, Howie—Detroit 1937
Mackell, Fleming—Toronto 1949, 1951
Mackell, Jack—Ottawa 1921
MacLean, John—New Jersey 1995
MacLeish, Rick—Philadelphia 1974, 1975
MacLellan, Brian—Calgary 1989
MacMillan, John—Toronto 1962, 1963
Macoun, Jamie—Calgary 1989; Detroit 1998
MacPherson, James "Bud"—Montreal 1953
MacTavish, Craig—Edmonton 1987, 1988, 1990; New York Rangers 1994
Madden, John—New Jersey 2000
Mahovlich, Frank—Toronto 1962, 1963, 1964, 1967; Montreal 1971, 1973
Mahovlich, Peter—Montreal 1971, 1973, 1976, 1977
Majeau, Fern—Montreal 1944
Maki, Ronald "Chico"—Chicago 1961
Malakhov, Vladimir—New Jersey 2000
Maley, David—Montreal 1986
Mallen, Ken—Vancouver 1915
Malone, Jeff—Quebec 1913
Malone, Joe—Quebec 1912, 1913; Montreal 1924
Maltby, Kirk—Detroit 1997, 1998
Mantha, Georges—Montreal 1930, 1931
Mantha, Sylvio—Montreal 1924, 1930, 1931
Marcetta, Milan—Toronto 1967
March, Harold "Mush"—Chicago 1934, 1938
Marcotte, Don—Boston 1970, 1972
Marini, Hector—New York Islanders 1981, 1982
Marker, Gus—Montreal Maroons 1935
Marks, Jack—Quebec 1912, 1913; Toronto 1918
Marshall, Don—Montreal 1956, 1957, 1958, 1959, 1960
Marshall, Grant—Dallas 1999
Marshall, Jack—Winnipeg Vics 1901; Montreal AAA 1902;
    Montreal Wanderers 1907, 1910; Toronto 1914
Martin, Clare—Detroit 1950
Masnick, Paul—Montreal 1953
Matteau, Stephane—New York Rangers 1994
Matvichuk, Richard—Dallas 1999
Matz, Johnny—Vancouver 1915
Mazur, Eddie—Montreal 1953
McAlpine, Chris—New Jersey 1995
McCaffrey, Bert—Montreal 1930, 1931
McCarty, Darren—Detroit 1997, 1998
McClelland, Kevin—Edmonton 1984, 1985, 1987, 1988

McCool, Frank—Toronto 1945
McCormack, John—Toronto 1951; Montreal 1953
McCreedy, John—Toronto 1942, 1945
McCrimmon, Brad—Calgary 1989
McDonald, Ab—Montreal 1958, 1959, 1960; Chicago 1961
McDonald, Jack—Quebec 1912
McDonald, Lanny—Calgary 1989
McDonald, "Bucko"—Detroit 1936, 1937; Toronto 1942
McDougall, A.—Montreal Victorias 1895
McDougall, Bob—Montreal Victorias 1895, 1896, 1897, 1898
McDougall, Hartland—Montreal Victorias 1895, 1896, 1897, 1898
McEachern, Shawn—Pittsburgh 1992
McEwen, Mike—New York Islanders 1981, 1982, 1983
McFadden, Jim—Detroit 1950
McFadyen, Don—Chicago 1934
McGee, Frank—Ottawa 1903, 1904, 1905
McGee, Jim—Ottawa 1904
McGriffen, Roy "Minnie"—Toronto 1914
McGimsie, Billy—Kenora 1907
McKay, Doug—Detroit 1950
McKay, Randy—New Jersey 1995, 2000
McKendry, Alex—New York Islanders 1980
McKenna, Joe—Montreal Shamrocks 1899, 1900
McKenney, Don—Toronto 1964
McKenzie, John—Boston 1970, 1972
McLea, Ernest—Montreal Victorias 1896, 1897, 1898
McLean, Jack—Toronto 1945
McLellan (first name unknown)—Montreal Victorias 1897
McMahon, Mike—Montreal 1944
McManus, Sam—Montreal Maroons 1935
McNab, Max—Detroit 1950
McNamara, George—Toronto 1914
McNamara, Howard—Montreal 1916
McNeil, Gerry—Montreal 1953, 1957, 1958
McPhee, Mike—Montreal 1986
McReavy, Pat—Boston 1941
McSorley, Marty—Edmonton 1987, 1988
Meeker, Howie—Toronto 1947, 1948, 1951
Meeking, Harry—Toronto 1918; Victoria 1925
Meger, Paul—Montreal 1953
Melanson, Roland—New York Islanders 1981, 1982, 1983
Melnyk, Larry—Edmonton 1985
Menard, Henri—Montreal Wanderers 1906
Merrick, Wayne—New York Islanders 1980, 1981, 1982, 1983

Merrill, Horace—Ottawa 1920
Merritt, George—Winnepeg Vics 1896
Messier, Mark—Edmonton 1984, 1985, 1987, 1988, 1990;
    New York Rangers 1994
Metz, Don—Toronto 1942, 1945, 1947, 1948, 1949
Metz, Nick—Toronto 1942, 1945, 1947, 1948
Michayluk, Dave—Pittsburgh 1992
Mikita, Stan—Chicago 1961
Miller, Bill—Montreal Maroons 1935
Miller, Earl—Toronto 1932
Mironov, Dmitri—Detroit 1998
Mitchell, Ivan "Mike"—Toronto 1922
Modano, Mike—Dallas 1999
Mogilny, Alexander—New Jersey 2000
Molson, Percy—Montreal Victorias 1897
Mondou, Armand—Montreal 1930, 1931
Mondou, Pierre—Montreal 1977, 1978, 1979
Moog, Andy—Edmonton 1984, 1985, 1987
Moore, Alfie—Chicago 1938
Moore, Art—Ottawa 1903, 1904, 1905
Moore, Dickie—Montreal 1953, 1956, 1957, 1958, 1959, 1960
Moran, Paddy—Quebec 1912, 1913
Morenz, Howie—Montreal 1924, 1930, 1931
Morris, Bernie—Seattle 1917
Morris, Elwin "Moe"—Toronto 1945
Morrow, Ken—New York Islanders 1980, 1981, 1982, 1983
Mortson, Gus—Toronto 1947, 1948, 1949, 1951
Mosdell, Kenny—Montreal 1946, 1953, 1956, 1959
Motter, Alex—Detroit 1943
Mowers, Johnny—Detroit 1943
Mullen, Joe—Calgary 1989; Pittsburgh 1991, 1992
Muller, Kirk—Montreal 1993
Mummery, Harry—Quebec 1913; Toronto 1918
Muni, Craig—Edmonton 1987, 1988, 1990
Munro, Dunc—Montreal Maroons 1926
Murdoch, Bob—Montreal 1971, 1973
Murdoch, Murray—New York Rangers 1928, 1933
Murphy, Joe—Edmonton 1990
Murphy, Larry—Pittsburgh 1991, 1992; Detroit 1997, 1998
Murphy, Ron—Chicago 1961
Murray, Troy—Colorado 1996
Murzyn, Dana—Calgary 1989
Mussen, Clare—Montreal AAA 1894

# N

Napier, Mark—Montreal 1979; Edmonton 1985
Naslund, Mats—Montreal 1986
Nattress, Ric—Calgary 1989
Needham, Mike—Pittsburgh 1992
Nemchinov, Sergei—New York Rangers 1994; New Jersey 2000
Nesterenko, Eric—Chicago 1961
Nevin, Bob—Toronto 1962, 1963
Nicholson, Billy—Montreal AAA 1902
Niedermayer, Scott—New Jersey 1995, 2000
Nieuwendyk, Joe—Calgary 1989; Dallas 1999
Nighbor, Frank—Vancouver 1915; Ottawa 1920, 1921, 1923, 1927
Nilan, Chris—Montreal 1986
Nilsson, Kent—Edmonton 1987
Noble, Reg—Toronto 1918, 1922; Montreal Maroons 1926
Nolan, Pat—Toronto 1922
Nolet, Simon—Philadelphia 1974
Noonan, Brian—New York Rangers 1994
Northcott, Lawrence "Baldy"—Montreal Maroons 1935
Nyrop, Bill—Montreal 1976, 1977, 1978
Nystrom, Bob—New York Islanders 1980, 1981, 1982, 1983

# O

Oatman, Eddie—Quebec 1912
O'Brien, E.—Montreal AAA 1894
O'Connor, "Buddy"—Montreal 1944, 1946
Odelein, Lyle—Montreal 1993
Olczyk, Ed—New York Rangers 1994
Oliver, Harry—Boston 1929
Oliwa, Krzysztof—New Jersey 2000
Olmstead, Bert—Montreal 1953, 1956, 1957, 1958; Toronto 1962
O'Neil, Tom "Windy"—Toronto 1945
Orlando, Jimmy—Detroit 1943
Orr, Bobby—Boston 1970, 1972
Osgood, Chris—Detroit 1997, 1998
Otto, Joel—Calgary 1989
Owen, George—Boston 1929
Ozolinish, Sandis—Colorado 1996

# P

Paek, Jim—Pittsburgh 1991, 1992
Palangio, Pete—Chicago 1938
Pandolfo, Jay—New Jersey 2000
Pappin, Jim—Toronto 1964, 1967
Parent, Bernie—Philadelphia 1974, 1975
Paton, Tom—Montreal AAA 1893
Patrick, Frank—Vancouver 1915
Patrick, Lester—Montreal Wanderers 1906, 1907; New York Rangers 1928
Patrick, Lynn—New York Rangers 1940
Patrick, Muzz—New York Rangers 1940
Patterson, Colin—Calgary 1989
Pavelich, Marty—Detroit 1950, 1952, 1954, 1955
Pederson, Barry—Pittsburgh 1991
Peluso, Mike—New Jersey 1995
Peplinski, Jim—Calgary 1989
Persson, Stefan—New York Islanders 1980, 1981, 1982, 1983
Peters, Garry—Boston 1972
Peters, Jim—Montreal 1946, Detroit 1950, 1954
Pettinger, Gordon—New York Rangers 1933; Detroit 1936, 1937; Boston 1939
Phillips, Bill—Montreal Maroons 1926
Phillips, Tom—Kenora 1907
Picard, Noel—Montreal 1965
Pietrangelo, Frank—Pittsburgh 1991
Pike, Alf—New York Rangers 1940
Pilote, Pierre—Chicago 1961
Pitre, Didier—Montreal 1916
Plamondon, Gerry—Montreal 1946
Plante, Derek—Dallas 1999
Plante, Jacques—Montreal 1953, 1956, 1957, 1958, 1959, 1960
Plasse, Michel—Montreal 1973
Poile, Bud—Toronto 1947
Polich, Mike—Montreal 1977
Portland, Jack—Boston 1939
Potvin, Denis—New York Islanders 1980, 1981, 1982, 1983
Potvin, Jean—New York Islanders 1980
Poulin, Skinner—Montreal 1916
Pouzar, Jaroslav—Edmonton 1984, 1985, 1987
Power, "Rocket"—Quebec 1913
Pratt, Babe—New York Rangers 1940, Toronto 1945
Price, Noel—Montreal 1966
Priestlay, Ken—Pittsburgh 1992

Primeau, Joe—Toronto 1932
Prodgers, "Goldie"—Quebec 1912; Montreal 1916
Pronovost, Andre—Montreal 1957, 1958, 1959, 1960
Pronovost, Marcel—Detroit 1950, 1952, 1954, 1955; Toronto 1967
Provost, Claude—Montreal 1956, 1957, 1958, 1959, 1960, 1965, 1966, 1968, 1969
Prystai, Metro—Detroit 1952, 1954
Pulford, Bob—Toronto 1962, 1963, 1964, 1967
Pulford, Harvey—Ottawa 1903, 1904, 1905
Pullan, William—Montreal Victorias 1895
Pushor, Jamie—Detroit 1997
Pusie, Jean—Montreal 1931

# R

Racicot, Andre—Montreal 1993
Rafalski, Brian—New Jersey 2000
Ramage, Rob—Calgary 1989, Montreal 1993
Randall, Ken—Toronto 1918, 1922
Ranford, Bill—Edmonton 1988, 1990
Rankin, Norman—Montreal Victorias 1895
Reardon, Kenny—Montreal 1946
Reay, Billy—Montreal 1946, 1953
Recchi, Mark—Pittsburgh 1991
Reddick, Eldon "Pokey"—Edmonton 1990
Redmond, Mickey—Montreal 1968, 1969
Reibel, "Dutch"—Detroit 1954, 1955
Reid, Dave—Dallas 1999
Reise, Jr. Leo—Detroit 1950, 1952
Resch, Glenn "Chico"—New York Islanders 1980
Ricci, Mike—Colorado 1996
Richard, Henri—Montreal 1956, 1957, 1958, 1959, 1960, 1965, 1966, 1968, 1969, 1971, 1973
Richard, Maurice "Rocket"—Montreal 1944, 1946, 1953, 1956, 1957, 1958, 1959, 1960
Richardson, Frank—Montreal Victorias 1898
Richer, Stephane—Montreal 1986; New Jersey 1995
Richter, Mike—New York Rangers 1994
Rickey, Roy—Seattle 1917
Ridpath, Bruce—Ottawa 1911
Riley, Jim—Seattle 1917
Risebrough, Doug—Montreal 1976, 1977, 1978, 1979
Rivers, Gus—Montreal 1930, 1931

Roach, John "Ross"—Toronto 1922
Roberge, Mario—Montreal 1993
Roberto, Phil—Montreal 1971
Roberts, Gary—Calgary 1989
Roberts, Gord—Pittsburgh 1991, 1992
Roberts, Jimmy—Montreal 1965, 1966, 1973, 1976, 1977
Robertson, Earl—Detroit 1937
Robertson, Fred—Toronto 1932
Robinson, Earl—Montreal Maroons 1935
Robinson, Larry—Montreal 1973, 1976, 1977, 1978, 1979, 1986
Rochefort, Leon—Montreal 1966, 1971
Rodden, Eddie—Boston 1929
Rollins, Al—Toronto 1951
Rolston, Brian—New Jersey 1995
Romnes, Elwin "Doc"—Chicago 1934, 1938
Ronan, Ed—Montreal 1993
Ronan, Skene—Montreal 1916
Rooney, Steve—Montreal 1986
Rooney, Walter—Quebec 1912
Ross, Art—Kenora 1907, Montreal Wanderers 1908
Rothschild, Sam—Montreal Maroons 1926
Roulston, William "Roly"—Detroit 1937
Rouse, Bob—Detroit 1997, 1998
Rousseau, Bobby—Montreal 1965, 1966, 1968, 1969
Routh, Harvie—Montreal AAA 1893, 1894
Rowe, Bob—Seattle 1917
Roy, Patrick—Montreal 1986, 1993; Colorado 1996
Ruotsalainen, Reijo—Edmonton 1987, 1990
Russell, Ernie—Montreal Wanderers 1906, 1907, 1908, 1910
Rychel, Warren—Colorado 1996

# S

St. Laurent, Dollard—Montreal 1953, 1956, 1957, 1958; Chicago 1961
Sakic, Joe—Colorado 1996
Saleski, Don—Philadelphia 1974, 1975
Samis, Phil—Toronto 1948
Samuelsson, Kjell—Pittsburgh 1992
Samuelsson, Ulf—Pittsburgh 1991, 1992
Sanderson, Derek—Boston 1970, 1972
Sands, Charlie—Boston 1939
Sandstrom, Tomas—Detroit 1997
Savard, Denis —Montreal 1993

Savard, Serge—Montreal 1968, 1969, 1971, 1976, 1977, 1978, 1979
Sawchuk, Terry—Detroit 1952, 1954, 1955; Toronto 1967
Scanlon, Fred—Montreal Shamrocks 1899, 1900
Schmidt, Milt—Boston 1939, 1941
Schneider, Mathieu—Montreal 1993
Schriner, David "Sweeney"—Toronto 1942, 1945
Schultz, Dave—Philadelphia 1974, 1975
Scott, Laurie—New York Rangers 1928
Seaborn, Jimmy—Vancouver 1915
Seibert, Earl—New York Rangers 1933, Chicago 1938
Semenko, Dave—Edmonton 1984, 1985
Sevigny, Richard—Montreal 1979
Shack, Eddie—Toronto 1962, 1963, 1964, 1967
Shanahan, Brendan—Detroit 1997, 1998
Sheehan, Bobby—Montreal 1971
Sheppard, John—Chicago 1934
Sherf, John—Detroit 1937
Shewchuk, Jack—Boston 1941
Shibicky, Alex—New York Rangers 1940
Shields, Allan—Montreal Maroons 1935
Shill, Jack—Chicago 1938
Schock, Dan—Boston 1970
Shore, Eddie—Boston 1929, 1939
Shore, Hamby—Ottawa 1905, 1911
Shutt, Steve—Montreal 1973, 1976, 1977, 1978, 1979
Siebert, Babe—Montreal Maroons 1926; New York Rangers 1933
Sims, Jim—Dallas 1999
Simmons, Donald—Toronto 1962, 1963, 1964
Simms, Percy—Ottawa 1903
Simon, Chris—Colorado 1996
Simon, John "Cully"—Detroit 1943
Simpson, Craig—Edmonton 1988, 1990
Skinner, Alf—Toronto 1918
Skov, Glen—Detroit 1952, 1954, 1955
Skrudland, Brian—Montreal 1986; Dallas 1999
Sloan, Blake—Dallas 1999
Sloan, Tod—Toronto 1951; Chicago 1961
Smaill, Wally—Montreal Wanderers 1908
Smith, Alex—Ottawa 1927
Smith, Alf—Ottawa 1904, 1905
Smith, Billy—New York Islanders 1980, 1981, 1982, 1983
Smith, Bobby—Montreal 1986
Smith, Clint—New York Rangers 1940

Smith, Dallas—Boston 1970, 1972
Smith, Des—Boston 1941
Smith, Geoff—Edmonton 1990
Smith, Normie—Detroit 1936, 1937
Smith, Reginald "Hooley"—Ottawa 1927; Montreal Maroons 1935
Smith, Rick—Boston 1970
Smith, Sid—Toronto 1948, 1949, 1951
Smith, Stan—New York Rangers 1940
Smith, Steve—Edmonton 1987, 1988, 1990
Smylie, Rod—Toronto 1922
Soetaert, Doug—Montreal 1986
Somers, Art—New York Rangers 1933
Sorrell, John—Detroit 1936, 1937
Speer, Bill—Boston 1970
Spittal, Charles—Ottawa 1903
Stackhouse, Ted—Toronto 1922
Stanfield, Fred—Boston 1970, 1972
Stanley, Allan—Toronto 1962, 1963, 1964, 1967
Stanley, Barney—Vancouver 1915
Stanowski, Wally—Toronto 1942, 1945, 1947, 1948
Stanton, Paul—Pittsburgh 1991, 1992
Starr, Wilf—Detroit 1936
Stasiuk, Vic—Detroit 1952, 1955
Stemkowski, Pete—Toronto 1967
Stephenson, Wayne—Philadelphia 1975
Stevens, Kevin—Pittsburgh 1991, 1992
Stevens, Scott—New Jersey 1995, 2000
Stewart, Gaye—Toronto 1942, 1947
Stewart, John "Black Jack"—Detroit 1943, 1950
Stewart, James—Montreal AAA 1893, 1894
Stewart, Nels—Montreal Maroons 1926
Stewart, Ron—Toronto 1962, 1963, 1964
Strachan, Billy—Montreal Wanderers 1906, 1907
Stuart, Billy "Red"—Toronto 1922
Stuart, Bruce—Montreal Wanderers 1908; Ottawa 1909, 1911
Stuart, Hod—Montreal Wanderers 1907
Suter, Gary—Calgary 1989
Sutter, Brent—New York Islanders 1982, 1983
Sutter, Duane—New York Islanders 1980, 1981, 1982, 1983
Svoboda, Petr—Montreal 1986
Sydor, Darryl—Dallas 1999
Sykora, Petr—New Jersey 2000

# T

Taglianetti, Peter—Pittsburgh 1991, 1992
Talbot, Jean-Guy—Montreal 1956, 1957, 1958, 1959, 1960, 1965, 1966
Tambellini, Steve—New York Islanders 1980
Tansey, Frank—Montreal Shamrocks 1899, 1900
Tardif, Marc—Montreal 1971, 1973
Taylor, Billy—Toronto 1942
Taylor, Bobby—Philadelphia 1974
Taylor, Fred "Cyclone"—Ottawa 1909; Vancouver 1915
Taylor, Harry—Toronto 1949
Taylor, Tim—Detroit 1997
Terreri, Chris—New Jersey 1995, 2000
Thompson, Cecil "Tiny"—Boston 1929
Thompson, Paul—New York Rangers 1928; Chicago 1934, 1938
Thomson, Jimmy—Toronto 1947, 1948, 1949, 1951
Tikkanen, Esa—Edmonton 1985, 1987, 1988, 1990; New York Rangers 1994
Timgren, Ray—Toronto 1949, 1951
Tocchet, Rick—Pittsburgh 1992
Tonelli, John—New York Islanders 1980, 1981, 1982, 1983
Tremblay, Gilles—Montreal 1966, 1968
Tremblay, J.C.—Montreal 1965, 1966, 1968, 1969, 1971
Tremblay, Mario—Montreal 1976, 1977, 1978, 1979, 1986
Trihey, Harry—Montreal Shamrocks 1899, 1900
Trottier, Bryan—New York Islanders 1980, 1981, 1982, 1983;
    Pittsburgh 1991, 1992
Trottier, Dave—Montreal Maroons 1935
Trudel, Louis—Chicago 1934, 1938
Turek, Roman—Dallas 1999
Turner, Bob—Montreal 1956, 1957, 1958, 1959, 1960

# V

Vachon, Rogie—Montreal 1968, 1969, 1971
Vadnais, Carol—Montreal 1968; Boston 1972
Van Impe, Ed—Philadelphia 1974, 1975
Vasko, Elmer—Chicago 1961
Verbeek, Pat—Dallas 1999
Vernon, Mike—Calgary 1989; Detroit 1997
Vezina, Georges—Montreal 1916, 1924
Voss, Carl—Chicago 1938

# W

Walker, Jack—Toronto 1914; Seattle 1917; Victoria 1925
Wall, Frank—Montreal Shamrocks 1899, 1900
Wallace, W.—Montreal Victorias 1896
Walsh, Marty—Ottawa 1909, 1911
Walter, Ryan—Montreal 1986
Walton, Mike—Toronto 1967; Boston 1972
Wamsley, Rick—Calgary 1989
Wand, A.C. "Toad"—Montreal AAA 1899
Ward, Aaron—Detroit 1997, 1998
Ward, Jimmy—Montreal Maroons 1935
Wares, Eddie—Detroit 1943
Wasnie, Nick—Montreal 1930, 1931
Watson, Harry—Detroit 1943; Toronto 1947, 1948, 1949, 1951
Watson, Jimmy—Philadelphia 1974, 1975
Watson, Joe—Philadelphia 1974, 1975
Watson, Phil—New York Rangers 1940, Montreal 1944
Weiland, Cooney—Boston 1929, 1939
Wells, Jay—New York Rangers 1994
Wentworth, Cy—Montreal Maroons 1935
Westfall, Ed—Boston 1970, 1972
Westwick, Harry—Ottawa 1903, 1904, 1905
Wharram, Kenny—Chicago 1961
White, Frank—Ottawa 1905
White, Colin—New Jersey 2000
Wiebe, Art—Chicago 1938
Willet, Stanley—Montreal Victorias 1896
Wilson, Cully—Toronto 1914; Seattle 1917
Wilson, Johnny—Detroit 1950, 1952, 1954, 1955
Wilson, Larry—Detroit 1950
Wilson, Murray—Montreal 1973, 1976, 1977
Wiseman, Eddie—Boston 1941
Woit, Benny—Detroit 1952, 1954, 1955
Wolanin, Craig—Colorado 1996
Wood, Burke—Winnipeg Vics 1901
Wood, F.H.—Ottawa 1903
Worsley, Lorne "Gump"—Montreal 1965, 1966, 1968, 1969
Wregget, Ken—Pittsburgh 1992

# Y

Yelle, Stephane—Colorado 1996
Young, Doug—Detroit 1936, 1937
Young, Scott—Pittsburgh 1991; Colorado 1996
Young, Wendell—Pittsburgh 1991, 1992
Yzerman, Steve—Detroit 1997, 1998

# Z

Zeidel, Larry—Detroit 1952
Zelepukin, Valeri—New Jersey 1995
Zubov, Sergei—New York Rangers 1994; Dallas 1999